Contents

List of tables and figures

Tables

Figures

Acknowledgements

I would like to thank all those associated with the three books on New Labour (I always wanted to write a trilogy!). This includes current and former staff of The Policy Press, and the contributors (some of whom have been in all three books). I would also like to thank colleagues at the University of Birmingham. Finally, of course, the books would not have been possible without New Labour!

Notes on contributors

Mark Baldwin is Senior Lecturer in Social Work at the University of Bath. His research interests lie predominantly in exploring the part played by professional discretion in the implementation of public policy. He is interested in the use of critical reflection for organisational learning and jointly edited the book *Social work, critical reflection and the learning organization* (Ashgate, 2004) (with Nick Gould). He is a founder member of the South West Social Work Activists Network.

Sarah Charman is Principal Lecturer in Criminology at the Institute of Criminal Justice Studies, University of Portsmouth. She has published in the areas of both policing and criminal justice policy and was the co-author (with Stephen Savage and Stephen Cope) of *Policing and the power of persuasion* (Blackstone Press, 2000).

David Denney is Professor of Social and Public Policy at Royal Holloway, University of London. He has previously held academic appointments at Bangor University, Wales, and at the University of Kent at Canterbury. His main research interests have been in race and the criminal justice system, and aspects of nationalism. He was part of the ESRC Violence Research programme and has written extensively on violence and abuse in the workplace since 2002. He has also investigated differential treatment in the Canadian criminal justice system. He is the author of a number of single-authored books including *Risk and society* (Sage, 2005) and *Social policy and social work* (Oxford University Press, 1998).

Alexandra Dobrowolsky is Professor and Chair of Political Science at Saint Mary's University, Halifax, Canada. She has recently co-edited *Women, migration, and citizenship: Making local, national, and transnational connections* (Ashgate, 2006) (with Evangelia Tastsoglou) and *Women Making constitutions: New politics and comparative connections* (Palgrave Macmillan, 2003) (with Vivien Hart). She has also authored *The politics of pragmatism: Women, representation, and constitutionalism in Canada* (Oxford University Press, 2000). She is currently publishing articles that examine shifts in citizenship discourses and practices, and is preparing a volume on women and recent policy trends in Canada.

Mark Drakeford is Professor of Social Policy and Applied Social Sciences at the University of Cardiff. Since 2000 he has also been the Cabinet's health and social policy adviser at the Welsh Assembly Government, and Senior Special Adviser to the First Minister. Recent publications include *Scandal: Social policy and social welfare* (2nd edn) (The Policy Press, 2005) (with Ian Butler).

Peter Dwyer is Professor of Social Policy in the Graduate School, Business, Law and Social Sciences at Nottingham Trent University. His work focuses on issues related to social citizenship and also migration. To date he has published three books and a number of journal articles and papers on these themes. He is managing editor of *Social Policy and Society*.

Ian Greener is a Reader in Social Policy at Durham University. He has written widely on health policy, education policy and public sector management, and has published in a wide range of journals including *Public Administration, Governance, Policy and Politics* and *Administration and Society*. He is currently carrying out fieldwork in hospitals and in primary care to try and work out the effect of New Labour's policy on them. When not worrying about the welfare state he likes trying to persuade PC owners to get Macs instead, and watching Spongebob with his children.

Ruth Lister is Professor of Social Policy in the Department of Social Sciences, Loughborough University and was, until recently, the first Visiting Donald Dewar Professor of Social Justice at the University of Glasgow. She was previously Professor of Applied Social Studies at Bradford University and is a former Director of the Child Poverty Action Group. She has published widely in the areas of: poverty; social security; welfare reform; gender; children and young people; and citizenship. Her latest books are: *Citizenship: Feminist perspectives* (2nd edn) (Palgrave, 2003); *Poverty* (Polity, 2004); *Gendering citizenship in Western Europe* (The Policy Press, 2007) (with others); and *Why money matters* (co-edited for Save the Children, 2008).

Brian Lund is Principal Lecturer in Social Policy at the Manchester Metropolitan University. His publications on housing and social policy include *Understanding state welfare* (Sage, 2002) and *Understanding housing policy* (The Policy Press, 2006).

Susan Martin is Senior Lecturer in the Department of Education at the University of Bath. Her main research interests are in assessment and learning, and supporting learners in different contexts, such as Initial Teacher Education and pupils in Key Stages 2–4. Her publications include: S. Martin, A.D. Reid, K. Bullock and K.N. Bishop, *Student Voices, Teacher Choices* (Geographical Association, 2002) and L. Stoll, G. Stobart, S. Martin, S. Freeman, E. Friedman, P. Sammons, and R. Smees, *Preparing for Change: Evaluation of the Implementation of the KS3 Pilot Programme*, Final Report to the DfES (2002).

Stephen McKay is Professor of Social Research at the University of Birmingham, within the new School of Social Policy. He conducts research on family change, income inequality and the labour market. His publications include *Lone parent families: Gender, class and state* (Pearson, 2002), *Attitudes to inheritance* (JRF/The Policy Press, 2005) and *Women's financial assets and debts* (The Fawcett Society, 2007).

Yolande Muschamp is Senior Lecturer at the University of Bath, where she is Head of the Department of Education. Her research interests are in educational policy and the pedagogy of the primary school. She publishes in these areas, focusing on the impact of educational policy on the classroom and the transition of pupils between schools. Her publications include *Work and identity in the primary school* (Open University Press, 1996) and, more recently, *Parenting, caring and educating for the Primary Review* (University of Cambridge, 2008).

Catherine Needham is Lecturer in Politics at Queen Mary, University of London. She is the author of *The reform of public services under New Labour: Narratives of consumerism* (Palgrave, 2007) and *Citizen consumers: New Labour's marketplace democracy* (Catalyst, 2003).

Calum Paton is a political scientist. He is Professor of Health Policy at Keele University, and editor-in-chief of the *International Journal of Health Planning and Management* (Wiley Blackwell). He was until recently Chairman of the University Hospital of North Staffordshire NHS Trust. He is author of 10 books and many articles on politics, the politics of health policy and health systems. His most recent book is *New Labour's state of health: Political economy, public policy and the NHS* (Ashgate, 2006). He is a frequent commentator in the media and on national platforms.

Martin Powell is Professor of Health and Social Policy at the Health Services Management Centre, School of Social Policy, University of Birmingham. He has written widely on social and health policy, and has edited two previous books on New Labour: *New Labour, new welfare state?* (The Policy Press, 1999) and *Evaluating New Labour's welfare reforms* (The Policy Press, 2002). He is the editor of *Social Policy and Administration*.

Karen Rowlingson is Professor of Social Policy and Director of Research at the Institute of Applied Social Studies, University of Birmingham. Her research interests lie in the financial security of individuals, families and households, including: assets and asset-based welfare; poverty, wealth and inequality; social security policy; and financial planning and management (including savings, pensions, credit and debt). She has recently published a Fabian pamphlet on inheritance tax (with Rajiv Prabhakar and Stuart White) and a JRF report on attitudes to inequality (with Michael Orton).

Stephen P. Savage is Director of the Institute of Criminal Justice Studies and Professor of Criminology at the University of Portsmouth. He founded the Institute in 1992 and has published extensively in the areas of policing, criminal justice policy and miscarriages of justice. His most recent publication, *Police reform: Forces for change* (Oxford University Press, 2007), considers the factors driving policing policy in Britain over the last three decades.

Martin Seeleib-Kaiser is Reader in Comparative Social Policy and Politics at the University of Oxford, and Fellow of Green College. Prior to his appointment at Oxford University in 2004, he held appointments at the Universities of Bremen and Bielefeld, Germany, as well as at Duke University, North Carolina, US. His research focuses on comparative welfare state analysis, with a special focus on the role of political parties and ideas, and the relationship between globalisation and welfare systems, as well as the interplay between 'public' and 'private' social policies. Recent book publications include *The dual transformation of the German welfare state* (Palgrave Macmillan, 2004) (co-authored with P. Bleses), *Party politics and social welfare* (Edward Elgar, 2008) (co-authored with S. van Dyk and M. Roggenkamp) and *Welfare state transformations* (Palgrave Macmillan, 2008) (editor). His journal articles have been published in, among others, *American Sociological Review, German Politics, Social Policy and Administration* and *West European Politics*.

ONE

Introduction: modernising the welfare state

Martin Powell

'A new dawn has broken. Isn't it wonderful?...We have been elected as New Labour and we will govern as New Labour.'
(Tony Blair, election night, 2 May 1997)

Introduction

This is the third book in what I am terming my 'New Labour trilogy'. The first book, *New Labour, new welfare state* (Powell, 1999), was one of the first books to examine the social policy of New Labour's 'Third Way'. The second book, *Evaluating New Labour's welfare reforms* (Powell, 2002), focused on manifesto promises and Annual Reports. This third book, *Modernising the welfare state*, looks back at the longest-serving Labour government and Labour Prime Minister in British history, to examine 'the Blair legacy'.

This book examines the 'hand of history' on Tony Blair's shoulders, and there is no shortage of material on his legacy. For example, websites such as Blairwatch.co.uk and BlairLegacy.org.uk have been set up, and a search for the term 'Blair + Legacy' brings about 541,000 hits on Google (04/02/08).

This book examines the main changes to the welfare state since New Labour came to power in 1997, updating existing accounts, as they tend to focus on the first term of government up to 2001. The main focus of the book, however, is to examine the degree of change that has occurred in the welfare state – the book's analytical template is New Labour's modernisation of the welfare state. The elements of modernisation are examined to see whether there was a coherent modernisation package in different sectors, or whether modernisation actually means different things in different sectors. Similarly, the trajectory of change is examined to determine when the major changes occurred, and whether later changes built on earlier ones, or conflicted with them. Finally, the importance of change is examined using Hall's (1993) orders of change.

Modernising the welfare state and the party of welfare reform

The 1997 Labour election manifesto stated that 'We will be the party of welfare reform'. Blair's introduction to the manifesto claimed that: 'in each area of policy a new and distinctive approach has been mapped out, one that differs from the old left and the Conservative right'. Labour made large claims about welfare reform (Powell, 1999, pp 281-2): in the first Queen's Speech, Blair launched a crusade for welfare reform, singling out modernisation of the £90 billion-a-year welfare system as the 'big idea' of the Labour government. Frank Field was appointed Minister of Welfare Reform to 'think the unthinkable'. Blair claimed, 15 months after the election, that Labour had accomplished more welfare reform in those 15 months than the Conservatives had done in 15 years. Indeed, in Labour's first Annual Report they claimed that it had been 'a year of welfare reform'. In the Queen's Speech in November 1998 Blair claimed that the measures undertaken amounted to the largest programme of change in public services for many years – it is claimed that 'the process of modernisation began on May 2nd, the day after the election' (DH, 1997, para 1.9). And, according to Blair, in May 1997 'we started on the road of modernisation at a cracking pace' (Foreword, quoted in Kelly, 1999, p 1).

Subsequent manifestos promised that this fast pace would continue. The main aims of the 2001 manifesto (Labour Party, 2001) were: prosperity for all, world-class public services, a modern welfare state and strong and safe communities. Investment and reform in public services were at the heart of the manifesto. The 2005 manifesto (Labour Party, 2005) claimed that the UK had changed for the better because Labour had fulfilled its promises of 1997 and 2001, including welfare reform and a modern welfare state. And Gordon Brown's first speech to the Labour Party conference as Prime Minister spoke of the 'next stage in the transformation of public services', and of taking the NHS 'into a new era' (Brown, 2007a). Brown's New Year message claimed that 2008 would be a year of 'real and serious changes' (Brown, 2007b).

The meaning of modernisation

If modernising the welfare state is an important aim of the New Labour government, then its actual meaning should be examined. Unfortunately, the term is rarely or poorly defined by government or commentators, and it appears to have many different meanings, which results in no generally accepted definition.

It is claimed that 'the Government has a mission to modernise, renewing our country for the new millennium' (Introduction by Blair, quoted in Cabinet Office, 1999), and that 'Modernisation is a hallmark of the Government' (Cabinet Office, 1999, p 9). Blair and Schroeder (1999, p 29) claimed that constraints on 'tax and spend' forced radical modernisation of the public sector and reform of public services to achieve 'better value for money', and 'a new programme for changed realities'.

The importance of 'new' and 'modern' can be seen in the titles of key government documents: *The new NHS: Modern, dependable* (DH, 1997); *Modernising social services* (DH, 1998a); *Modernising mental health services* (DH, 1998b); *Modern public services* (HMT, 1998); *Modern local government* (DETR, 1998); *New ambitions for our country* (DSS, 1998); and *Modernising government* (Cabinet Office, 1999). In the Fabian series on 'Modernising Britain' (Kelly, 1999), it was claimed that the Prime Minister made the modernisation of Britain a key theme of the New Labour administration. Finlayson (2003, p 66) states that if there is a single word that might capture the essence of New Labour's social and political project, then it is 'modernisation'. Miller (2004, p 29) writes that Labour entered government committed to the modernisation of welfare provision. I would assert (2002, p 12) that this theme of modernisation, achieving traditional objectives by modern means, is central to the Third Way. Newman (2001, pp 52, 173) argues that New Labour's reform programme was driven by a commitment to modernisation, and modernisation was a programme of public sector reform around principles closely linked to the politics of the Third Way. So, does modernisation put the 'new' into New Labour (Newman, 2001, p 46)?

The theme of 'modernising' government is not new, however, and has been used in connection with the Conservatives in the early 1960s (Lowe, 1997) and in the 1980s (Hoggett, 1990). For example, in the 1960s, Harold Wilson's Labour Party conference speech was of the 'white heat' of a scientific revolution, with no place for restricted practices or for outdated methods (Marr, 2007, p 238). And in the 1980s, modernisation of the Conservative Party was the key theme (Gould,

1998). After being successful in this, the modernisers then turned their attention to the nation.

Before becoming leader of the Labour Party, in 1993 Blair wrote an article entitled 'Why modernisation matters', which spelled out the early themes of the Third Way: the failure of left and right, and change in the modern world. The label of modernisation then, pre-dated the 'Third Way' for New Labour (see Gould, 1998). From the start Blair had wanted to make the UK a renewed and modern country, and the project of renewal for Labour mirrored that for Britain (Gould, 1998, p 235). Blair believed that modernisation would construct a new model of social democracy (Gould, 1998, p 251). Although Blair's book *New Britain* (1996) contained little on modernisation, with no index entry, it did emphasise rebuilding and renewing modern public services and the 'young country'. These themes fit with the Third Way. In *The Third Way* (1998, p 1), Blair stated that it stood for a modernised social democracy for a changing world. Other writers of the time concur with this view, for example, Giddens (1998) regarded the Third Way as the renewal of social democracy, while Gould (1998, p 237) wrote that the Third Way was a label, but it was also an approach that was rooted in the modernising tradition. Finlayson (2003, p 106) has pointed out, however, that the very name of the Third Way automatically implies that the old ways are no longer relevant, and that something new is required.

According to Fairclough (2000, pp 18-19), 'new' occurs 609 times in 53 of Blair's speeches between 1997 and 1999 (cf modern: 89; modernise/modernisation: 87; reform: 143). Despite the impression picked up by satirists that 'new' applied to everything and anything ('New Labour, new underwear'), it is used quite selectively for national, political and governmental renewal in 'new times', which generates new opportunities and challenges and calls for new approaches, ideas and attitudes. It is perhaps 'modernise' that tends to be used more indiscriminately: 'modernisation' applies to the Labour Party, the constitution, the health service, education and schools, the welfare state, defence, the Common Agricultural Policy and so on. In 25 cases in Blair's speeches, 'modernisation' (or, in a few cases, 'modernise') is used in a general way without reference to a specific domain (for example, 'money for modernisation': 3; or 'modernisation for a purpose': 5). A striking contrast between 'modernisation' and 'reform' is that the former is overwhelmingly used with reference to the UK, whereas the latter is used roughly equally with reference to the European Union (EU), but 'welfare reform' is used more frequently in the UK than 'modernisation'. According to 6 and Peck (2004a, p 4), a search on 'modernisation' using the (now superseded) Webcat search engine www.open.gov.uk (13/07/01) produced 5,399 government documents in which the word appeared on the first page. A search on www.official-documents.gov.uk (04/02/08) produced 638 documents with diverse subjects such as modernising education and training for over-16s; modernising our procurement of criminal legal aid; modernising the Right to Buy; modernising medical careers; modernising marine fisheries management; and modernising our service delivery footprint. A search on the Department of Health website (04/02/08) produced more than 500 results, including: NHS Modernisation Agency; NHS Modernisation Board; modernisation of A&E departments; workforce modernisation; modernisation fund; modernisation of pathology services; modernising radiography; Local Modernisation Reviews; the modernisation agenda in social care; and that a 'fair and affordable pay rise is part and parcel of modernisation'. It also helpfully suggested 'also try building upgrading'.

Finlayson (2003, ch 3) provides one of the most detailed explorations of modernisation. Dictionaries, rather unhelpfully, define the word 'modernisation' in thoroughly tautological terms. Finlayson points to a number of competing interpretations of New Labour's meaning of modernisation: adopting a Thatcherite agenda; a simple continuation, perhaps culmination, of the party reforms first attempted by Gaitskell; and an empty term hiding the single sin of having nothing to say. However, he adds that modernisation is a word that attempts to structure thinking and action. It can be understood in three ways: its rhetorical function, its concrete reference and its deployment as a strategy of governance (2003, pp 66-7).

According to 6 and Peck (2004a, pp 3-5), the term is used to describe a vast array of activities. Policy analysts might treat this term as the petty flotsam of political rhetoric, a matter of no great consequence. This would be an unwise approach due to the importance of political language and rhetoric. Modernisation is not some general slogan used to describe the whole New Labour project. Rather, having been first used to brand the reform of the party in opposition, it quickly became a specific term for the changes demanded by New Labour in the organisation of the public sector. From 1998 onwards, modernisation has become the preferred noun for New Labour's reform of client-facing, service-orientated parts of government. 6 and Peck explore four programmatic texts – DH (1997, 1998a); DETR (1998); Cabinet Office (1999) – but nowhere are we presented with a definition of modernisation. None of the papers sets out generic principles from which specific applications to its own field can be derived. Each presents its own concerns separately, and although there are indeed important overlapping themes, they are left implicit. None sets out the problems.

Flynn (2007, p 38) states that 'modernisation' meant many different things. Scourfield (2006, p 19) claims that identifying a single, clear and coherent philosophy in modernisation is problematic – it is characterised by its pragmatism. Toynbee and Walker (2001, p 202) write that, as a theme, 'modernisation' wafted in and out of hearing range, audible when the forces of conservatism were being excoriated at Labour's 1999 conference, faint whenever it was seeking to pacify Middle England. Never explicitly defined, it shaded into democratisation, meaning an effort to breathe new life into participative government by bringing its institutions physically or figuratively closer to the people. The usually acute Timmins (2001, p 584) states that modernisation included making services more responsive, more pleasant and quicker to use. Finlayson (2003, p 77) comments on Blair's speech to the 1997 Labour Party conference: 'You can have the education revolution, the health revolution, the welfare revolution. But it means hard choices. It means us all getting involved. And it means modernisation … [as] perhaps the clearest statement of what modernisation means'. (I would hate to see the most opaque statement!)

In addition to the unclear definition, it is far from clear whether the term has any coherence. Finlayson (2003, pp 77–8) remarks that modernisation seems to be a kind of code word for what needs to be done, and whatever the education and health system require can be called modernisation. Many things can be, and have been, 'modernised': capital modernisation; payment systems in the NHS; licensing laws; the post office; Home Office; Training Standards Officers; and even gambling – 'The main thrust of the modernisation of the duty structure is to change the way of calculating the amount of general betting duty' (Finlayson, 2003, pp 77–8). But the most large-scale and directed 'modernisations' are in the primary public services of health, welfare and education (Finlayson, 2003, p 92). Any institution or practice that is perceived as not working perfectly is held to require 'modernisation' (p 96) (the compilation of intelligence dossiers, for example?). This appears to suggest that modernisation is a catch-all term that can be applied to any situation. There is, to New Labour, a consistency and coherence across policy areas; the way in which themes repeat themselves is also indicative of New Labour's tendency to justify a diverse range of actions through an unstable rhetorical trope such as 'modernisation'. This means that developing a single theory or single perspective on New Labour is probably a mistake (Finlayson, 2003, p 10). Yet Finlayson claims that because the same word is used to describe constitutional reform, changes to the police force, health service and education system, it seems that some sort of coherent approach is underpinning policy (2003, p 67).

It is possible to examine a number of different approaches to modernisation. The first approach is that modernisation simply means *improvement*. The term 'modern' is a redundant qualifier, adding emphasis as 'doubleplusgood' in George Orwell's *1984*. Blair (Foreword, quoted in Kelly, 1999, p 2) states that we are determined to deliver our programme of modernisation and reform – applying our values to improve Britain. Consider whether the term could be removed without altering the meaning in the following: 'Best, modern clinical practice is identified' (DH, 2000, p 59); 'modernised and more accountable professional regulatory arrangements' (p 91); 'making NHS dentistry a modern and truly national service again' (p 102); and 'government services must use the best and most modern techniques' (Jack Cunningham, Minister for the Cabinet Office, quoted in Cabinet Office, 1999).

Second, modernisation is a *process*. Modernised things are technically advanced, they make use of the latest information and communication technologies (ICT) and are networked, lean, flexible, efficient and knowledge friendly (Finlayson, 2003, p 68). There will be no slowing down on the pace of change. If anything, the speed of the modernisation programme will be accelerated. By definition, modernisation has to be a continuous process – improvement is not just reached and then achieved. Modernisation and improvement have to be a permanent drive to ensure that things are really getting better (Blair, quoted in Kelly, 1999, p 1). According to Gould (1998, p xii), his book is called *The unfinished revolution* because modernisation can never be completed; it is a process that never ends; the need to change will never cease. In other words, modernisation is a state of permanent revolution.

Third, it is an updated version of *Croslandite revisionism*, separating means and ends. According to John Prescott, former Deputy Prime Minister, New Labour represents 'traditional values in a modern setting' (quoted in Finlayson, 2003, p 2). In Blair's article in 1996, he saw the task as determining 'how the enduring values of 1945 can be applied to the very different world of today'. The 1997 Labour Party manifesto stated that the policies of 1997 'cannot be those of 1947 or 1967, but our values are the same' (quoted in Powell, 2002, p 12).

Fourth, it represents *private sector methods for the public sector*. Finlayson (2003, p 89) writes that Blairism looks to cutting-edge management and business theory for its guidelines on what is modern. Ultimately, the objects on which modernisation will be imposed are state institutions. Where Wilson's form of modernisation entailed the full introduction of the state into the economy and engaged with society, Blairite modernisation affects the public only in as much as they (when at school, in hospital or on welfare) are the 'customers' of public services. Blairism seeks to modernise the state by bringing it into line with business best practice. For example, the role of public–private partnership (PPP)/private finance initiative (PFI) is not simply private capital, but private sector methods and culture (Finlayson, 2003, p 97). In his introduction to the White Paper on modernising government (Cabinet Office, 1999), Jack Cunningham, Minister for the Cabinet Office, wrote that government services must use the best and most modern techniques, to match the best of the private sector. Cunningham later claimed that people are exercising choice and demanding higher quality. In the private sector, service standards and service delivery have improved as a result. People are rightly demanding a better service not just from the private sector, but from the public sector too (Cabinet Office, 1999, p 10; cf the discussion of 'fit1' that follows).

Fifth, modernisation is a measure of fit in terms of *time* (fit1). According to the Department of Social Security (1998, p iv), the welfare system has not kept pace with change; it has failed to keep pace with profound economic, social and political changes. The machinery of welfare has the air of yesteryear (DSS, 1998, p 9). Modern services have to meet the changing context of changing work, working women, changing families, an ageing society, people with disabilities, increased individual and collective welfare provision and rising expectations (DSS, 1998, pp 13-16). Similarly, the National Health Service (NHS) is too much the product of the era in which it was born. In its buildings, its ways of working, its very culture, the NHS bears too many of the hallmarks of the 1940s, while the rest of society has moved on. On 5 July 1948, the day the NHS was founded, the high street banks were open between 10am and 3pm. Today the public has 24-hour access to banking services. In 1948 women formed a third of the workforce. Today they make up nearly half. We now live in a diverse, multi-cultural society. Family lives, social structures and public expectations have also moved on. In 1948 deference and hierarchy defined the relationships between citizens and services. In an era of mass production, needs were regarded as identical and preferences were ignored. Today, successful services thrive on their ability to respond to the individual needs of their customers. We live in a consumer age. Services have to be tailor-made not mass-produced, geared to the needs of users not the convenience of producers. The NHS has been too slow to change its ways of working to meet modern patient expectations for fast, convenient, 24-hour, personalised care. Staff efforts to modernise services all too often founder on the fault lines in the NHS that are a hangover from the world of 1948 (DH, 2000, p 26). Blair (2002, pp iv, 9) wrote that it was time to acknowledge that the 1945 settlement was a product of its time and we must not be a prisoner to it. Our task is to give modern expression to our values in a time of unprecedented aspirations, declining deference and increasing choice, of diverse needs and greater personal autonomy. This is a major theme in Giddens' work (1998, pp 31-2): Britain lags behind other industrial nations in various key aspects, with crusty old institutions that have lost their relevance to the modern world. There is now a new individualism, associated with the retreat of tradition and custom, where all of us have to live in a more open and reflective manner than previous generations. Modernisation is presented as a necessary response to both an ever more demanding public and a fast-changing world (Scourfield, 2007, p 110).

Sixth, modernisation represents a second sense of fit between *problems and solutions* (fit2). According to Finlayson (2003), modernisation serves as a mechanism for diagnosing errors in the organisation and management of public services and for establishing the cure. It follows that different solutions are required for different problems, and so if the problems in healthcare, education and local government are different, then the solutions (see the themes below) will also differ.

The elements or themes of modernisation are also elusive. For example, *Modernising government* (Cabinet Office, 1999) has six elements (services 24/7; joined-up government; a new drive to remove unnecessary regulation; electronic delivery; incentives for staff; and a new focus on delivery: p 6), three aims (ensuring that policy making is more joined up and strategic; making sure that public service users, not providers, are the focus, by matching services more closely to people's lives; and delivering public services that are high quality and efficient: p 6) and five key components (policy making will be forward-looking; responsive public services; quality public services; information age government; public services will be valued, not denigrated: p 7). Finlayson (2003, p 90) regards *Modernising government* as a long-term project, which will transform the face of public services: putting citizens first; joined-up government (JUG); and information age approaches (www.cabinet-office.gov.uk/moderngov/index.htm). The chapter headings of the White Paper on modernising government (Cabinet Office, 1999) are themselves an indication of what modernisation means: 'Vision', 'Policy making',

'Responsive public services', 'Quality public services' and 'Information age government (consumers not producers)'.

A number of commentators have suggested various themes. Perri 6 (1998) suggested that tomorrow's government would be based on three principles: prevention (rather than cure); integration (joined-up government); and intervening to change cultures. Finlayson (2003, p 91) suggests JUG and the delivery of responsive public services.

According to Poole and Mooney (2006, pp 566-7), we can hypothesise that while throughout Britain New Labour has presented the 'modernisation' of public services in terms of 'what works', 'best value', 'partnership' and 'consumer choice', this is something of a smokescreen for its managerialist and privatisation-centred agenda. Scourfield (2007, pp 109-10) views much of the blueprint for New Labour's modernisation programme as coming from Clinton's administrations of the 1990s, particularly in respect of linking rights to responsibilities and to the notion of active welfare systems. The principle of 'person-centredness' is key to modernisation. According to Flynn (2007, p 38), detailed diagnoses of problems in local government, the Civil Service and the NHS varied. The solutions followed a pattern of trying to assert control over organisations that were seen variously as too bureaucratic, too professionally dominated and in some cases self-interested and self-serving. The methods used were chosen eclectically. 'Modernisation' of government was closely connected to the modernisation of the party and especially the abandonment of the commitment to public ownership. It was also about the methods of service delivery and service design, about getting access to services through the internet and call centres.

Blair (2001) stated that it was on the basis of sustained investment, a frank appraisal of the good and the bad in our public services and a non-ideological approach to reform that we were embarking on the most ambitious programme of change since the 1940s. Investment was being backed with reform around four key principles: high national standards and full accountability; devolution to the front line to encourage diversity and local creativity; flexibility of employment so that staff were better able to deliver modern public services; and the promotion of alternative providers and greater choice. All four principles have one goal – to put the consumer first. Blair (2002) gave four slightly different key principles of reform: national minimum standards; earned autonomy; the reform of public service professionals; and greater choice.

6 and Peck (2004a, 2004b) have given the most detailed exploration of the themes of modernisation. The New Labour signature in public

management has 10 key commitments: inspection; central standard setting; area-based initiatives; coordination and integration; devolution but limited decentralisation; earned autonomy as a settlement between centralism and decentralisation; an extended role for private capital; a modest increase in citizen obligations; access; and e-government. They claim that it is the combination – rather than the mere presence – of these features that is distinctive (6 and Peck, 2004a, p 3), and that some elements can be found in other countries' reform programmes, but not necessarily together. What is distinctive is the particular combination of commitments. Moreover, they claim, New Labour's signature in public management has evolved since 1997 (p 15).

6 and Peck (2004b, pp 90-1) write that there are five basic themes and elements in almost every area of New Labour's public management: regulation (inspection, central standard setting and evidence-based policy); structure (phase I: 1998–2001, area-based initiatives, horizontal coordination, devolution and limited decentralisation; phase II: 2000 to date, earned autonomy and local planning); sector (expanded role for the private sector and compacts); citizenship (citizen's obligations and participation); and interface (access and e-government). This is a slightly different list of 15 different strands of reform (6 and Peck, 2004b, p 83), but actually adds up to 11 in phase I and 13 in phase II.

Newman (2001, p 35) writes that the initiatives linked to Labour's modernisation programme tend to draw on a mix of approaches – delegation and central control, long-term capacity building and short-term targets – producing tensions in the process of institutional change. Modernisation was a label attached to a wide range of institutional reforms, including those of government, party and the political process itself (Newman, 2001, p 40), and is a loose term applied to widely different programmes of reform or restructuring (p 48). In relation to both health and welfare, the meaning of modernisation went through subtle shifts as the programme evolved, with further cycles of modernisation launched in each year of Labour's term of office (p 53). Modernising public services was based on a series of very different models of change, with a number of emergent tensions within the implementation of the modernisation agenda (pp 95-7). Newman concludes that at first sight it seems possible to map different elements of Labour's programme of modernisation as 'belonging' to a particular model in terms of its dominant focus or orientation. But it quickly becomes apparent how different modes of governance might coexist within discrete policy areas. For example, the centrally driven modernisation of services such as health, education and criminal justice belongs predominantly to the rational goal model, but it also includes elements of the open system and self-governance models where services are linked to 'cross-cutting' initiatives, policy innovation or the development of new forms of collaboration with users or communities (Newman, 2001, p 164).

Analysing the modernisation of the welfare state

There are many problems in exploring the dependent variable of welfare change (Powell and Hewitt, 2002; Powell, 2004; Clasen and Siegel, 2007). Bonoli and Powell (2004) and Powell and Barrientos (2004) have examined policy change with reference to discourse, values, policy goals, policy mechanisms and outcomes. Powell and Hewitt (2002, p 67) searched for welfare change in terms of aims, mechanisms, inputs, outputs and outcomes. However, any analysis of change must cover the two basic dimensions of what, and how much.

The 'what' dimension is examined in terms of the themes of modernisation (see above), while the 'how much' dimension is explored in terms of Hall's (1993) orders of change. Hall (1993) presents three central variables of policy making: the overarching goals that guide public policy in a particular field; the techniques or policy instruments used to attain those goals; and the precise settings of those instruments. First order change on levels or settings (for example, to the annual budget) tend to occur frequently. Second order change of techniques or instruments and settings (for example, the development of 'cash limits' for public spending control in 1976) occur less frequently. Third order changes involving simultaneous change in all three components of goals, techniques and settings (for example, from Keynesianism to monetarism) are rare. Following Kuhn (1962), first and second order change can be seen as cases of 'normal policy making', namely, of a process that adjusts policy without challenging the overall terms of a given policy paradigm. Third order change, by contrast, is likely to reflect a very different process, marked by radical changes in the overarching terms of policy discourse associated with a 'paradigm shift'. If first and second order changes preserve the broad continuities usually found in patterns of policy, third order change is often a more disjunctive process associated with periodic discontinuities in policy. This framework can be criticised, however. It is possible that step-order changes in budgets rather than incremental change may be more important than third order change. There is no place for policy outcomes, and it is possible that a radically healthier country might be achieved by large first order change, but not by third order change. Nevertheless, it is a useful heuristic framework for analysis.

In other chapters in this book the contributors examine the content and extent of change. They explore which of the elements of modernisation has resonance for their area, and the extent or 'order' of change – which sectors saw the greatest degree of change? They also examine change over time with reference to the terms of the government – was reform a fairly continuous event, or was it concentrated in certain periods? Analyses of Thatcherism claim that it was the third (1987–92) term that was the most radical (see Powell and Hewitt, 2002). New Labour has served three terms; however, the first and third may be termed 'short'. Toynbee and Walker (2001, p 3) claim that in a sense the Labour government did not start until April 1999, when Conservative Party spending ended and Gordon Brown's own spending plans came in. Similarly, Blair's signal that he would not serve a full third term in 2005 arguably undermined his authority, and slowed down modernisation. Did later reforms build on earlier ones, or were they changes in course meaning that later reforms conflicted with earlier ones (cf Greener, 2004)?

The contributors also give a brief assessment of future policy direction – would Brown or Cameron carry on the Blair legacy (cf Giddens, 2007, ch 2)? Some commentators such as Jenkins (2007) use the term 'Blatcherism' to imply that there are few policy differences between Blair and Thatcher. Are we now in a period of 'Camrownism' (Cameron/Brown)? In an article in the *Daily Telegraph* in 2007, David Cameron stated that New Labour had expended a huge amount of time and energy abolishing Conservative reforms in their first term, before reinstating many of them after the 2001 General Election. He claimed that he would keep many of Blair's flagship reforms, including city academies, foundation hospitals and payment by results in the NHS (*Daily Telegraph*, 'We will keep some of Blair's reforms, insists Cameron', 27/1/07, p 14). Similarly, Brown has delivered his clearest endorsement yet of the Blairite agenda of choice, competition and the use of the private sector to improve public services. In a letter to the Confederation of British Industry (CBI) he referred to 'continued modernisation' (quoted in Timmins, 2007). His first speech to the Labour Party conference as Prime Minister used a number of Blairite themes: 'as the world changes so we must change too'; crime and disorder policy is 'to both punish and prevent'; 'rights and responsibilities'; 'those who work hard and play by the rules'; and a NHS 'personal to you' (Brown, 2007a).

The chapters that follow examine the main service sectors (the NHS, housing, social security, social care, education and criminal justice), major overarching themes (the social investment state, risk, conditionality, privatisation and choice), the different phases of New Labour, and a comparison with 'Die Neue Mitte' ('New Centre') of the German Social Democrats. This allows the claim of the 1997 election manifesto that New Labour would be 'the party of welfare reform' (Powell, 1999, p 8) to be examined. Will the Blair legacy be a 'modernised welfare state'?

References

6, P. (1998) 'Problem-solving government', in I. Hargreaves and I Christie (eds) *Tomorrow's politics*, London: Demos.

6, P. and Peck, E. (2004a) 'Modernisation: the ten commitments of New Labour's approach to public management', *International Public Management Journal*, vol 7, no 1, pp 1–18.

6, P. and Peck, E. (2004b) 'New Labour's modernization in the public sector: a neo-Durkheimian approach and the case of mental health services', *Public Administration*, vol 82, no 1, pp 83–108.

Blair, T. (1993) 'Why modernisation matters', *Renewal*, vol 1, no 4.

Blair, T. (1996) *New Britain. My vision of a young country*, London: Fourth Estate.

Blair, T. (1998) *The Third Way*, London: Fabian Society.

Blair, T. (2001) Prime Minister's speech on public service reform, 16 October.

Blair, T. (2002) *The courage of our convictions: Why reform of the public services is the route to social justice*, Fabian Ideas 603, London: Fabian Society.

Blair, T. and Schroeder, G. (1999) *The Third Way*, London: Labour Party.

Bonoli, G. and Powell, M. (2004) 'One third way or several?', in J. Lewis and R. Surender (eds) *Welfare state change: Towards a Third Way?*, Oxford: Oxford University Press.

Brown, G. (2007a) Speech to Labour Party conference, 24 September (www.labour.org).

Brown, G. (2007b) New Year message, 30 December (www.pm.gov.uk/output/Page14099.asp).

Cabinet Office (1999) *Modernising government*, London: The Stationery Office.

Clasen, J. and Siegel, N. (2007) *Investigating welfare state change: The 'dependent variable problem' in comparative analysis*, Cheltenham: Edward Elgar.

DETR (Department of the Environment, Transport and the Regions) (1998) *Modern local government*, London: The Stationery Office.

DH (Department of Health) (1997) *The New NHS: Modern, dependable*, London: The Stationery Office.

DH (1998a) *Modernising social services*, London: The Stationery Office.

DH (1998b) *Modernising mental health services*, London: The Stationery Office.

DH (2000) *The NHS Plan: A plan for investment, a plan for reform*, London: The Stationery Office.

DSS (Department of Social Security) (1998) *New ambitions for our country*, London: The Stationery Office.

Fairclough, N. (2000) *New Labour, new language?*, London: Routledge.

Finlayson, A. (2003) *Making sense of New Labour*, London: Lawrence and Wishart.

Flynn, N. (2007) *Public sector management* (5th edn), London: Sage Publications.

Giddens, A. (1998) *The Third Way: The renewal of social democracy*, Cambridge: Polity Press.

Giddens, A. (2007) *Over to you, Mr Brown*, Cambridge: Polity Press.

Gould, P. (1998) *The unfinished revolution: How the modernisers saved the Labour Party*, London: Little, Brown and Co.

Greener, I. (2004) 'The three moments of New Labour's health policy discourse', *Policy & Politics*, vol 32, pp 303-16.

Hall, P.A. (1993) 'Policy paradigms, social learning and the state: the case of economic policy making in Britain', *Comparative Politics*, vol 25, no 3, pp 275-96.

HMT (Her Majesty's Treasury) (1998) *Modern public services*, HM Treasury and Cabinet Office, London: The Stationery Office.

Hoggett, P. (1990) *Modernisation, political strategy and the welfare state*, Bristol: SAUS Publications, University of Bristol.

Jenkins, P. (2007) *Thatcher and sons: A revolution in three acts*, Harmondsworth: Penguin.

Kelly, G. (ed) (1999) *Is New Labour working?*, London: Fabian Society.

Kuhn, T. (1962) *The structure of scientific revolutions*, Chicago, IL: Chicago University Press.

Labour Party (2001) *New ambitions for our country* (election manifesto), London: Labour Party.

Labour Party (2005) *Britain: Forward not back* (election manifesto), London: Labour Party.

Lowe, R. (1997) 'The core executive, modernization and the creation of PESC, 1960-64', *Public Administration*, vol 75, no 4, pp 601-15.

Marr, A. (2007) *A history of modern Britain*, London: Macmillan.

Miller, C. (2004) *Producing welfare*, Basingstoke: Palgrave Macmillan.

Newman, J. (2001) *Modernising governance. New Labour, policy and society*, London: Sage Publications.

Poole, L. and Mooney, G. (2006) 'Privatising education in Scotland? New Labour, modernization and "public services"', *Critical Social Policy*, vol 26, no 3, pp 562-86.

Powell, M. (ed) (1999) *New Labour, new welfare state? The 'third way' in British social policy*, Bristol: The Policy Press.

Powell, M. (ed) (2002) *Evaluating New Labour's welfare reforms*, Bristol: The Policy Press.

Powell, M. (2004) 'In search of the dependent variable: welfare change in Europe', Paper presented at COST A15 Conference, Nantes, 21-22 May.

Powell, M. and Barrientos, A. (2004) 'The route map of the Third Way', in S. Hale, W. Leggett and L. Martell (eds) *The Third Way and beyond*, Manchester: Manchester University Press, pp 9-26.

Powell, M. and Hewitt, M. (2002) *Welfare state and welfare change*, Buckingham: Open University Press.

Scourfield, P. (2006) 'What matters is what works: how discourses of modernisation have both silenced and limited debate on domiciliary care for older people', *Critical Social Policy*, vol 26, no 1, pp 5-30.

Scourfield, P. (2007) 'Social care and the modern citizen: client, consumer, service user, manager and entrepreneur', *British Journal of Social Work*, vol 37, pp 107-22.

Timmins, N. (2001) *The five giants*, London: HarperCollins.

Timmins, N. (2007) 'Blair's reforms win Brown's backing', *Financial Times*, 7 June.

Toynbee, P. and Walker, D. (2001) *Did things get better?*, Harmondsworth: Penguin.

TWO

The NHS after 10 years of New Labour

Calum Paton

Introduction

With the accession to the premiership of Gordon Brown, the record of New Labour under Tony Blair's premiership from 1997 to 2007 can be viewed in perspective. As regards health and the NHS, Brown has affirmed the importance of services to suit the patient (Labour Party conference speech, 24 September 2007; Speech at King's College London, 7 January 2008), and therefore at one level is continuing the focus on 'the consumer'. Some of the institutions created by the Blair reforms to the NHS – including foundation trusts, about which Brown was initially sceptical – will continue. But the emphasis has changed slightly, with less ideologically based policy discourse (about 'markets' and 'choice' as understood by neoliberal economists), although the policy of giving budgets for care directly to individuals in particular areas of health as well as in social care (seen as a totemic Blairite policy) was recently re-emphasised by Brown.

We can put New Labour's health policy – from Blair or Brown – into context by considering what 'modernisation' has actually meant. It has been the generic term applied by New Labour to diverse policy areas, where different things have been happening on the ground despite a generic New Labour orientation to applying the tenets of neoliberalism in social policy as well as wider areas. 'Modernisation' has had political utility for signalling and symbolic purposes: it is part-technical or a descriptive term and part-ideological or a prescriptive term, and New Labour leaders have been able to shift ground from one to the other as has suited them. Where change is essentially non-ideological, or where New Labour policy varies only incrementally from its predecessors, this prosaic fact can be disguised by the rhetorical poetry of 'technological modernisation' (which is essentially as phoney as Harold Wilson's 'white heat of the technological revolution' in 1964). And yet where change is ideologically rooted in a manner unappealing to mainstream Labour supporters (as with the neoliberal drift of New Labour's later health policy, towards 2008), the actual ideology can be disguised in the rhetorical gush of 'necessary modernisation', thus redefining opponents left and right (but mostly left) as 'old-fashioned' or 'conservative'.

6 and Peck's (2004) 'themes of modernisation' (see Table 2.1) may be interpreted in this way, although at the outset it must be stressed that their framework is dated: it fails to capture the neoliberal hard edge of later New Labour, with all the 10 themes concerned either with centrally mandated policies (including the 'extended role for private capital', which is centrally controlled and administered, and including 'devolution', which is centrally determined and adjudicated) or with earlier 'Third Way' themes (such as 'coordination and integration' between agencies and 'area-based initiatives'). Furthermore, most of the themes are, if anything, more 'Brownite' than 'Blairite' – as with 'inspection', 'standard setting', 'earned autonomy', 'access' and 'e-government' – reflecting the fact that Brown drove most domestic policy from the Treasury between 1997 and 2007, with Blairite 'outriders', such as Alan Milburn in health (1999–2003), operating as dilettantes at the edges of policy, as well as reflecting the fact that 6 and Peck's framework misses the ideological thrust of the last Blair years as he sought to redefine his legacy in ever more neoliberal terms.

In terms of the Blair legacy as regards the 'new public management' (NPM) in health, I would argue that it is a term best replaced in this case with a tailor-made neologism – 'the new public administration'. While some of the classic tenets of NPM (Hood, 1991) are aspirationally present in (some of) New Labour's policy statements, NPM on its own cannot characterise either the policy complexity or the administrative and managerial cultures spawned in the NHS. There are more examples of overloaded public bureaucracy than of 'business-like management', and these are part of the face of Blairism – the face Blair did not see as his self-image when he looked in the mirror to rehearse speeches about the 'forces of conservatism' (1999) and the 'scars on his back' associated with trying to reform public services.

New Labour arrived at the Department of Health in 1997 pledging to 'abolish the internal market' (long since reversed, see below). They had an ambivalent attitude, however, to NPM in a number of ways. They continued the 'managerialist' institutions that they inherited from the Conservatives, such as the 'purchaser–provider split', and even extended the 'total purchasing pilot' projects of the mid-1990s into primary care groups (later trusts). Yet they supplanted the last surviving pretensions of NPM towards diminished political interference and devolution of responsibility to and down the management chain. Many of the senior managers who had been close to the implementation of Conservative policy now became close to New Labour (and arguably were partly responsible for the eventual re-emergence of the 'market NHS', as they fed upwards, along with special advisers, the view that 'there was no alternative' in pursuit of efficiency). Yet by 2000 the 'central admin' culture was more compelling than it had ever been in the 1990s. And the apotheosis of central command came with the merging of the jobs of the Permanent Secretary to the Department of Health with that of the Chief Executive of the NHS, when Nigel Crisp was appointed in October 2000, removing the last vestiges at central level of Sir Roy Griffiths' NPM reforms set out in 1983.

During the period from 2000 to 2006, the new public administration was characterised by the phenomenon of 'l'état, c'est moi', with the 'moi' in this period variously and confusingly being either the Prime Minister (Blair) or the Chancellor of the Exchequer (Brown), with only one Health Secretary (Alan Milburn, 1999–2003) muscling in on the 'moi'. Instead of the Weberian tramlines of traditional 'public administration', we have had directives, targets and 'standards' that are both centrally set and almost (were it not for New Labour's earnestness in believing its own rhetoric) whimsically changing. This is not just a rhetorical point: changing targets – and, for example, separate and often inconsistent targets for purchasers/commissioners of care, on the one hand, and providers such as hospitals, on the other hand – have specifically affected both behaviour and outputs/outcomes in local health economies across England (much of this, although not all, is an English analysis).

The high noon of Alan Milburn's centralism (1999–2002 – when he thought or pretended that he was beginning to devolve) was, on my reading, the apotheosis of Thatcherite centralism as described by Jenkins (1995). And Brown, 'son' of Thatcher (Jenkins, 2006), is likely to go further. Furthermore, Chancellor Brown was much more enthusiastic about the private finance initiative (PFI) in health than its godfather, Norman Lamont, and PFI requires central political and bureaucratic control to impose contracts and payback on local health economies.

The New Labour approach, especially from 2002 on, was to preach (and seemingly believe in) what was called 'devolution' (actually de-concentration, not even decentralisation) – for example, the misleadingly named *Shifting the balance of power to the frontline* (DH, 2002). Yet this abolished the 'meso'-level regional institutions that were the only way centralism could be mitigated while at the same time health services could be coherently planned or even steered. Thus Milburn's centralism really came into its own at the very time he thought he had recanted on the road to Damascus for his centralist past.

New Labour's approach to the NHS

This section reviews NHS 'modernisation' using the themes suggested by 6 and Peck (see Table 2.1 below) and the additional theme of 'neoliberalism in the public sector'.

Table 2.1: Modernisation themes in health/NHS reform

Area	Health/NHS reform
Inspection	NICE/CHI/CG, CHAI and HCC; unified governance; Monitor; CHRE; targets etc (internal inspection); standards; Audit Commission
Central standard setting	Move from targets to standards; mix of national and local 'standards' (and targets); myth of 'external assurance of internal control'
Area-based initiatives	HAZ; Sure Start (including health); StBoP/PCTs; targets on inequality etc
Coordination and integration	'Joint commissioning'; otherwise *dis*integration; decline of coordinated planning
Devolution but limited decentralisation	Four UK national health services; decentralisation of responsibility, not power; market versus decentralisation; PFI versus decentralisation
Earned autonomy as a settlement between centralism and decentralisation	On paper: FTs; star ratings (three-star trusts had more freedom on paper); reality of Monitor and FTs; rhetoric of decentralisation but reality of centralism, for example, 'new model contract' from Department of Health in 2007
An extended vote for private capital?	Yes. PFI has increased under New Labour
A modest increase in citizen obligations	Mostly rhetoric, concerning rationing by PCTs of services treating self-caused ill health
Access	– Targets but most targets are utilitarian rather than egalitarian – Symbolic things like walk-in centres and NHS Direct
E-government	NPfIT; NHS information centre

Notes: NICE = National Institute for Clinical Excellence; CHI = Commission for Health Improvement (later CHAI); CG = clinical governance; CHAI = Commission for Healthcare Audit and Inspection (later HCC); HCC = Healthcare Commission; CHRE = Council for Healthcare Regulatory Excellence; HAZ = Health Action Zone; StBoP = *Shifting the balance of power*; PCT = primary care trust; PFI = private finance initiative; FT = foundation trust; NPfIT = National Programme for Information Technology.

Inspection, central standard setting and earned autonomy

Soon after New Labour's election victory in 1997, the government set out a vision for the NHS which combined local collaboration (packaged as part of the 'Third Way' – allegedly neither hierarchy nor market) with increasingly external inspection (DH, 1997). At the national level, the National Institute for Clinical Excellence (NICE) (now the National Institute for Health and Clinical Excellence, having absorbed the Health Development Agency) was to set standards for care. At this time, NICE's 'standards' basically meant recommending to the Secretary of State for Health whether or not particular drugs, treatments or technologies should be provided on the NHS. Additionally, 'national service frameworks' were to set out appropriate guidelines, clinical pathways and (less frequently) protocols for delivering services, for example, for stroke, coronary heart disease and mental ill health. At the local level, health providers were to use 'clinical governance' – defined by Scottish Health Minister at the time, Sam Galbraith, as 'corporate governance of the clinical process' – to assure quality of care as well as compliance with such national guidance.

The newly created Commission for Health Improvement (CHI) would inspect local quality and compliance. CHI was initially seen by many, including its first chief executive, as being in the peer review mould, that is, facilitative and developmental, but by the time it mutated into the Commission for Healthcare Audit and Inspection (CHAI), and later the Healthcare Commission (HCC) (soon to be the Care and Quality Commission, which also took over the inspection of social care and mental health from other, outgoing agencies), it had become an 'external inspector'. This approach was in line with the growing trend to 'regulation of the new market' in the English NHS, with the return to the market approach prefigured in 2002 and implemented from 2006 onwards.

The idea was that a 'market' required – in order to strengthen the 'invisible hand' – the visible fist of external regulation rather than a more collaborative approach to compliance, as with the 'Third Way'.

As well as clinical standards, the government (especially after 1999) relied on national targets for a whole range of service aspects, most famously waiting times. These were successful in many respects (Alvarez-Rosete et al, 2005), but were also criticised for creating perverse incentives. For example, it was alleged that hospitals admitted patients out of Accident and Emergency (A&E) into wards so that they could comply with the 'target' that 98% of patients should spend less than four hours in A&E. There is no direct evidence that this happened (the indirect evidence comes from rising admissions during the same period, which could be explained in many alternative ways), but it may be that clinical priorities were distorted at the margin (that is, admitting easier cases within the target waiting time rather than treating other cases, already to be seen within the target time, even sooner).

In terms of inspecting these 'standards', there was a panoply of 'command and control' measures, operating via parallel hierarchies for different targets (which frequently failed to communicate and be 'joined up') from the Department of Health through the regional, then strategic, health authorities (SHAs), to local NHS provider trusts and primary care trusts (PCTs) (the bodies which purchased and commissioned care from the NHS trusts, mostly hospitals). One of New Labour's mantras was 'joined-up' policy, but the culture of the bureaucracy (Department of Health) and the breathless, short-termist nature of targets made this very difficult. The SHAs were often left as mere 'postboxes', monitoring performance rather than managing it, sometimes asking the impossible of local providers, with confusingly different targets for PCTs and NHS trusts which made local collaboration to achieve meaningful outcomes difficult.

The 'star ratings' system (at first internally administered and later handled by the HCC, although the regulator did not set the rules: it assessed against a governmentally defined amalgam of 'core targets') was used inter alia for granting 'earned autonomy' to the better (that is, 'three star') performers. But this was small beer: small amounts of capital could be used without direct SHA control. Given the 'apparatchik' culture of performance management (using military terminology, for example, the weekly 'sitrep' – situation report – for trusts facing 'breaches' of the target rules, to the extent of even one solitary patient for example waiting longer than the inpatient, outpatient or emergency waiting time target allowed), earned autonomy was mostly rhetoric.

Perhaps the later policy of foundation trusts (FTs) (passed in parliament in 2003 but only implemented meaningfully from 2005 onwards) can be seen as the apotheosis of 'earned autonomy', but FTs – like other NHS trusts – depend for their income on PCTs, and their 'regulation' (or arguably close control) by Monitor, the FT 'regulator', is just as tight as the regulation of NHS trusts (without foundation status) by the traditional bureaucracy. Additionally, the Department of Health and SHAs create frameworks for implementation of policy that constrain nominally 'free' actors such as FTs. For example, the 'new model contract' of 2007 mandated sliding scales of payment for 'over-performing' hospitals (that is, those who saw, or had to see, more patients than the intended contractual limits of PCTs).

Later (in 2005) the (quantitative) target regime was allegedly replaced by a regime of wider, qualitative standards, with a mix of national and local standards to be developed against which providers and commissioners would be assessed. This was a slight change of emphasis, however, rather than a radical departure. National targets remained (only 'reduced' in number by failing to count already-extant targets, now assumed to be met and still policed). What is more, local 'standards' were justified as allowing local flexibility in making priorities (and arguably a means of measuring 'value added' rather than absolute benchmarks, as in education), but this did not gel with the new inspection regime that assumed a common national framework.

In terms of inspection, one should also mention the Audit Commission. Like all regulators, especially in the turbulent years of the 2000s, the Commission found difficulty in disentangling 'technical audit' from the effects of NHS budgetary politics on financial regimes and actual finance. In a nutshell, the near-anarchy in contracting (and paying bills) occasioned by the ill-fated *Shifting the balance of power* (2002–06, when the small PCTs it had spawned were abolished) meant that financial regimes were of necessity imperfect (with hospitals, for example, often unable to confirm budgets until near the end of the financial year, owing to the unwillingness or inability of PCTs to confirm payment even for necessary care which they could not provide themselves outside hospital). When 'things worked out at year end', District Audit (the local arm of the Audit Commission) usually gave a clean bill of health. If things went wrong, however, District Audit might then draw attention to 'technical' shortcomings (for example, failure to set a budget on time) that were, in fact, a consequence of the politics of the contracting and budgetary process (Paton, quoted in House of Commons Select Committee on Health, 2006).

This raises a wider point, regarding the approach of external regulation of a market system (whether the Financial Services Authority for banking, or the Audit Commission and HCC for healthcare), the devil will be in both the detail and the politics surrounding the regulatory regime. Internal management of quality and financial performance may spawn 'scandals' (for example, 'Bristol' in the NHS, where poor performance in paediatric surgery was concealed), but external regulation may fall short, as with Northern Rock.

Area-based initiatives and coordination and integration

The early approach after 1997 was to focus on local 'blackspots', in line with the 'Third Way' approach derived from the conclusions of the Commission on Social Justice (1994) of eschewing national redistribution and emphasising opportunity rather than 'levelling'. The main approach was Health Action Zones (HAZs), as well as Sure Start programmes that included health, with the latter more durable than the former – although, as ever, with evaluation suggesting that they sometimes failed to reach those in greatest need.

More recently, joint commissioning by PCTs and local authorities has revived a long-playing theme which can be traced back to Barbara Castle's initiatives when Social Services Secretary from 1974 to 1976. The aim of 'joined-up' approaches to tackle area-based health and social problems is re-emphasised in the health reform programme from 2007 onwards, with 'strategic commissioning' by PCTs and others allegedly the glue which would bind together the often centripetal institutions spawned by New Labour's neoliberal lurch towards recreating a market-based mixed economy for health.

Devolution but limited decentralisation and an extended role for private capital

Political devolution within the UK has led to four divergent national health services (Greer, 2003, 2004), each with a different ethos. For example, Scotland has eschewed England's neoliberal turn, and has abolished the last institutional vestiges of the 1990s' Thatcher reforms. Wales stresses public health and local community control.

Regarding private capital, the move to a mixed public–private system is sometimes (wrongly) seen as an example of devolution of power from government. In fact PFI in health has thoroughly centralised power in the Department of Health and Treasury, with decisions as to where to allow capital investment centralised upwards from regions. PFI was a Conservative policy initially opposed (in health) by Labour in opposition before being Treasury-driven in government, with Gordon Brown the main driver.

Citizen obligation and access

A New Labour theme has been 'responsibilities as well as rights': in health, this might have translated into balancing access with obligations on citizens to keep healthy. This could well have been an authoritarian slippery slope, however, and short of 6 and Peck's debating whether George Best deserved his second liver transplant or not, has not been a New Labour theme in practice. Access has concerned both more traditional utilitarian targets (waiting times for the population, for example) and limited egalitarian ambitions (for example, targets to reduce social class health differentials in areas such as low birthweight, life expectancy and teenage pregnancy).

The record is one of improving health for most of the population except the bottom cohort, yet widening differentials. The law of inverse care – whereby those more in need access services less – still applies, and there is now debate about whether tailored 'choice' initiatives will worsen the situation or provide a mechanism whereby the poor can get to know their rights better.

New Labour's first term saw the twin initiatives of walk-in centres and NHS Direct, geared to making access more user-friendly. Risk-aversion by the latter (after publicised cases in which NHS Direct's telephone advice led to delay in necessary treatment) mean that its effect is probably peripheral, and walk-in centres have probably added a tier of access rather than substituted for another tier. The policy of 'out-of-hours' access to better quality general practitioner (GP) care – Brown's first initiative in health – reflects the perverse effects of a new GP contract in 2005 which reduced GPs' obligations to offer out-of-hours care, putting it in the hands of the PCTs, whose financial pressures at the time did not help.

E-government

This self-evident symbol of modernisation saw, in the NHS, the National Programme for Information Technology (NpfIT) (Connecting for Health), a multi-billion pound scheme to put medical and health records online and to link them. Unfortunately, major delays and cost overruns in procurement in what is the biggest public IT procurement in British history have discredited the policy, and fears about data safety following debacles in other ministries have taken the shine off this manifestation of 'technical' modernisation.

Neoliberal policies

6 and Peck omit arguably the most significant trend in New Labour's health policy – the acceptance from 2002 (DH, 2002) and especially from 2007 of neoliberal approaches to steering the NHS (for example, the assumption that providers and managers are 'knaves' rather than 'knights'; see Le Grand, 2007), and that trust and professionalism are not adequate to ensure good outcomes. Later in this chapter I discuss the implications of this in terms of the 'multiple policy streams' down which New Labour has paddled in the English NHS.

The story of the NHS under New Labour has been one of some solid achievement, partially undermined by persistent re-(dis)organisation, occasioned by a queasy mixture of ideology and media spin obsession. 6 and Peck's themes of modernisation, which they admit are not distinctive individually but which they claim make a distinctive whole, are in fact an ad hoc combination of apolitical technicalia (for example, 'e-government' and even 'inspection') and 'Third Way'-esque exhortation rather than 'delivery', ironically, a favourite New Labour word (see Barber, 2007) (for example, 'coordination and integration').

New Labour's policy mantras were 'what counts is what works', 'joined-up government' and 'SMART' (specific, measurable, achievable, relevant, timed). Yet the major structural and institutional initiatives regarding the NHS (referring respectively to architecture and incentives; see Tuohy, 2004) have been largely evidence-free and occasioned by the 'politics of the rubbish bin' (Cohen et al, 1972; Kingdon, 1984; Paton, 2006) rather than by a 'rational' approach to using means (for example, 'joined-up government') to achieve clear ends. The latest 'answer' to the NHS's problems of architecture and incentives – practice-based commissioning – is an example: it is an answer begging a clear question (Paton, 2006).

Thus 6 and Peck's claim that New Labour's modernisation themes make an original package perhaps deserves the riposte made to the apocryphal student: that his thesis was both valid and original, but that unfortunately the original bits were not valid and the valid bits were not original! The collective distinctiveness is, to this author, the distinctiveness of the contents of the rubbish bin – arguably different to that of any other bin, but not substantively or analytically interesting by virtue of this.

The nature of change

In Hall's terminology of the three orders of change (1993), many of New Labour's health policies have been 'second order' (see Table 2.2) – not challenging the goals of policy but seeking (endlessly) new instruments through which to deliver those (very general, aspirational) ends. Yet there has been a circularity as well as political plagiarism about these instruments, which leaves New Labour the restless magpie rather than the crusading eagle. Different policy instruments have emerged from the 'rubbish bin' of ideas and associated mechanisms – networked collaboration; multiple yet individually devised central directives; agent-led markets in which the 'principal', the patient, is not paramount (commissioning); principal-led markets (consumerism and choice) – at different times in the political cycle, from 1997 to 2007.

Table 2.2: Assessment of health policy against Hall's orders of change

Theme	Policy	First order	Second order	Third order
Access	Level of expenditure on the NHS (2000–08)	(Significantly) higher expenditure	'Reform to accompany investment'	(Tacitly) changing mission for NHS, influenced by political economy
Integration (limited)	The new NHS: Modern, dependable (DH, 1997)	Builds on institutions created at erc of Conservative tenure		
Inspection; access	The NHS Plan (DH, 2000)	Sets targets for increased 'investment'	New framework for codifying initiatives and investments	
Devolution (in theory)	Shifting the balance of power (StBoP) (DH, 2001)		Devolution (of responsibility, not power) to local commissioners	
'Neoliberalism'	The NHS Plan: Next steps for investment, next steps for reform (DH, 2002)		'The new market'	
Coordination	Commissioning a patient-led NHS (DH, 2005)		Reverses StBoP (DH, 2001)	
Citizen obligations	Our health, our care, our say (DH, 2006a)		Shifting to primary and community services (aspirational/normative)	
'Neoliberalism'	Health reform in England (DH, 2006b) (July 2006)		Yes	
Standard setting	The future regulation of health in England (DH, 2006c) (November 2006)		Yes	
Variety	Overall NHS/health priorities and provision	Incremental/evolutionary (some)	Targets to prioritise new outputs (outcomes)	Tripartite NHS mission: services for middle classes, pro-poor and in support of the economy

Note: Many of the second order changes are about processes rather than outputs or outcomes, for example, concerning policy instruments. The problem is that the implementation of policy has often been symbolic and/or transitory

Table 2.2 only begins to convey the constantly changing structure of the NHS. New Labour inherited the purchaser–provider split in 1997, and preserved it by creating new primary care groups (PCGs), with PCGs as purchasers of services from hospitals, mental health units and community service trusts. By 2001, 100 health authorities had been replaced by about 350 PCTs, with 29 new SHAs replacing eight regional offices – and above the SHAs, four new regional departments of health and social care (DHSCs) – as system managers or regulators (it was never made clear which). Within a year, the four DHSCs had been abolished, and almost immediately it was seen that there were far too many purchasers (PCTs) to allow coherent commissioning and purchasing and also that having 29 SHAs instead of eight regional offices diminished the capacity for strategic planning. Thus in 2005, in a major reversal, the White Paper *Commissioning a patient-led NHS* (DH, 2005) heralded the 2006 reversal of StBoP, with now around 150 PCTs and 10 SHAs. There was also a move to split off the 'provider arm' of PCTs (to solve an alleged conflict of interest whereby PCTs could otherwise favour their own internal service providers and 'starve' hospitals and external providers), which has led up to 2008 to ongoing 're-(dis)organisation' whereby more autonomous 'provider units' are created – incidentally repeating the history of the early 1990s when self-governing community NHS trusts were created. Furthermore new practice-based commissioning organisations – consisting of merged GP practices, often similar in size to the small PCTs which had just been abolished – were set up from 2006 onwards to complicate the chain further, with individual GP practices, to boot, now responsible for administering the 'Choose and Book' patient choice policy, 'rolled out' in April 2008 to allow patients to go to any accredited provider in the country (thus returning to the situation which pertained, albeit imperfectly, from 1948 to 1991).

I surmise that all this, often circular, structural chopping and changing cost upwards of £3 billion in non-recurring costs, and that the recurrent costs of more cumbersome administrative structures are more than £1 billion (Paton, 2007b). Where policy has had overtones of Hall's 'third order' change is in the more recent 'neoliberal turn'. The difference between New Labour's market pretensions in the closing Blair years and at the beginning of the original (Thatcher) internal market in 1990 was well summed up by Paul Corrigan, successively Health Secretary Alan Milburn's and Prime Minister Tony Blair's special health adviser – "they bottled out; we're not going to". Even here, however, policy is on the cusp of third and second order change: to a large measure, the neoliberal route is seen as a more radical means to the same end, that is, a publicly funded, universal NHS. The third order dimension is more indirect: neoliberal means have a habit of changing ends, being the tiger from which it is hard to dismount (Paton, 2007a). And pressure from international as well as national political economy can surreptitiously change the mission of the NHS from social equity to economic investment (Paton, 1997).

Influenced by 'postmodern' thinkers such as Geoff Mulgan, founder of the Demos think-tank and then head of Blair's Strategy and Innovations Units – described by John Humphries (2004) as the man who 'told Blair what to think' – New Labour policy makers have almost subconsciously assumed that the NHS should mirror in its organisational forms what they assume the 'postmodern organisation' to look like. But this is a psychological rather than logical approach: to play its role in a post-Fordist political economy, the NHS arguably has to be neo-Fordist (Paton, 2006). Many of the second order changes (see Table 2.2) (instruments believed to be [post]modern as opposed to of the industrial era) are subconsciously perceived as aiding third order change (a more complex mission for the NHS in a post-Fordist economy), but may in practice be a distraction and a source of great administrative overhead (Paton, 2007b).

The 'bottom line' of the story of New Labour's 10 years is: much new money, only partial achievement and limited cost effectiveness (Paton, 2006; Wanless et al, 2007). The Right use this generalisation to suggest that 'state medicine' is intrinsically flawed (they mean the NHS itself, although think-tanks such as Reform seek to have their cake and eat it here, sometimes talking of replacing the NHS with 'social insurance' and sometimes talking of improving it). But the real lesson is less ideological, or indeed arguably more friendly to the Left: more could have been done with the money if it had been spent on services.

One symptom of this was the 'deficit crisis' of 2005–07. Those who argue that the national (English) NHS deficit was a small percentage of the NHS budget miss the point. Apart from the fact that the official deficit in 2005/06 was less than half of the real operating deficit (House of Commons Select Committee on Health, 2006; Paton, 2006), the fact that so much extra money for the NHS still resulted in a widespread deficit – alongside a failure to do as much with the money as expected – was a major political own goal. It provided grist to the mill of the enemies of 'state medicine' and put the government on the defensive. Add to this the fact that Blair's leitmotif – of chastising the 'forces of conservatism' (Blair, 1999) in the public sector, causing the 'scars on his back' – raised expectations as to the dividend of reform, which, when it came, was not 'too little' but endemically confused (Paton, 2007b); and the result was to put the ideology and political creed underpinning the NHS on the defensive.

A distinctive New Labour approach?

Health policy and the NHS always provided a less likely location for the apotheosis of New Labour as a distinctive creed or practice. For as Blair rightly said (Foreword, quoted in DH, 2000), 'the NHS was the greatest act of modernization ever undertaken by a Labour government'. But as Toynbee and Walker (2005) have pointed out, New Labour has undersold its progressive achievements – and, I would argue in the case of the NHS, diminished these – by apologising for the public sector rather than bolstering it.

The overt part of the 'ideology' of New Labour was derivative in two senses. Firstly, it was not based on values per se but derived from the dictates of political strategy. Secondly, this strategy was derived from the Clinton campaigns in the US. The Blair 'project' sought to 'triangulate' between two polar opposites – defining itself by what it was not. Clinton had rejected not only Republicanism but also 'traditional tax-and-spend Democratic policy'. The Blair project rejected not only (Thatcherite) Conservatism (at least on paper) but also the social democracy of what the Blairites were the first to call Old Labour.

Anything that was to the left of New Labour or based on the institutional interests of the Labour coalition was conveniently called Old. It was a short step in the world of spin, therefore, to adopt the word 'modernisation' as New Labour's mantra. But, just as Herbert Morrison had defined socialism in the 1940s as what Labour does, 'modernisation' could now be described as everything New Labour governments do – and everything that they disapproved was 'old' (whether Old Labour or – to try to keep the party faithful onside – the Old Tories).

But modernisation also had a harder edge – it was not just the pragmatism, or opportunism, of Morrison in a modern setting. 'Modernisation' was part of the (initially) more covert part of New Labour ideology: it was at root a term alluding to political economy – in particular, the need for New Labour policy to conform to the dictates and constraints of capitalist globalisation.

New Labour talked of 'old values in a new setting', but this was just rhetoric for the party faithful. When elected as party leader in 1994, Blair had still used the word 'socialism', but inserting a hyphen, that is, 'social-ism' (Blair, 1994). At a postmodern stroke of a pen, he had reduced the 'hard' ideology of Labour to a woolly belief in the 'social' (who could differ, apart from the Aunt Sally version of Margaret Thatcher quoted out of context by her enemies as believing that there is 'no such thing as society'?).

Later, social democracy also fell by the wayside, to be replaced by the 'triangulated' concept of the Third Way. It was this concept that was initially applied to health policy – mechanistically and again derivatively, as a political strategy rather than a policy development. (This belief in 'politics as policy', with implementation looking after itself, to boot, would come back to haunt Blair and New Labour, in general and especially on the NHS.)

The NHS was different, however, from many other areas of the economy and even of social policy: as quoted above, Blair had described the NHS per se as modernisation. The logic then was that radical change was not necessary. Yet in his desire to be 'businesslike', Blair confused policy hyperactivism with business efficiency. And indeed the fall of the Department of Health's reputation, from 'hero to zero' (Greer, 2006) shows how tenuous reputation can be.

New Labour has moved through a number of policy regimes – or steering devices – not all of which were new but which were emphasised at different times between 1997 and 2007. It started with exhortations to collaborate (the NHS 'Third Way'), from 1997 to 1999; then central control, the heyday of which was from 1999 to 2002 (although de facto central control continued to 2006 and arguably to this day); and – trailed in 2002 yet only really implemented in 2006/07 – the 'new market' of patient choice buttressed allegedly by a new system of reimbursing healthcare providers. The backdrop to all these was – and is – the purchaser-provider split inherited from the Conservatives and justified theoretically by popularised versions of neoliberal public choice theory.

Taken together, these stages have been presented by the ideologists and advisers of the Blair regime as a 'cunning plan' to move through central standards, to 'pull up the NHS by the scruff of its neck', towards the relaxation of central control and reliance on consumerism and the new market to ensure standards (and financial control).

I have offered a different explanation, however, based on the 'rubbish bin' approach to interpreting New Labour's first 10 years (Paton, 2006). This depicts each of these policy regimes as short-termist in origin and deriving most of its justification ex post. Moreover, and crucially, the four regimes – old and new markets, local collaboration and central command and/or control – have coexisted, and still do, to an extent that causes confusion – certainly in implementation of policy and arguably in policy itself.

After Blair: emerging consensus on the NHS?

With the publication in June 2007 of the Conservative Party's paper, *NHS autonomy and accountability*, it is worth exploring whether there is a consensus emerging around health policy between the main parties (in England). Are any areas of consensus based on evidence – about past failures (and successes) – and what are the reasons for any significant differences?

Firstly, both Labour and the Conservatives (and certainly the Liberal Democrats) are committed to a universal health service, free at the point of need and funded by taxes, with it interestingly being the Liberal Democrat leader, Nick Clegg, who is identified both with alternative funding possibilities and the use of the private sector (adopting the Conservatives' abandoned 'patient passport' policy), as part of the Liberals' discovery of neoliberalism. To emphasise their own transformation, the Conservatives dropped their 2005 proposal for a 'patient passport', in effect a subsidy for private healthcare. This differed from the Labour government's use of private providers, which uses the private sector in the context of NHS financing and NHS 'rules of access'.

The second area to explore is the use of markets and competition. At the broad level, both main parties now favour markets – 'provider plurality' and competition by hospitals and others to win contracts from commissioners and/or choice by patients (not the same thing). Labour learned from some of the flaws of the original Conservative internal market in the 1990s, in particular, price competition that threatened clinical quality and even lives (Propper et al, 2004). After a meandering route through the 'Third Way' then central targets, the government reintroduced a market policy (DH, 2002) but eschewed price competition for 'quality competition' via the tariff ('payment by results', or rather by activity) which outlawed price competition, while the Conservatives have returned to price competition, establishing continuity with their 1990s' internal market.

The third area concerns central control. The Conservatives say they will abolish targets, and New Labour claims to have diminished them significantly. Both claims can be taken with a pinch of salt. The Conservatives have taken up the idea of an NHS board – like the Bank of England or the BBC – to take the politics out of health. Health Minister Andy Burnham was among those floating the same in September 2006, but Labour has cooled to the idea on the grounds that much of the NHS's providing, regulatory and even commissioning framework has already been devolved or 'floated off'. That is, what would the board do, other than jockey with ministers for general policy rights?

Conclusion

New Labour has influenced levels of NHS expenditure for the future by its financial settlements for the NHS since 2000. In turn it has been influenced by neoliberal (originally Conservative) ideas for running the NHS. It had stronger public health pretensions in 1997 but lost much of the impetus through destabilising and marginalising the public health function as a result of persistent reorganisation, as well as the superseding of public health concerns through economic choices (in terms of drinking hours and gambling, for example, as well as the wider absence of macro-redistribution) – with the 'no smoking' policy the major exception. Many New Labour themes have resonances with those of 6 and Peck (2004), but they tend to form a list rather than a pattern or a theory driven (or indeed evidence-based) programme, and the politics of the policy process, rather than issue pragmatism, has created and added to this list.

References

6, P. and Peck, E. (2004) 'Modernisation: the ten commitments of New Labour's approach to public management?', *International Public Management Journal*, vol 7, no 1, pp 1-18.

Alvarez-Rosete, A., Bevan, G., Mays, N. and Dixon, J. (2005) 'Effects of diverging policy across the NHS', *British Medical Journal*, vol 331, pp 946-50.

Barber, M. (2007) *Instruction to deliver: Tony Blair, public services and the challenge of achieving targets*, London: Politico's.

Blair, T. (1994) Address to the launch of the report of the Commission on Social Justice.

Blair, T. (1999) Speech to the Labour Party conference.

Cohen, M., March, J.G. and Olsen, J.P. (1972) 'A garbage can model of rational choice', *Administrative Science Quarterly*, vol 1, pp 1-25.

Commission on Social Justice (1994) *Social justice: Strategies for national renewal*, London: Vintage.

DH (Department of Health) (1997) *The New NHS: Modern, dependable*, London: The Stationery Office.

DH (2000) *The NHS Plan: A plan for investment, a plan for reform*, London: The Stationery Office.

DH (2001) *Shifting the balance of power to the frontline in the NHS*, London: DH.

DH (2002) *Delivering the NHS Plan: Next steps for investment, next steps for reform*, London: DH.

DH (2005) *Commissioning a patient-led NHS*, London: DH.

DH (2006a) *Our health, our care, our say*, London: The Stationery Office.

DH (2006b) *Health reform in England: Update and commissioning framework*, London: DH.

DH (2006c) *The future regulation of health in England*, London: DH.

Greer, S. (2003) *Four way bet*, London: UCL Constitution Unit.

Greer, S. (2004) *Territorial politics and health policy*, Manchester: Manchester University Press.

Greer, S. (2006) *The Department of Health*, London: Nuffield Trust.

Hall, P.A. (1993) 'Policy paradigms, social learning and the state: the case of economic policy making in Britain', *Comparative Politics*, vol 25, no 3, pp 275-96.

House of Commons Select Committee on Health (2006) *Report on NHS deficits*, London: The Stationery Office.

Humphries, J. (2004) *Lost for words*, London: Hodder and Stoughton.

Jenkins, S. (1995) *Accountable to none: The Tory nationalization of Britain*, London: Hamish Hamilton.

Jenkins, S. (2006) *Thatcher and sons: A revolution in three acts*, Harmondsworth: Penguin.

Kingdon, J. (1984) *Agendas, alternatives and public policies*, Boston, MA: Little, Brown.

Le Grand, J. (2007) *The other invisible hand*, London and Princeton, NJ: Princeton University Press.

Paton, C. (1997) 'Necessary conditions for a socialist health service', *Health Care Analysis*, vol 5, no 3.

Paton, C. (2006) *New Labour's state of health: Political economy, public policy and the NHS*, Aldershot: Ashgate.

Paton, C. (2007a) 'He who rides a tiger can never dismount: six myths about reform in the English NHS', *International Journal of Health Planning and Management*, vol 22, no 3, pp 97-111.

Paton, C. (2007b) Interviewed on Dispatches, Channel 4, 'The NHS: where did all the money go?', 26 February.

Propper, C., Burgess, S. and Green, K. (2004) 'Does competition between hospitals improve the quality of care? Hospital death rates and the NHS internal market?', *Journal for Public Economics*, vol 88, no 7-8, pp 1247-82.

Toynbee, P. and Walker, D. (2005) *Better or worse? Has New Labour delivered?*, Harmondsworth: Penguin.

Wanless, D., Appleby, J., Harrison, A. and Patel, D. (2007) *Our future health secured?: A review of NHS funding and performance*, London: King's Fund.

THREE

Housing policy: coming in and out of the cold?

Brian Lund

Introduction

Unlike health and education and, to a lesser extent, social security and social care, the state never attained a dominant role as a direct housing supplier. Moreover, between 1979 and 1997, state involvement in housing provision was 'rolled back' so that New Labour inherited a social housing stock − council housing plus state-supported and regulated housing association property − comprising 23% of total housing supply compared with 32% in 1979. Nonetheless, a 'residual' provider role does not necessarily mean limited state action to influence the supply and distribution of housing. Thus, in examining Blair's housing legacy it is necessary to consider how the market domain in housing has been managed alongside the policies relating to the social housing sector.

Adjustments to the social housing sector under Blair reflected the new public management (NPM) agenda identified by 6 and Peck (2004) to which 'choice' can be added. Policy adjustments, albeit expressed in a new political language, were at the 'settings' and 'instruments' levels (Hall, 1993). Changes in the regulation of the 'market' domain were also at the lower levels, but, post-2003, under Brown's influence and trends in the supply–demand balance, a policy goal change of potential 'third order' dimensions can be identified (Hall, 1993).

New Labour, old housing policy?

The tone of New Labour's approach to housing policy was set by Blair in a speech made to a 1995 Labour Party housing conference:

> But Labour is back in touch − the party of social housing, but the party of private housing too....And in government I am

firmly committed to encouraging the housing association movement and in ensuring a diversity of providers in rented housing. Part of that diversity must be to encourage the private rented sector. (Blair, 1996, pp 190, 198)

This speech constructed a symbolic distance from 'old' Labour's preoccupation with council housing and its distaste for private landlords but, as Kemp (1999, p 134) commented, 'Apart from a few specific manifesto commitments on housing, it was not clear what Labour's housing policy objectives would be, nor what instruments it would use to pursue them'. There was no 'third order' housing policy change (Hall, 1993) in New Labour's first term in office. Housing policy marked time, albeit expressed within a novel political language. Indeed, there was an interlude in which it appeared that housing policy had been mislaid, appearing, if at all, under New Labour's social exclusion agenda.

Housing and social exclusion

In his first speech as Prime Minister, delivered at the Aylesbury Estate in Southwark, Blair said:

> There is a case not just in moral terms but in enlightened self interest to act, to tackle what we all know exists – an underclass of people cut off from society's mainstream, without any sense of shared purpose…. The basis of this modern civic society is an ethic of mutual responsibility or duty. (Blair, 1997)

This 'underclass'/rights attached to obligations agenda – a development of Major's 'back to basics' discourse – was incorporated into the broader notion of 'social exclusion' when a social exclusion unit, reporting directly to the Prime Minister, was established. Housing featured in two of its first three reports.

Deprived neighbourhoods

The Social Exclusion Unit was given a remit to examine how to develop integrated and sustainable approaches to the problems in the 'worst housing estates', but its report *Bringing Britain together: A national strategy for neighbourhood renewal* (SEU, 1998a) concentrated on deprived neighbourhoods not just on council estates. It was claimed that in the past there had been too many initiatives governed by too many centrally imposed rules; programmes had not been 'joined up'; community commitment had not been harnessed; and there had been too much concentration on buildings and not enough on people. A new programme emerged from these conclusions – New Deal for Communities was launched in 1998 with 39 'pathfinder partnerships'. It concentrated on enhancing 'social' capital by community involvement in shaping a neighbourhood's future. It was enhanced by other area-based initiatives including the Neighbourhood Renewal Fund, available to the most deprived local authorities to generate neighbourhood renewal schemes involving local strategic partnerships, coordinating mainstream services and local neighbourhood managers.

Evaluating the overall impact of New Labour's first wave area-based initiatives is hampered by a dearth of neighbourhood-level information but the general consensus of opinion is that the deprivation tide is slowly turning (Page, 2006; Tunstall and Coulter, 2006; New Deal for Communities National Evaluation, 2008). In its internal evaluation of success, New Labour relied on local authority-level indicators comparing the 88 most deprived local government areas with the rest of England. Even on these indicators the overall impact has been, at best, modest. The gap between the national average and the 88 most deprived local government areas had increased on two indicators and had declined by less than 2.5 per cent on seven indicators. Only on the 'Key Stage 2: level 4 maths' indicator had the gap been reduced by more than 3% (ODPM, 2005a).

Rough sleeping

Rough sleeping (SEU, 1998b) assembled evidence to demonstrate that the causes of sleeping rough rested in the rough sleepers' 'personal biographies', with their histories of disturbed childhoods, institutionalisation and drug and alcohol abuse. Accordingly, the solution could be found in 'joined-up' action that addressed these deep-seated problems. However, whereas the report was symbolic in indicating Blair's emphasis on enhancing 'capabilities', subsequent policies were a development of Michael Heseltine's 1990 Rough Sleepers' Initiative, a programme to appoint outreach workers to make contact with people sleeping rough plus an increase in the supply of night shelters, hostels and 'move on' accommodation. New Labour's initiative placed emphasis on getting homeless people off the streets into some form of shelter, day and night. *Coming in out of the cold* (DETR, 1999), so it was argued, would break the rough sleeping 'street culture' and enable opportunities for treatment, occupation and work to be offered. Measured in terms of a reduction in the visible and counted rough sleeping problem, New Labour's Rough Sleepers Initiative has been a success. The target, set in 1998, to reduce the number of people sleeping rough by two thirds was met. In England, only 498 people were counted as sleeping rough in 2006 although, in making the national count, if a council estimates that it has between zero and ten rough sleepers, then zero is recorded.

Statutory homelessness

Statutory homelessness refers to households, 75% with children, who are entitled to assistance from local authorities. When measured by the number of households in temporary accommodation arranged by local authorities statutory homelessness increased rapidly from 45,290 households in 1997 to 101,020 in 2005. Part of this increase can be attributed to new categories of 'priority need' but, between 1996/97 and 2003/04, social housing supply declined (Hills, 2007, p 44), a consequence of accelerating council house sales and low levels of new social housing construction.

The government's response to the escalating 'headline' homelessness statistic was to restrict the terms under which council housing could be bought, helping to reduce Right to Buy sales from 69,577 in 2003/04 to 16,816 in 2006/07 and to promote a 'new approach' to tackling homelessness. This focused on 'people's personal problems' rather than just structural 'bricks and mortar causes', a recognition that:

> ... the provision of housing alone cannot solve homelessness.
> Underlying problems which led to homelessness in the first
> place have to be addressed in order to provide long-term
> solutions. (ODPM, 2005b, p 13)

Local authorities were encouraged to prevent homelessness by a target to reduce the use of temporary accommodation by 50% by 2010 and new 'best value' indicators relating to performance in preventing homelessness applications. In response, local authorities set up a number of schemes such as 'housing options' — interviews prior to a formal homelessness assessment from which ways of dealing with an accommodation problem, other than designation as homeless, might emerge — and tenancy support. These schemes were remarkably successful in reducing the number of households in temporary accommodation, producing a decline of 15,100 between 2005 and 2007 following a long-term upward trend (National Statistics, 2007).

Choice and housing

Towards the end of New Labour's first term a specific 'Blair agenda' for public service 'modernisation' started to emerge. According to Diamond, a special adviser in Blair's Policy Unit, this agenda was a consequence of 'a journey as ministers, government departments and public service agencies have sought to learn from their mistakes.... It was argued that choice and competition would ensure greater equity in public service outcomes, as well as stronger efficiency and responsiveness to customer demands' (Diamond, 2007, p 9). Home information packs, giving prospective buyers information on which they might make an informed choice on their housing purchase, were heralded in the 2004 Housing Act and a diluted version started to be introduced in late 2007. However, stock transfer, choice-based lettings, Housing Benefit reform and encouraging the private landlord sector were the principal choice-enhancing mechanisms injected into the housing domain. These were supplemented by 'top-down' measures such as new inspection regimes, 'earned autonomy' (6 and Peck, 2004) and the enhanced use of targets and performance indicators aimed at improving the social housing sector's capacity to respond to consumer wants. These measures could be represented as a 'third order' change (Hall, 1993) but, taking a longer perspective, they were borrowed 'first and second order' changes in techniques and settings and represented a modified version of John Major's policy orientation (Lund, 2008).

Stock transfer

The 1988 Housing Act had allowed council tenants, either individually or collectively, to transfer their homes to an 'approved' landlord, but only 1,470 homes were transferred via 'tenants' choice'. However, by the time New Labour had acquired office, stock transfer was gaining momentum through 'voluntary' stock transfer. 'Voluntary' stock transfer involves a local authority initiating and supporting the sale of its stock to an existing registered social landlord or one specifically created to receive the dwellings. New Labour encouraged stock transfer via the promotion of 'decent homes', setting a target to ensure that all social housing met the decent homes standard by 2010. In order to be 'decent' a home should be warm, weatherproof and have 'reasonably modern facilities', defined in terms of the age of the bathroom and kitchen.

Attaining the decent homes target would require local authorities to allocate substantial capital resources to council housing. To secure these resources local authorities had to investigate various avenues set out by central government. Some selected the private finance initiative (PFI) and others picked an arm's-length management organisation, available as 'earned autonomy' if the local authority achieved a two- or three-star rating from the Housing Inspectorate – established in 2000 to promote good practice in housing management. Whether by choice or necessity, many local authorities opted to transfer their stock to a registered social landlord. Despite tenant resistance, in some areas, coordinated by 'Defend Council Housing', 459,578 dwellings were transferred from local government between 2001 and 2006 (DCLG, 2007a). This stock transfer, with its associated private finance injection, has contributed to a fall in the number of 'social' sector homes failing to meet the decent homes standard – down by over a million since 1996 (DCLG, 2007b).

Choice-based lettings

Heralded in the 2000 housing Green Paper (DETR/DSS), a policy objective that all local authorities should be running a choice-based lettings system by 2010 was set. Choice-based lettings schemes usually involve allocating 'currency' in the form of priority bandings and then advertising vacant properties on websites or local newspapers. Prospective tenants 'bid' for a property, often using a website, and, if unsuccessful, are informed of their relative priority for a particular property type in a particular area. Thus, using 'electronic service delivery' (6 and Peck, 2004, p 13), choice-based lettings mimic the market, with 'consumers' learning about supply and demand in the social rented sector. Choice-based lettings appear not to have reduced the rehousing opportunities of the most vulnerable applicants (Pawson and Watkins, 2007) but, in many areas, choice is severely constrained by lack of supply. It is hardly surprising, then, that the proportion of households saying that they did not have enough choice or were given no choice in the allocation process remained static, at 61% between 2001/02 and 2004/05 (DCLG, 2007c).

Housing Benefit reform

Building choice and responsibility: A radical agenda for Housing Benefit (DWP, 2002) announced a standard local housing allowance – means tested and variable according to household size and the local rented market – paid directly to tenants in the deregulated private rented sector. It argued that:

The new approach means tenants who rent a property at below the standard allowance, or who move to a cheaper property in their local area, or who negotiate to keep the rent below the standard allowance, will be able to keep the difference – putting the decision in their hands. (DWP, 2002, p 4)

The standard local housing allowance was tested in nine 'pathfinders' and will be 'rolled out' into a national scheme – less generous than that piloted in the 'pathfinder' areas – from 2008. The 2004 Budget statement announced that a standard local allowance would be extended to social tenants 'when conditions were right', but no final decision on such an extension has been made, with the Department for Work and Pensions declaring:

> We are aware that there are significant differences between the private rental market and social housing, and between the social housing sectors of the UK devolved administrations.... Proposals need to be developed with caution and over a longer timescale. (DWP, 2006, p 89)

Blair's 'conditional welfare' agenda (see Chapter Twelve, this volume) was reflected in clauses in the 2007 Welfare Reform Act that provided for a reduction in Housing Benefit when a person has been evicted on grounds of anti-social behaviour and has refused to cooperate with the support offered to improve this behaviour.

Private landlord sector

Between 1997 and 2005, 347,000 dwellings were added to the private landlord sector, far more than the 102,000 in the 18 years of Conservative government. In part, this expansion was the outcome of New Labour adopting a welcoming approach to private landlords, thereby securing the necessary political consensus for long-term investment. Although New Labour's 1997 manifesto had promised to 'provide protection where most needed' by 'a proper system of licensing by local authorities which will benefit tenants and responsible landlords alike' (Labour Party, 1997), this did not become law until the 2004 Housing Act and, when it happened, the regulation was 'light touch' and targeted on 'bad' landlords (Cowan and McDermont, 2006, p 152) in low demand areas.

'Buy-to-let' was the principal driver in the growth of private landlordism. In 1996 a consortium of mortgage lenders launched 'buy-to-let', that is, lending to private landlords on terms close to those offered to owner-occupiers and, whereas home owners had lost the right to offset their mortgage interest against their tax liability in 2000, private landlords continued to be to able balance their mortgage payments against their rental income. By June 2007, the number of buy-to-let loans outstanding had reached 938,500, up from 28,700 in 1998 and, between 2004 and 2006, the number of dwellings rented from private landlords increased by more than the number of dwellings that were owner-occupied − 236,000 compared to 181,000 (DCLG, 2007d).

Devolution

Given the suspension of the Northern Ireland Assembly in 2002 and, until 2007, New Labour's dominance in the Scottish Parliament and the Welsh Assembly, it is not surprising that housing policy in Scotland, Wales and Northern Ireland has trailed the English pattern. Scotland was granted the most power to develop a distinct housing path with the opportunity for 'third order' change, but, despite overall public expenditure being 18% above the level in England, Scotland tended to follow England's policy direction, albeit expressed in different terminology. Thus, for example, the 2006 Housing (Scotland) Act introduced 'purchasers' information packs', analogous to the English 'home information packs', plus a tenancy deposit scheme for the private landlord sector, similar to the system in England introduced under the 2004 Housing Act. Scotland's 'Homestake' replicates England's 'Homebuy' and the Scottish Executive has promoted stock transfer but with different procedures and with the Scottish Housing Quality Standard used as the benchmark for assessing investment requirements (Smith, 2006). Stock transfer process outcomes have tended to reflect 'bottom-up' pressures from local government and tenants rather than the policies promoted by the devolved administrations.

Homelessness policy offers the sharpest contrast between England and Scotland. The definition of priority need is broader in Scotland and the 'priority need' obstacle to securing permanent accommodation is due to be abolished in 2012. In the meantime, those deemed 'not in priority need' have been given entitlement to temporary accommodation. A consequence of this more liberal approach has been that, in contrast to England, the number of households in temporary accommodation has continued its upward trajectory, increasing by 21% between 2005 and 2007 (Scottish Government, 2007a).

The impact of devolution 'politics', 'structural determinants' such as global markets, or the influence of the new public sector managerialism (6 and Peck, 2004, p 3) may become clearer now that the Northern Ireland Assembly has been restored and the Scottish National Party has formed a minority government. The Scottish National Party's first document on housing policy (Scottish Government, 2007b) announced a new housing target, higher in percentage terms than New Labour's ambition for England, the abolition of the Right to Buy on new social sector homes and enhanced local authority housing supply.

Blair, Brown, Cameron and housing policy

Much has been written on the alleged succession 'settlement' between Blair and Brown made at the Granita restaurant on 31 May 1994. Peston's account states:

> So if the promise on the succession was freely offered by Blair, what then were Brown's actual conditions for withdrawing from the contest? Well they stemmed from Brown's fundamental lack of trust in Blair's commitment to an agenda based on social justice.... His ostensible motive was that he saw his destiny as the protector of the Party's traditional values. (Peston, 2005, p 65)

There is a good fit between Peston's version of the Blair Brown settlement and the aetiology of housing policy between 1997 and 2007. Initially, Blair had a strong impact on housing policy via the Social Exclusion Unit, and his emphasis on individual and community 'capabilities' was reflected in New Deal for Communities and the Rough Sleepers Initiative. Blair's influence can also be detected in the 'choice' agenda incorporated into housing policy in 2000 that, in many ways, anticipated its later injection into the education, health and personal social services domains. Under Cameron, the Conservatives have adopted Blair's approach. For example, the Conservatives' Public Services Improvement Policy Group (2007) praised choice-based lettings and suggested that homeless people should be allocated 'mentors' because homelessness is mainly a consequence of 'personal troubles'. It also recommended that social housing should be rebranded 'community housing' with limited security of tenure, 'counsellors' available to guide tenants out of the sector and a £10,000 equity stake conditional on good behaviour.

In contrast to Blair's preference for 'agency' explanations, Brown adopted a more structural, social democratic approach. He intervened directly in housing policy in 2003 when the Treasury identified volatility in the UK housing market as a barrier to joining the eurozone (HM Treasury, 2003), and was instrumental in introducing the Housing Market Renewal Fund, with its emphasis on physical capital rather than the social capital of New Deal for Communities. Post-2003, promoting housing supply became a joint Treasury/Office of the Deputy Prime Minister/Department for Communities and Local Government mission and represented the start of a potential 'third order' change in housing policy. Boosting housing supply was elevated in New Labour's 'hierarchy of goals' (Hall, 1993, p 279). Infrastructure investment to support housing construction in four growth areas was announced, housing associations received extra resources and Brown appointed Kate Barker to examine ways to deliver stability to the housing market. Her final report (Barker, 2004) recommended a step-change in housing supply to be achieved by setting national and regional affordability targets that, if unmet, would trigger land release and a tax on planning gain to be used for infrastructure investment.

Stimulating housing supply

Despite stimulating housing supply after 2003 New Labour's overall housing construction record in England has been disappointingly poor – 190,000 less houses in its first 10 years of office than in the last 10 years of the Conservative government (DCLG, 2007e) – and this at a time when demand has been rising fast due to net migration, increased household formation, low interest rates and sustained economic growth.

Building homes was not a Blair priority – housing was not included in the programme of 'delivery' targets to be achieved by the Prime Minister's Delivery Unit set up in 2001 (Barber, 2007) – but it is now a Brown priority. In his first speech as Prime Minister, Brown placed affordable housing alongside the NHS and schools in his list of priorities (Brown, 2007):

> ... as Prime Minister I will continue to listen and learn from the British people – I have heard the need for change: change in our NHS; change in our schools; change with affordable housing; change to build trust in government;

change to protect and extend the British way of life. (Brown, 2007)

The Green Paper *Homes for the future: More affordable, more sustainable* (DCLG, 2007f) indicated why and how Brown's government intended to boost overall housing construction in England and to deliver more affordable houses. It stated that overall housing supply needed to be increased because the latest household projections showed that the number of households was anticipated to grow by 223,000 a year until 2026, and housing supply had not kept pace with household formation, with the result that 'house prices have doubled in real terms over the last 10 years' (DCLG, 2007f, p 17). Moreover:

> Nearly 40% of first-time buyers aged under 30 now depend on help from family or friends to get them started on the housing ladder. In London an assisted young first-time buyer had an average deposit of £57,000 compared to £12,500 for unassisted young first-time buyers. (DCLG, 2007f, p 19)

The Green Paper also endorsed enhanced social housing construction because the number of households in temporary accommodation has increased and 'the number of households waiting for social housing has risen from 1 million to 1.6 million over the last ten years, both as the number of households has grown and as more families have found they cannot afford a home' (DCLG, 2007f, p 21).

Housing supply is scheduled to increase over time to 240,000 in 2016, then continue at about 240,000 per annum until 2020. Seventy thousand 'affordable' homes a year will be provided by 2010/11, with 45,000 of these homes in the social housing sector. New 'instruments' and amended 'settings' will help to accelerate overall housing supply. 'Eco-towns' – with balanced communities and zero carbon emissions – will be created and there will be continuing infrastructure finance for 'growth areas' (with a new one in the North) and for 'growth points'. Additional land for housing will come from abolishing Regional Assemblies, which, with their elected councillor representation, have proved troublesome in releasing land, designating surplus government sites for housing, encouraging local authorities to allocate land by a Housing and Planning Delivery Grant, plus a threat that, if a local authority does not allocate sufficient land for a rolling five-year house building programme, developers will find it easy to obtain planning permission. Social housing will be augmented by additional government finance and allowing local government to have a larger role in house building via local housing companies, arm's-length management organisations and direct building. Existing low-cost home ownership schemes will be boosted and a new Homes and Communities Agency will be created, bringing together The Housing Corporation, English Partnerships and the community development role of the Department for Communities and Local Government.

Public sector managerialism and orders of change

During Blair's premiership, housing policy was marked by the combination of the attributes identified by 6 and Peck (2004) (see Table 3.1). These initiatives were concerned with 'people change', managing the demise of the 'local state' housing sector, sponsoring choice and promoting a more pluralistic rented housing supply.

The 2007 Green Paper was very different in tone to New Labour's 2000 Green Paper – then aptly described by Shelter as 'an avalanche of new procedures for every nook and cranny of the housing sector' (Shelter, 2000, p 2). The 2007 Green Paper marked a partial return to 'old' Labour's housing agenda: a concern with supply; new towns

Table 3.1: The 10 commitments of New Labour's approach to public management (plus 'choice'): housing example

The 10 commitments	Housing examples
Choice	Choice-based lettings; Local Housing Allowance
Inspection	Housing inspectorate
Central standard setting	Decent homes standard; performance indicators
Area-based initiatives	New Deal for Communities; Housing Market Renewal pathfinders
Coordination and integration	Neighbourhood Renewal Fund
Devolution but limited decentralisation	No directly elected regional authorities with housing powers; proposed abolition of Regional Assemblies with their nominated local councillors
Earned autonomy	Arm's-length management organisations
An extended role for private capital	Stock transfer, expansion of private rented sector, private finance initiative (PFI)
A modest increase in citizen obligations	Rough Sleepers Initiative, conditional Housing Benefit
Access	Choice-based lettings, neighbourhood management
E-government	Choice-based lettings

(eco–towns); public housing; and taxing planning gain – an agenda that can be seen as a paradigm shift (see Table 3.2). Nonetheless, 'New Labourism' has remained influential. The 2007 Pre-Budget Report and Comprehensive Spending Review abandoned the proposed planning

Table 3.2: Assessment of housing policy against Hall's orders of change

	First order Levels or settings changed	Second order Policy instrument altered, goals unchanged	Third order 'Paradigm shift'
Owner-occupation	Phasing out of tax relief on mortgage interest	Home information packs	Post-2003 emphasis on supply culminating in 2007 housing Green Paper (issued under Brown)
Social housing	Stock transfer; housing inspectorate; restrictions on terms of sale under the Right to Buy	Choice-based lettings	
Private landlords	2004 Housing Act: licensing of multi-occupied dwellings and landlords operating in 'low-demand' areas	Local Housing Allowance	
Homelessness	Rough Sleepers Initiative extended; new homeless 'priority need' categories; stronger obligations on local authorities to tackle homelessness; post-2005 emphasis on prevention		
Area-based policies		New Deal for Communities; Neighbourhood Renewal programme; Housing Market Renewal pathfinders	
Devolution		Welsh Assembly; Northern Ireland Assembly	Scottish Parliament

gain tax and, although the proposals in the Green Paper have been described as marking 'the return of the council house' (Hencke, 2007), the transfer of existing stock will continue and new direct building by councils will be subject to 'rigorous criteria' (DCLG, 2007f, p 77). The overall house building target is modest, with 240,000 houses per annum set as the target for 2016. In 2006 160,761 new homes were constructed in England (DCLG, 2007f) leaving a current shortfall of 62,239. Thus, even if housing production is gradually ratcheted towards the 2016 target – a doubtful outcome given the dwindling confidence in the housing market following the crisis in the US sub-prime mortgage sector and the demise of Northern Rock PLC – there will still be a large housing deficit when compared to current household formation projections plus the houses required now to alleviate homelessness and overcrowding. The National Housing and Planning Advice Unit, set up by the government to provide the data on which house building targets can be set, has estimated that building 277,000 houses per year is necessary to make a significant impact on the affordability problem (National Housing and Planning Advice Unit, 2007). Moreover, following the Conservative Party's electoral revival on a social agenda with a distinctive Blairite flavour, Brown appears to have pressed the back button on the rights/obligations agenda. The Neighbourhood Renewal Fund has been renamed the Working Neighbourhood Renewal Fund and Caroline Flint, Minister for Housing, has floated the idea that new tenants who could work should sign commitment contracts when getting a tenancy, agreeing to actively seek work (Flint, 2008).

Conclusion

Three phases can be identified in New Labour's housing policy. In the first phase the dearth of specific housing commitments in New Labour's 1997 manifesto produced a vacuum in housing policy until the publication in 2000 of the housing Green Paper *Quality and choice: A decent home for all* (DETR/DSS, 2000), with its emphasis on supply diversity and choice and the application of 'new public sector management'. In stage three a new emphasis on supply culminated in *Homes for the future: More affordable, more sustainable* (DCLG, 2007f), with its promise to boost housing supply in both the market and the social sectors. For a time it appeared that a political consensus was developing on the need for such a step-change in housing construction. In March 2006 David Cameron claimed that 'the failure to provide an adequate number of new homes in Britain has contributed to the affordability problem. This situation is bananas. I say it's bananas because one of the problems we've faced is a system that encourages people to believe we should Build Absolutely Nothing Anywhere Near Anyone' (Cameron, 2006). In June 2007 the Conservative Shadow Housing Minister, Michael Gove, described Gordon Brown's housing target as 'displaying a poverty of ambition' (Gove, quoted in Murray, 2007), and declared that a huge increase in new home supply was needed. However, in July 2007, Gove was replaced by Grant Shapps, a strong supporter of a local campaign to stop 10,000 homes being built in his Welwyn Hatfield constituency. In contrast to New Labour's 2007 Green Paper, the Conservatives' Public Services Improvement Policy Group set no target for future social housing production. The Quality of Life Policy Group warned of a 'battle in every locality which is threatened with environmentally damaging development will be fierce and hard-fought' (Quality of Life Policy Group, 2007, p 122), and, although the Conservatives' Economic Competitiveness Policy Group claimed that the existing planning system limited housing supply and hence economic competitiveness, its main recommendation for increasing supply consisted of the designation of unspecified 'new communities' in 'sparsely populated areas, preferably with a high proportion of brownfield sites' (Economic Competitiveness Policy Group, 2007, para 9.4). Perhaps Brown's prudent housing target reflects the competition for the voters of 'Middle England' – their support is necessary to form a government but they are deeply resistant to any intrusion in their backyards.

References

6, P. and Peck, E. (2004) 'Modernisation: the ten commitments of New Labour's approach to public management', *International Public Management Journal*, vol 7, no 1, pp 1-18.

Barber, M. (2007) *Instruction to deliver: Tony Blair, public services and the challenge of achieving targets*, London: Politico's.

Barker, K. (2004) *Review of housing supply: Delivering stability: Securing our future housing needs, Final report, Recommendations*, London: HM Treasury (www.hm-treasury.gov.uk/consultations_and_legislation/barker/consult_barker_index.cfm).

Blair, T. (1996) 'Speech to a Labour Party housing conference', London, 5 March 1995, in T. Blair, *New Britain: My vision of a young country*, London: Fourth Estate.

Blair, T. (1997) Speech given by Tony Blair as Prime Minister, Aylesbury Estate, London (www.socialexclusionunit.gov.uk/news.asp?id=400).

Brown, G. (2007) First speech as Prime Minister, 27 June (www. timesonline.co.uk/tol/news/politics/article1995127.ece).

Cameron, D. (2006) 'We'll build more homes. And they will be beautiful: people must be given a bigger say. The current system is bananas', *Independent*, 26 March.

Cowan, D. and McDermont, M. (2006) *Regulating social housing: Governing decline*, Abingdon: Routledge-Cavendish.

DCLG (Department for Communities and Local Government) (2007a) *Completed large-scale voluntary transfers* (www.communities.gov.uk/ documents/housing/xls/completedlsvts.xls).

DCLG (2007b) *English House Conditions Survey 2005* (www.communities. gov.uk/publications/housing/englishhousesurveyannual).

DCLG (2007c) *English Housing Survey* (www.communities.gov.uk/ documents/housing/xls/139925).

DCLG (2007d) *Dwelling stock by tenure: England, historical series* (www. communities.gov.uk/documents/housing/xls/table-104.xls).

DCLG (2007e) *Housebuilding: Permanent dwellings started and completed: By tenure: England (quarterly)* (www.communities.gov.uk/documents/ housing/xls/140894).

DCLG (2007f) *Homes for the future: More affordable, more sustainable*, Cm 7191, London: The Stationery Office.

DETR (Department of the Environment, Transport and the Regions) (1999) *Rough sleeping: The Government's strategy: Coming in out of the cold*, London: DETR.

DETR/Department of Social Security (DSS) (2000) *Quality and choice: A decent home for all*, Housing Green Paper, London: The Stationery Office.

Diamond, P. (ed) (2007) *Public matters: The renewal of the public realm*, London: Politico's.

DWP (Department for Work and Pensions) (2002) *Building choice and responsibility: A radical agenda for Housing Benefit* (www.dwp.gov. uk/housingbenefit/publications/2002/building_choice/prospectus. pdf).

DWP (2006) *A New Deal for welfare: Empowering people to work*, Cm 6730, London: The Stationery Office.

Economic Competitiveness Policy Group (2007) *Freeing Britain to compete: Equipping the UK for globalisation: Submission to the Shadow Cabinet* (www.conservatives.com/getfile. cfm?file=ECPGcomplete&ref=GENERALFILE/3585&type=pdf).

Flint, C. (2008) Address to the Fabian Society (www.communities.gov. uk/speeches/corporate/fabiansocietyaddress).

Hall, P.A. (1993) 'Policy paradigms, social learning and the state: the case of economic policy making in Britain', *Comparative Politics*, vol 25, no 3, pp 275-96.

Hencke, D. (2007) 'Labour U-turn on council house building', *Guardian*, 14 July.

Hills, J. (2007) *Ends and means: The future roles of social housing in England*, CASEReport 34 (http://sticerd.lse.ac.uk/dps/case/cr/CASEreport34.pdf).

HM Treasury (2003) *Housing, consumption and EMU* (http://news8.thdo.bbc.co.uk/1/shared/spl/hi/europe/03/euro/pdf/4.pdf).

Kemp, P. (1999) 'Housing policy under New Labour', in M. Powell (ed) *New Labour, new welfare state?: The 'third way' in British social policy*, Bristol: The Policy Press.

Labour Party (1997) *New Labour because Britain deserves better: Britain will be better with new Labour* (www.psr.keele.ac.uk/area/uk/man/lab97.htm).

Lund, B. (2008), 'Major, Blair and the "Third Way" in social policy', *Social Policy and Administration*, vol 42, no 1, pp 43-58.

Murray, K. (2007) 'Gove: higher housing targets under Tory government: Conservative pledge to tackle Nimbyism', *Inside Housing*, 25 June.

National Housing and Planning Advice Unit (2007) *Developing a target range for the supply of new homes across England* (www.communities.gov.uk/publications/housing/supplynewhomes).

National Statistics (2007) Statistical Release, *Statutory homelessness, 2nd quarter 2007, England* (www.communities.gov.uk/news/corporate/468125).

New Deal for Communities National Evaluation (2008) *New Deal for Communities: A synthesis of new programme wide evidence 2006/7*, Research Report 39 (http://extra.shu.ac.uk/ndc).

ODPM (Office of the Deputy Prime Minister) (2005a) *Making it happen in neighbourhoods: The National Strategy for Neighbourhood Renewal – Four years on*, London: ODPM.

ODPM (2005b) *Sustainable communities: Settled homes – Changing lives – A strategy for tackling homelessness*, London: ODPM.

Page, D. (2006) *Respect and renewal: A study of neighbourhood social regeneration*, York: Joseph Rowntree Foundation.

Pawson, H. and Watkins, D. (2007) 'Quasi-marketising access to social housing in Britain: assessing the distributional impacts', *Journal of Housing and the Built Environment*, vol 22, pp 149-75.

Peston, R. (2005) *Brown's Britain*, London: Short Books.

Public Services Improvement Policy Group (2007) *Restoring pride in our public services: Submission to the Shadow Cabinet* (www.conservatives.com/pdf/psipg-report.pdf).

Quality of Life Policy Group (2007) *Blueprint for a green economy: Submission to the Shadow Cabinet* (www.conservatives.com/tile.do?def=news.story.page&obj_id=138484).

Scottish Government (2007a) *Operation of the Homeless Persons legislation in Scotland: National and local authority analyses 2005–06* (www.scotland.gov.uk/Publications/2005/11/0193147/31478).

Scottish Government (2007b) *Firm foundations: The future of housing in Scotland* (www.scotland.gov.uk/Publications/2007/10/30153156/0).

Shelter (2000) *Roof briefing No 39*, April.

Smith, R. (2006) 'Devolution and divergence in social-housing policy in Britain', in J. Adams and K. Schmueker, *Devolution in practice 2006: Public policy differences within the UK*, London: Institute for Public Policy Research.

Social Exclusion Unit (1998a) *Bringing Britain together: A National Strategy for Neighbourhood Renewal*, London: Cabinet Office.

Social Exclusion Unit (1998b) *Rough sleeping* (www.socialexclusionunit.gov.uk/downloaddoc.asp?id=240).

Tunstall, R. and Coulter, A. (2006) *Twenty-five years on twenty estates: Turning the tide?*, Bristol: The Policy Press.

FOUR

Social security and welfare reform

Stephen McKay and Karen Rowlingson

Introduction

The UK social security system is a huge, complex juggernaut that has grown in a largely incremental way over at least the last century (McKay and Rowlingson, 1998). Government spending on social protection (principally social security benefits) takes up around £159 billion, well over one quarter of all public spending and more than the total raised in income tax (£154 billion) (HM Treasury, 2007). Radical reform is rare as the system affects the lives of so many people: state support is received by 70% of households in the UK, with 30% receiving at least half their income from this source (Family Resources Survey 2005-06, Table 3.9 – see www.dwp.gov.uk/asd/frs/2005_06/index.asp). Changes in one part of the system impact, sometimes in unanticipated ways, on others. Even the (apparently) radical Beveridge reforms (1942), often cited as creating the foundations of the modern social security system, built heavily on the past. For example, the principle of collective social insurance had already been established by the reforms of the earlier Liberal governments, and Beveridge deliberately set out to preserve the role of the private sector, particularly in relation to saving for retirement. And while Beveridge hoped to reduce the long-established role of means testing in the social security system, his hopes were not realised, and means testing remains a key feature of the UK system.

So radical change, or 'third order' change (Hall, 1993), is rare in the social security system and 10 years of New Labour have, in the main, failed to achieve such change. There remains a large role for means-tested benefits, immersed in a system of flat-rate social insurance (especially for pensioners) with various universal benefits in particular for people with disabilities. Someone familiar with the benefits system in 1997 would understand much of the system prevailing in 2007. And in many respects, New Labour continued with similar policy goals to the previous Conservative government, particularly in relation to the focus on moving people from welfare to work. However, there have also been some significant changes in policy goals compared with previous administrations, not least making poverty reduction a top priority for government action.

One way of measuring the legacy is to consider any change in spending on social security. An increase in spending might be seen as a positive endorsement of the system and part of a poverty reduction agenda. However, increased spending can also be the result of economic recession and greater calls on the system. Given the positive economic climate under New Labour we can probably rule out the latter. But New Labour has not regarded spending on social security in a positive light – Tony Blair proudly declared in 2001 that Labour were 'cutting the costs of economic failure; with real terms social security spending falling for the first time in decades' (Blair, 2001). Instead, targets were set around people leaving benefits, thereby reducing benefits spend.

Measuring the overall size of spending on social security is complicated by the introduction of tax credits. Nevertheless, Phillips and Sibieta (2007) have attempted to piece together a consistent trend series of spending. As we show in Table 4.1, spending on social security benefits rose from 1996/97 to 2005/06 by over 50% in cash terms, and by nearly one quarter (22.5%) after adjusting for inflation. The proportion of gross domestic product (GDP) spent on social security did, however, fall back slightly, from 11.9% to 11.4%. Even so, the

Table 4.1: Benefits spending, 1996/97–2005/06

Year	Cash spending (£m)	Real terms spending (£m)	Real rise each year (%)	% of GDP
1997–98	93,346	112,896	–1.6	11.3
1998–99	95,554	112,702	–0.2	11.0
1999–2000	100,290	115,942	2.9	10.9
2000–01	106,016	120,863	4.2	11.0
2001–02	114,426	127,426	5.4	11.4
2002–03	120,460	130,120	2.1	11.3
2003–04	125,618	131,775	1.3	11.1
2004–05	132,449	135,256	2.6	11.2
2005–06	140,649	140,649	4.0	11.4
1996/97–2005/06	+52.5%	+22.5%		–0.5 percentage points

Source: Phillips and Sibieta (2007, p 60), itself based on various Department for Work and Pensions/Department of Social Security sources

record of much lower unemployment and generally benign economic conditions might lead one to have expected a larger reduction, given the cyclical nature of some social security spending.

In the areas of *policy change* that led to extra spending, the clearest changes were in extra benefits for families with children, in in-work benefits (and tax credits) and in additional spending on poorer pensioners. At the same time spending on Incapacity Benefit, other disability benefits and on Housing Benefit continued to rise – these continue to be future priorities for policy change.

This chapter discusses each of the most significant reforms in order to come to an assessment of New Labour's impact on the social security system. It then considers why New Labour has had this particular impact. We assess the kinds of reforms made against the yardsticks of Hall's (1993) orders of change (see Table 4.2). Hall characterises third order change as involving changes to *policy goals* and also involving a *paradigm shift*. The next, second, level of change involves keeping the same policy goals but changing *policy instruments*, and 'first order' change involves keeping the same policy instruments but changing the *levels or settings*. While this is a helpful framework to consider policy change, there are also problems applying it, which we discuss in the chapter.

Third order change: reclaiming the 'p-word'

Under the Conservative governments from 1979 to 1997, UK poverty levels rose dramatically (particularly during the 1980s) but there was no official definition of, and virtually no government discussion about, poverty. Research funded by the then Department of Social Security never directly addressed or mentioned 'poverty', focusing instead on 'low income', a much less emotive and politically resonant concept. One of New Labour's main claims to radical change in the field of welfare and social security has been to put poverty firmly back on the political, policy and public agendas, most visibly in relation to child poverty but also in relation to pensioner poverty.

The commitment to end child poverty

In 1999 Tony Blair made the following pledge: 'Our historic aim will be for ours to be the first generation to end child poverty forever, and it will take a generation. It is a twenty year mission, but I believe it can be done' (Blair, 1999). This pledge has set the agenda for much later policy change, and represents one of the boldest statements made

Table 4.2: Assessment of social security and welfare policy against Hall's orders of change

Areas of reform	First order Levels or settings changed	Second order Policy instrument altered, goals unchanged	Third order 'Paradigm shift'
Families with children	Higher levels of benefits for children Increase in maintenance disregards	Introduction of tax credits Asset-based welfare (Child Trust Fund)	Commitment to end child poverty by 2020
Working-age groups		New Deal policies Minimum Wage	
Pensioners	Higher rates of Pension Credit Tax simplification via A-day (new rules for tax treatment of pensions from 6 April 2006) Winter Fuel payments	Personal accounts (DWP, 2006b) Savings Credit within Pension Credit Gradually raising state pension age, reaching 68 by 2046 Linking the Basic State Pension to rises in earnings (DWP, 2006a)	Focus on reducing pensioner poverty
Child Support Agency		Move to Child Maintenance and Enforcement Commission, emphasis on voluntary arrangements	
People with disabilities		Equality agenda and the new Office for Disability Issues	
Delivery of social security		Increasing role of private and third sector in some areas of delivery Increasing use of call centres and electronic forms of delivery	

within social security (if not social policy as a whole, Walker, 1999). It is a commitment that came to be shared by the Conservative Party.

According to Hall (1993), 'third order' change involves a 'paradigm shift' which, itself, relates to major changes in discourse. The pledge, and subsequent emphasis, on child poverty certainly conforms to that definition. For example, in Figure 4.1 we show the number of days on which two leading quality newspapers (*The Guardian* and the *Financial Times*) have used the phrase 'child poverty', from the 1980s onwards. The frequency of such mentions was very low even in 1997 and 1998, before this commitment was made but still under New Labour. The Major years from 1990 to 1997 saw only infrequent mentions of child poverty – and many of these related specifically to covering statements from the Child Poverty Action Group. From 1999 onwards newspaper mentions of 'child poverty' have both been much higher, and generally on an upward trend – the apparent final downturn reflecting figures that are for less than a whole year in 2007 (at the time of writing), and consistent with a continuing upward trend.

Progress towards actually meeting this commitment has been clear, but agonisingly slow and hard-won, mostly through changes to existing policy instruments such as increasing the levels of Income Support and wage supplements for those in work. Tough challenges lie ahead, if it is to be met (Hirsch, 2006). In Figure 4.2 we chart progress to reduce child poverty. This is measured as the proportion of children

Figure 4.1: Newspaper mentions of the phrase 'child poverty'

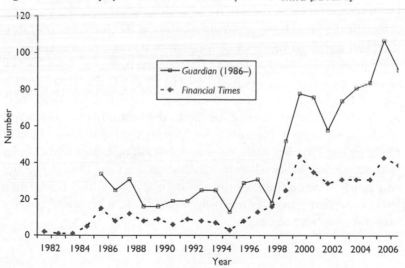

Source: Nexis-UK, LexisNexis database (2007 figures up to end of September)

Figure 4.2: Percentage of children in households below 60% of contemporary median income, UK

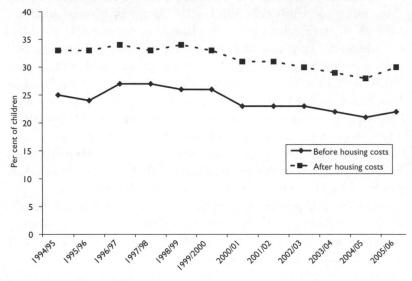

Source: DWP (2007, p 52)

living in families with incomes below 60% of the median, looked at both before and after housing costs (denoted as BHC and AHC). As the figure shows, child poverty actually rose between 2004/05 and 2005/06. The government has missed its first target for reducing child poverty, with half a million more children in poverty in 2006 than the target set for 2005.

Part of the issue here, although one less at the forefront of policy, has been trends in the level of inequality, as the official measure of child poverty is related to levels of inequality. In Figure 4.3 we show trends in income inequality from 1979 to 2005/06, the latest available figures. Inequality is measured both by the overall 'Gini coefficient', and by the ratio of incomes of the top to the bottom 10%. They reveal mostly similar trends. Inequality rose sharply during the *second half* of the Margaret Thatcher years (but was flat or falling before that). Under John Major inequality fell quite steadily. Under Tony Blair inequality rose slowly but consistently until about 2002, after which it has fallen back somewhat – perhaps reversing in 2005/06, when child poverty rates also rose very slightly.

Figure 4.3: Changes in overall income inequality, 1979–2005/06

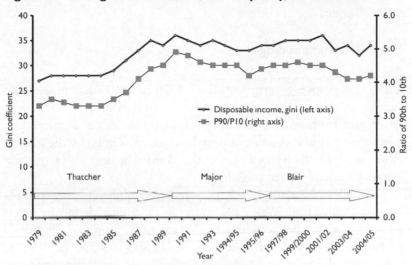

Note: Gini coefficient for equivalised disposable income.

Source: Jones (2007)

Pensioner poverty

Pensioner poverty has had a lower public profile than child poverty but levels of pensioner poverty have been significantly reduced. The proportion of pensioners living in low-income households (AHC) has been falling throughout the last decade, from 29% of all pensioners in 1996/97 to 17% in 2005/06. Pensioners are now *less* likely to be living in low-income households than non-pensioners (see www.poverty. org.uk/38/index.shtml?2).

The reduction in pensioner poverty has been mostly achieved through increases in the means-tested benefit, Pension Credit. This has been a controversial strategy in some ways as those pensioners who have made modest amounts of savings or occupational pensions are little, or no, better off than those who have not made such provision. This raises issues of fairness and (dis)incentives to save. The 'Saving Credit' part of Pension Credit was an attempt to address this problem but it has not been conspicuously successful.

Significant change: the National Minimum Wage and asset-based welfare

The introduction of the National Minimum Wage (in 1999) and the development of asset-based welfare policies, such as the Child Trust Fund and the Saving Gateway, constitute significant reforms by New

Labour, although, as we shall argue below, they fall short of 'third order' change.

National Minimum Wage

The Conservative governments from 1979 to 1997 championed the supremacy of the free market in all fields, not least industrial relations. A series of Employment Acts reduced the power of trade unions and employees' pay and conditions were increasingly settled by the market alone. In 1993, the limited protection afforded against low pay – the Wages Councils – were abolished.

The idea of dictating levels of wages to employers by setting a National Minimum Wage was therefore a radical departure from previous policy. The Conservative Party strongly opposed the policy and argued that the Minimum Wage would lead to wage inflation (as those above this level would demand wage rises to maintain differentials) and unemployment (as employers would be unable to afford the higher wages). In the event, it was set at a fairly modest level and a buoyant economic situation helped to avoid these outcomes. However, this modest start also meant that it failed to eradicate problems of low pay and in-work poverty. This is the reason we categorise it as a significant though not radical change. Hall's framework does not take into account the impact of policy change and this is an important aspect to bear in mind when categorising policy reforms.

Asset-based welfare

Arguably, one of the greatest 'paradigm changes' has been the concept of 'asset-based welfare'. The main idea behind this is to encourage and enable people to build up a stock of assets that they can then use during times when income is reduced (for example, if unemployed, sick or disabled, or retired). In theory, this form of welfare could replace existing 'income-based welfare' or become the third 'pillar' of the welfare state, alongside income-based policies and the provision of services (Paxton et al, 2006).

To date, however, this policy approach has mostly been manifested in two pilot programmes for the Saving Gateway, the full-scale introduction of the Child Trust Fund, and reforms to the treatment of capital and savings within the benefits system (especially Pension Credit and HMRC's [Her Majesty's Revenue & Customs'] tax credits). While these are interesting developments, their impact has been very modest and so this change has also been categorised as significant though not 'third order' change.

Second order change

This section turns to more modest, although still significant, 'second order' change, where the policy goals have largely remained unchanged but the policy instruments to achieve those goals have been altered.

Active labour market policies

The New Deal for Young People was one of New Labour's flagship policies, following on from its 1997 General Election pledge to reduce youth unemployment by 250,000. For working-age people, 'activation' became the key policy goal although, in some senses, it was a means of achieving broader goals of reducing poverty and cutting expenditure on social security in order to stick to previous Conservative tax and spend plans. A host of sound bites soon accumulated, most notably: 'work as the best form of welfare' and 'work for those who can, security for those who cannot' (although ideas of who could or could not work changed during the Blair years). This approach has been implemented through various New Deal policies, ultimately arriving at a system denoted by Kemp (2005, p 30) as a 'work-focused benefit regime'.

The government has been fortunate that the UK has had strong economic conditions and so a very high rate of employment among those of working age. It has set a long-term aspiration to increase this to 80% of the working-age population. This requires a particular focus on disadvantaged groups with lower than average rates of employment. Among lone parents rates of employment have risen from around 45% to 57% (Labour Force Survey figures, DWP, 2006c). However, further progress is needed, and especially for those minority ethnic groups and low-skilled groups for whom employment rates fall well below the national average.

But ideas and policies in relation to 'activation' were certainly not new. The introduction of Jobseeker's Allowance and the 'lone parent caseworker project' under the Major government are important precursors, and this may also reflect some policy transfer from the US. Changes to Invalidity Benefit (as was) under the Conservative government also sought to tighten up on eligibility criteria to ensure that only those who were 'genuinely' unable to work could claim it – as well as other changes to restrict entitlement and levels of award.

The current Labour government plans to extend activation policies still further. For example, lone parents with no children under the age of 11 will be treated as unemployed. This will then be extended to those with no children aged seven or younger. And unemployed people receiving Jobseeker's Allowance will have to attend a 'rights and responsibilities seminar' after eight weeks' unemployment. Presumably the prospect of this will form an added incentive to take a job, in addition to any value added by the seminar.

Tax credits

As part of both the poverty reduction and activation policy agendas, the government has introduced tax credits aimed primarily at families with children both in and out of work (the Child Tax Credit) and those in low-paid work (Working Tax Credit). This reform could, again, be considered as quite radical change, as it appears to introduce a fundamental shift from paying out benefits to giving people tax credits/cuts. However, this is not an entirely new policy approach. Family Income Supplement, introduced in 1971 by a Conservative government, and then Family Credit (1988), were the clear precursors to Working Families' Tax Credit (1999) and then to Working Tax Credit. While Working Tax Credit has innovative features (more closely integrated with the tax system), the basic principles are the same as for Family Credit.

If anything, the reform has removed some of the more successful features of Family Credit, such as the fixed six-month awards which gave people some certainty about their financial position. Working Tax Credit payments are made in advance but then reconciled at the end of the year when any overpayments are clawed back. This caused huge problems for many people who had to make repayments and has now been partially reformed. Working Tax Credit was also controversial for focusing on making payments through the wage packet rather than the purse. Within couples, this tended to involve giving the male worker the money rather than the female carer, and major concerns were raised about the impact on expenditure on children. The delivery of tax credits has also been controversial, with a move in responsibility from the Department of Social Security to the Inland Revenue (now HMRC). The Inland Revenue had traditionally collected taxes rather than paid money out and so lacked the experience to deal with this complex part of the welfare system. The disastrous loss, in November 2007, of the personal details of 25 million people – covering 7.25 million families overall – suggests that HMRC is still struggling in this area.

Saving for retirement

As part of its 'Third Way' approach, New Labour initially put its faith in the market providing a greater proportion of retirement income for pensioners in the future (DSS, 1998). But it soon became clear that employers were moving away from generous pension packages. This reflected changes in the legislation affecting defined benefit schemes, their tax treatment and the ending of a positive stock market run. Increasing longevity also placed a strain on pension funds and many accumulated large funding deficits. The government needed to rethink its strategy here and it decided to do so with the help of an independent pensions commission.

The Pensions Commission (2005) recommended a rise in the age at which people could first receive state pensions, alongside a renewed role for insurance-based state pensions (through restoring the link between increases in the state retirement pension and earnings) and more support for private saving. These proposals were received very positively across the political and public spectrum. It is, perhaps, surprising that the age for receipt of the state pension has been 65 since the birth of Beveridge's insurance-based pensions. It is therefore a major shift. Similarly, the decision to link rises in the state retirement pension to earnings reverses a policy change made in 1980 and one that successive campaigns by pensioner groups and members of the Labour Party (most notably, Barbara Castle) had failed to come close to achieving.

The greatest opposition to the Commission's proposed reforms may have come from Brown himself. At least, issues were raised about the credibility of the cost estimates made by the Pensions Commission, against the continuation of more of a means testing-based approach. In the government response, it is noticeable that restoring the link between the state retirement pension and earnings will be 'subject to affordability', and even if it is introduced, it will take many years to make much difference to the pockets of pensioners.

Child support reform

Labour inherited a Child Support Agency introduced four years earlier that had started disastrously, and seemed to be heading downhill. The Agency did not have a successful record of either setting maintenance accurately or collecting it regularly. It was widely and openly despised by clients, and most had no choice but to use its services. The intended centrepiece of reform was the 2000 Child Support, Pensions and Social

Security Act, which introduced a new system from 2003 (it had been delayed). This abandoned the complex calculation of the 1993 system and replaced it with a new formula operating in a much simpler way. This was designed to free up staff time from collecting data, to collecting child support. It only applied to new claims, however, meaning that two separate systems operated for a time – a time that continues and is projected to continue.

However, problems with delivery and technology meant that little improvement took place. In 2006 the government lost patience with trying to make child support – and especially the Child Support Agency – work as it was intended. Following an independent review (under Henshaw, 2006), the failure of its earlier reforms to make progress, and continued bad performance statistics, in December 2006 a White Paper set out a new direction for child support. This meant a greater emphasis on people making their own arrangements and the proposal for a new body with even stronger enforcement powers. The policy emphasis strongly shifted towards tackling child poverty as an objective, and away from the earlier focus on making people face responsibilities.

People with disabilities

New Labour has had a mixed set of policies towards people with disabilities. On one level, there has been considerable unease about the growing caseloads receiving Incapacity Benefit and other disability-related benefits. As mentioned above, this area of reform began in a faltering way, moved in a voluntarist direction with the New Deal for Disabled People, but continues with the agenda of welfare reform, and attempts to move more people with disabilities back into work.

However, it would be wrong to ignore the progress made on disability rights and, in particular, the introduction of the Office for Disability Issues (which tries to coordinate the development and delivery of government services for people with disabilities). It followed the approach set by the pivotal report of the Prime Minister's Strategy Unit to ensure that 'By 2025, disabled people in Britain should have full opportunities and choices to improve their quality of life, and will be respected and included as equal members of society' (PMSU, 2005, p 15). As with other areas, there are pre-New Labour precursors, such as the 1995 Disability Discrimination Act. From October 2007, the Equality and Human Rights Commission took over responsibility for equality issues.

Delivering benefits/tax credits

When assessing changes in the delivery of benefits (and now tax credits), it is useful to draw on 6 and Peck's (2004) '10 commitments' framework. Table 4.3 goes through each of these in detail. Many have changed very little, or are not particularly relevant to the social security system, but there is certainly a growing role for the private and third

Table 4.3: The modernisation of social security delivery

Area	Social security reform
Inspection	No relevant changes, aside perhaps from within the childcare setting
Central standard setting	The social security system remains highly centralised and continues standardised modes of delivery
Area-based initiatives	Remains common for piloting and pathfinder approaches. Sure Start is a particular example of area-based policies, although not squarely within social security
Coordination and integration	No relevant changes, although pilots have attempted to bring closer integration with Housing Benefit
Devolution but limited decentralisation	Most (if not all) social security powers reserved. Some important innovation, eg through commissioners for children, free prescriptions, free elder care in the devolved administrations
Earned autonomy as a settlement between centralism and decentralisation	No relevant changes
An extended role for private capital	Some introduction of new suppliers for matching jobseekers to work. Remains a large purchaser of IT systems from the private sector. Role for third sector in some areas of delivery
A modest increase in citizen obligations	In contrast, a strong increase and emphasis on rights and responsibilities, and a strong increase in the obligations of certain benefit recipients – those of working age receiving benefits
Access (eg call centres, drop-in centres, web-enabled services)	Some movements towards call centres and use of electronic information – spectacularly unsuccessful in the case of the Child Support Agency. Move to more electronic approaches as part of the Pensions Service
E-government	Limited access, some moves to increasing access to pensions information on a more routine basis. Tax credits claimable online, although suspended at one point after large-scale fraud

sector in relation to purchasing information technology (IT) and providing some forms of 'activation' services, or even advice/help on applying for benefits, in the case of Age Concern. There has also been 'modernisation' in relation to modes of delivery with an increase in call centres, particularly in relation to the Child Support Agency and the Pension Service. Electronic applications for benefit have also been introduced, such as in relation to tax credits for a time, although there have been concerns about fraud here.

Explaining New Labour's legacy

So far in this chapter we have argued that there have been some radical 'third order' changes in social security policy under Blair, but most of the change has been less substantial, often following on from the policy approaches of the previous Conservative government. This section continues to assess the New Labour legacy and also gives some tentative explanations for it.

Whose legacy?

This book focuses on Blair's legacy. But the detail of social security policy was never a particular concern for Tony Blair. It is rumoured that the famous 'Granita' deal between Blair and Brown was that Blair would become leader of the party in return for Brown having control over social policy. If so, one would expect that Brown, as Chancellor of the Exchequer, played a key role in relation to social security. Brown's dominance here not only related to control of the government purse strings but also his continuity in post. Social security is an extremely complex part of the welfare state and successive changes in Secretary of State did not offer those in charge of it much time to understand the system and propose important reforms. The 10 years of Blair in power saw seven different heads of the Department running social security (see Table 4.4). This represents a period in office of barely 18 months on average, in what is one of the more complex areas of policy and among the most detailed with which to become acquainted. Table 4.4 provides a litany of would-be welfare reformers.

Political pragmatism and ideology

The primary goal of the New Labour project was to win power following 18 years in the political wilderness. Central to achieving this goal was to shed Old Labour's 'tax and spend' image. So New

Table 4.4: Secretaries of State at the Department for Work and Pensions (and Department of Social Security) under New Labour, 1997–2007

	Person	Appointed	Months in office	Destination
1	Harriet Harman	3 May 1997	15	Removed, along with deputy, Frank Field
2	Alistair Darling	27 July 1998	46	Went to Transport
3	Andrew Smith	29 May 2002	27	Resigned
4	Alan Johnson	8 September 2004	8	Went to Trade and Industry
5	David Blunkett	6 May 2005	6	Resigned
6	John Hutton	2 November 2005	19	Moved to Business, Enterprise and Regulatory Reform
7	Peter Hain[a]	28 June 2007	7	Resigned

Note: [a] Post-Blair, but continuing the theme, Peter Hain resigned on 24 January 2008, to be replaced by James Purnell.

Labour foreswore any increase on the Conservatives' published and stringent spending plans for 1997–99. Thus 'Prudence' might also be said to be responsible for social security policy, alongside the various political figures involved. This approach led to politically unpopular cuts made to One Parent Benefit, and press unease at potential benefit cuts for people with disabilities,[1] some of whom went on to chain themselves to the railings outside Downing Street and throw red paint described as 'Blair's blood'.[2] The reductions in benefits for lone parents were particularly surprising in the light of the substantial increases in spending on lone parents and their families that would later be made. They also seemed to have set back attempts at reforming benefits for working-age people with disabilities.

Brewer et al (2002) also point out that the first New Labour government began with few strong or explicit ideas about welfare reform – their creative energies lay elsewhere. The pledge to reduce youth unemployment through the New Deal was an exception here.

However, both Blair and Brown share common ideological convictions in this arena (stemming partly from broadly Christian socialist values): not least concern about poverty but also the importance of individual 'responsibility' and 'hard' work as the route out of poverty. The emphasis on 'work' also chimes with traditional concerns of the Labour Party, although Brown would only commit himself to providing 'full employability' rather than the Old Labour commitment to 'full employment'. We might expect the emphasis on 'work' to lead to a strengthening of the insurance-based elements of the social security system but Brown has resisted this in favour of apparently cheaper means-tested approaches. Thus political pragmatism appears to triumph over ideology here.

Political pragmatism also appears to lead New Labour to follow public opinion and this is certainly the case in relation to social security policy. In 1983, evidence from the British Social Attitudes Survey showed the balance of opinion was to maintain levels of tax and spending. In each subsequent year the policy of taxing and spending more (on particular social areas) has proved the more popular view. There was a sizeable dip in 2000, however, and a decline over much of Labour's first term. More recent data on public attitudes suggest that, if anything, attitudes towards state spending on welfare have hardened still further between 2002 and 2006 (Orton and Rowlingson, 2007; Taylor-Gooby and Martin, 2008). Some commentators have taken to believing that the approach is one of 'doing good by stealth' (Lister, 2004), an approach that leaves change quite vulnerable to being undone by stealth.

Policy change ahead?

David Cameron's Conservatives have said relatively little about welfare reform. Until recently their main lines of attack have been to express frustration with the administrative difficulties with the tax credit system, with the slow pace of reform of the Child Support Agency, and to raise the issue of how marriages (and couples) are undermined by the social security system. However, in October 2007, Cameron gave a major speech about 'Making British poverty history' (Cameron, 2007), in clear reference to campaigns around international development. The policy tools were not fully described, but seemed to involve a greater use of the private and third sectors in providing services to help people return to work. In addition, changes to Working Tax Credit were promised to promote couples remaining together rather than separating, as they suggest happens under the existing system.

Gordon Brown stands squarely behind pledges to eliminate child poverty. He has also been generally seen as the most supportive of means-tested approaches to tackle poverty, and less interested in more universal solutions. It has not escaped attention that both Prime Minister Brown and the Leader of the Opposition have families and disabled children, and hence are sympathetic to the needs of parents. Given his dominant role in shaping social security policy under Blair, it seems highly unlikely that there will be any major changes in direction under his premiership.

Conclusion

Radical change in social security policy is always likely to be rare as the system is huge and complex. Nevertheless, Blair achieved a 'paradigm shift' by putting 'poverty' back on the policy agenda. His pledge to eradicate child poverty was a major turning point in welfare reform although the failure to achieve even the interim targets in poverty reduction may come back to haunt his successor(s). The emphasis on poverty was a radical departure from the previous governments but the focus on children and pensioners draws on traditional views about the 'deserving poor'. Poverty rates among working-age adults without children are now particularly high and yet not the basis for much discussion or action.

Other highly significant changes include the National Minimum Wage, asset-based welfare approaches and, perhaps, changes in state retirement pensions. Other changes, although significant, have tended to follow on from older approaches of activation (welfare-to-work) and the introduction of tax credits. Delivery mechanisms have also changed but, again, this was likely to have happened under a Conservative government due to technological change and the accompanying opportunity to realise cost savings through cutting face-to-face interactions.

The reasons for the New Labour legacy in relation to social security are complex. They relate to the key players involved here (notably Blair, Brown and successive Secretaries of State) and their ideological underpinnings. Concern about the public purse strings has undoubtedly affected the extent of any legacy as has concern about public attitudes to redistribution. The caution of the first term in office can, perhaps, be better understood than the relative caution of the second term. Following years in the political wilderness, Labour's 'prudent' approach to tax and spend was clearly a vote winner. But after a second election landslide, it is surprising that the government was still so cautious and unwilling to lead, rather than simply follow, public opinion.

The 'Blair' legacy appears to have formed a new consensus on social security policy as there appears to be very little difference between Brown and Cameron in this area, although the recent rise in poverty levels and the claim that New Labour's anti-poverty strategy is 'largely exhausted' (Palmer et al, 2007, p 9) may spur more radical policy proposals to come forward if the government is truly committed to achieving its historic aim to eradicate child poverty.

Notes

[1] For instance, *The Observer*, 21 December 1997: 'Tony Blair has called a special crisis meeting of the Cabinet to discuss welfare reform amid a growing revolt led by Education Secretary David Blunkett against Treasury plans to cut benefits for the disabled.'

[2] See BBC news, 'Protesters throw "Blair's blood"' (http://news.bbc.co.uk/1/hi/uk/41746.stm).

References

6, P. and Peck, E. (2004) 'Modernisation: the ten commitments of New Labour's approach to public management?', *International Public Management Journal*, vol 7, no 1, pp 1-18.

Beveridge, W. (1942) *Social insurance and allied services*, London: HMSO.

Blair, T. (1999) Beveridge lecture, given at Toynbee Hall, 18 March.

Blair, T. (2001) Speech to the Confederation of British Industry, 5 November.

Brewer, M., Clark, T. and Wakefield, M. (2002) 'Social security under New Labour: what did the third way mean for welfare reform?', *Fiscal Studies*, vol 23, no 4, pp 505-37.

Cameron, D. (2007) 'Making British poverty history', Speech at Chance UK, 26 October.

DSS (Department for Social Security) (1998) *New ambitions for our country: A new contract for welfare*, Cm 3805, London: HMSO.

DWP (Department for Work and Pensions) (2006a) *Security in retirement: Towards a new pension system*, Cm 6841, London: The Stationery Office.

DWP (2006b) *Personal accounts*, Cm 6975, London: The Stationery Office.

DWP (2006c) *A new deal for welfare*, Green Paper, Cm 6730, London: HMSO.

DWP (2007) *Households Below Average Income 1994/95–2005/06*, London: DWP.

Hall, P.A. (1993) 'Policy paradigms, social learning and the state: the case of economic policy making in Britain', *Comparative Politics*, vol 25, no 3, pp 275-96.

Henshaw, D. (2006) *Recovering child support: Routes to responsibility*, Cm 6894, London: The Stationery Office.

Hirsch, D. (2006) *What will it take to end child poverty? Firing on all cylinders*, York: Joseph Rowntree Foundation (www.jrf.org.uk/bookshop/eBooks/9781859355008.pdf).

HM Treasury (2007) *Meeting the aspirations of the British people: 2007 Pre-Budget report and Comprehensive Spending Review*, October, London: HM Treasury.

Jones, F. (2007) *The effects of taxes and benefits on household income, 2005/06*, London: Office for National Statistics.

Kemp, P. (2005) 'Social security and welfare reform under New Labour', in M. Powell, L. Bauld and K. Clarke (eds) *Social Policy Review 17: Analysis and debate in social policy, 2005*, Bristol: The Policy Press, pp 15-32.

Lister, R. (2004) *Winning the argument on poverty*, London: Catalyst.

McKay, S. and Rowlingson, K. (1998) *Social security in Britain*, Basingstoke: Macmillan.

Orton, M. and Rowlingson, K. (2007) *Public attitudes to economic inequality*, Bristol: The Policy Press.

Palmer, G., MacInnes, T. and Kenway, P. (2007) *Monitoring poverty and social exclusion*, York: Joseph Rowntree Foundation.

Paxton, W., White, S. and Maxwell, D. (2006) *The citizen's stake: Exploring the future of universal asset policies*, Bristol: The Policy Press.

Pensions Commission (2005) *A new pension settlement for the twenty-first century: The second report of the Pensions Commission*, London: The Stationery Office.

Phillips, D. and Sibieta, L. (2007) *A survey of the UK benefit system*, London: Institute of Fiscal Studies.

PMSU (Prime Minister's Strategy Unit) (2005) *Improving the life chances of disabled people*, London: Cabinet Office.

Taylor-Gooby, P. and Martin, R. (2008) 'Trends in sympathy for the poor', in A. Park, J Curtice and K. Thomson (eds) *British social attitudes*, London: Sage Publications, pp 59-88.

Walker, R. (ed) (1999) *Ending child poverty: Popular welfare for the 21st century?*, Bristol: The Policy Press.

FIVE

Social care under Blair: are social care services more modern?

Mark Baldwin

Introduction

From a lukewarm beginning (Baldwin, 2002), New Labour's social care policy has come to the boil, with the changes introduced symbolic of their ambiguous approach to public policy – full of rhetoric on individual empowerment, but relentless in the unshackling of private capital to develop services. In this chapter I will look at what has changed in social care over the Blair years and how much it has changed. I will look at whether policy development reflects modernisation as conceptualised by 6 and Peck (2004), and evaluate the order of change, if any, from Conservative social policy using the Hall (1993) model.

The law relating to social care has always been different in England and Wales from Scotland and Northern Ireland, but devolution has made changes in the social care arena in the four countries that have not always been congruent. These differences need to be acknowledged, and some will be addressed.

Policy developments under New Labour

Since coming to power in 1997 New Labour has been active in the social care arena, producing a White Paper in 1998, *Modernising social services* (DH, 1998), and major policy initiatives for children and families, in the shape of the Green Paper *Every Child Matters* (DfES, 2003), and the White Paper *Our health, our care, our say* (DH, 2006) (see Table 5.1).

I shall look at the way in which these policy developments have reflected the themes of modernisation as classified by 6 and Peck (2004). The first is *coordination and integration*, which is also defined in the social care context as partnership, inter-agency working and inter-professional practice. These are concepts debated elsewhere (see

Table 5.1: The main policy changes in New Labour's social care

1998	White Paper *Modernising social services* (DH, 1998)	Tackling the Berlin Wall between health and social care; regulation of workforce
1999	Health Act	Removes demarcation between health and social care services
2001	White Paper *Valuing people: A new strategy for learning disability for the 21st century* (DH, 2001b)	Involves people with learning difficulties in developing policy for their needs
2001	Race Relations (Amendment) Act	Duty on public bodies to promote racial equality
2002	Fair access to care services (FACS)	National eligibility criteria to tackle the 'postcode lottery'
2003	Laming report *The Victoria Climbié Inquiry* (Laming, 2003)	Comments on the failures of management and inter-organisational practice in the death of a child
2003	Green Paper *Every Child Matters* (DfES, 2003)	Paves way for integrated Children's Trusts
2005	Disability Discrimination Act	Duty on public bodies to promote disability equality
2006	Equality Act	Brings age, religion and sexuality into the equality framework
2006	White Paper *Our health, our care, our say* (DH, 2006)	Introduces the personalisation agenda and Individual Budgets

Ovretveit et al, 1997; Onyett, 2003; Barrett et al, 2005; Glendinning et al, 2005; Quinney, 2006), and I will look at them as attempts to tackle the 'Berlin Wall' (DH, 1998) between social care and other services. *An extended role for private capital* has been argued as one way of ensuring choice for service users. In the social care context the latter theme would also include user involvement, and empowerment, within a consumerist framework. Central standard setting, with its emphasis on *regulation and quality*, will be discussed along with *inspection* – also a 6 and Peck theme. There are further themes argued in government policy as modern, which I will explore. These are firstly *prevention* and secondly *resource management, eligibility and prioritisation*. Another aspect of policy that is not argued as modern but has been a notable aspect of New Labour's policy is social justice. If empowerment has been located within the consumerist paradigm, then anti-discrimination legislation is located more within a rights perspective.

Coordination and integration

Before New Labour came to power in 1997 there were statutory powers for local authorities and health services to commission services together, but the notion of integration was absent, and partnership was more sound bite than coherent policy. There were localised health and social care staff in community mental health teams, co-located in the same buildings but employed by different organisations (Onyett, 2003).

Frank Dobson, the first New Labour Secretary of State at the Department of Health, declared, in the White Paper *Modernising social services* (DH, 1998), that the government would break down the 'Berlin Wall' between health and social care, although expressed no intention of integrating services within single organisations. Partnership was intended to tackle government inefficiency in response to growing demand in a modern welfare state (Rummery, 2006). It is a response that sits within the 'Third Way' (Powell, 2002), designed to manage tensions between market and bureaucracy. Government intentions rapidly slipped along the continuum from joint working to integration post-White Paper, with the formation of primary care trusts. The 1999 Health Act, with its 'flexibilities' (for example, Glendinning et al, 2005), indicates how fast New Labour moved. The Act dismantled the demarcation between health and social care, allowing either side to provide services delivered by the other (Edwards and Miller, 2003).

The 1999 Health Act removed barriers to joint working by introducing powers to enable health and local authorities to bring resources together in a pooled budget accessible to both commission and provide services (DH, 2001a, p 63).

Partnership is also a theme in children's policy, shifting to an integration model, following the publication of the Laming report into the death of Victoria Climbié (Laming, 2003). The Green Paper *Every Child Matters* (DfES, 2003) moves beyond urging organisations to work together effectively and lays the foundation for integration (Churchill, 2007) through Children's Trusts. This mirrors the shift from partnership and co-location in adult services. Most local authorities now organise their children and families services, formerly located in social services departments, within broader departments, dominated by education.

Although partnership was seen as a device for effective working across organisational and professional barriers, it was also argued as an alternative to the Conservative government's market in care (Rummery, 2007). Partnership should avoid obsession with managerialism and should not be seen as favouring any particular type of organisation and so is argued as ideologically neutral. Managerialism, however, has continued as the organisational device for social care (Beresford et al, 2007; Cowden and Singh, 2007), and partnership has not been reflected in equality between organisations (Glendinning and Means, 2006).

There are two major questions to address in evaluating coordination and integration as a theme. Firstly, if the aim is to get people working together more effectively, how can you make them do that? The second is, even if you could, would that make services more effective? An answer to the first question suggests that it is more than just reorganisation that is required to ensure better practice. Karen Newbigging argues that 'merely bringing together a group of different professionals and ... non-professionally aligned staff, in the hope that they can work it out together, leaves much to chance' (Newbigging, 2004, p 145).

On the second question, the evidence is not strong that such approaches are valued by service users (Brown et al, 2003), and the only positive aspect for which there is any evidence is that it saves money (Rummery, 2007). Glendinning et al (2005) note the problems of measuring outcomes in partnership, mainly because of the absence of agreed definitions. They conclude that 'on the basis of the evidence currently available, it is far from certain whether partnerships between health and social care "work" and, therefore, whether they should count' (2005, p 376).

Partnership is also criticised for being a misnomer (Sadd and Baldwin, 2006) when 'partners' have different levels of power within the relationship. Even with relationships between large organisations such as social services and health, or education, the more powerful organisation's aims and ethos are likely to hold sway (Churchill, 2007). This can result in the undermining of professional values such as social work, despite it being more attuned to policy aspirations such as user empowerment (Churchill, 2007).

Much recent policy assumes integration will have already led to effective inter-professional practice (DH, 2006, p 24), although academic studies continue to indicate that problems exist with differing ethos (Churchill, 2007), different aims (Warin, 2007) and problematic power relationships (Rummery, 2007). The Department of Health clearly recognises these problems with a recent document – *Modernising adult social care: What's working* – noting the continuing tension between 'different professional cultures' (DH, 2007, p 17) and the 'barrier to partnership or service integration' (2007, p 17).

Our health, our care, our say (DH, 2006) indicates the twin themes of partnership and competition within social markets in successive sections without any acknowledgement of potential conflicts of aims. So, 'better joining up of local services' is argued as 'encouraging innovation' (DH, 2006, p 9), but three pages later the policy is about 'allowing different providers to compete for services' (p 12). Trying to mitigate competition through urging partnership is a strange policy. Competitors in social care markets will not want to work in partnership with potentially competing providers, nor will they be keen on getting close to organisations that commission and regulate their service.

Glendinning et al (2005) conclude with a warning that the 'energetic promotion' of partnership as a form of governance while retaining quasi-markets undermines 'government claims for a distinctive "Third Way" strategy of governance through partnership', and that 'substantial challenges remain in demonstrating its effectiveness' (2005, p 378).

An extended role for private capital

Much has been written elsewhere (for example, Page, 2007) about New Labour and its desire to embrace markets as potential methods for achieving choice, quality and responsiveness. In the case of social care markets, New Labour may utilise a different language from crude neoliberalism (Farnsworth, 2006), but market ideology is argued as 'far more deeply embedded into social policy' than it was under the previous conservative administration (Farnsworth, 2006, p 820).

We can see this in the White Paper (DH, 2006), which argues that the Commission for Social Care Inspection (CSCI) should work closely with the Department of Health and local government to 'develop better the various social markets' (DH, 2006, p 170) to ensure choice from a range of services. While the imperative for developing social markets emphasises the part to be played by voluntary, community and 'values-driven organisations such as co-operatives' (DH, 2006, p 175), the possibility of privatising more social care (and even health – 2006, p 174) services is noted.

New Labour does not have a problem with private capital in social care provision, although its assertion that its policy is non-ideological needs investigation. There are arguments that business involvement undermines the 'democratic accountability of services' (Farnsworth, 2006, p 831). Farnsworth also suggests such involvement weakens the public service ethos so that it is ability to pay and maintaining profitability that counts, not meeting need. Drakeford (2006) adds that the residential care market has not proved responsive and user-focused but tended towards monopolisation and standardisation. Private business maintains its position in the market by reducing costs such as wages. The tendency to low-paid, low-skilled working practices does not square with the government's modernising quest for a highly skilled workforce (DH, 1998, 2006).

The White Paper states 'more powerful users of social care' will be able to stimulate the market, 'opening up the range and availability of services to match need' (DH, 2006, p 83). This is empowerment through choice within a consumerist framework. The policy instrument to achieve this is the individual budget, located within the Department of Health's new 'personalisation agenda'. All service users will have an individualised budget that will be calculated to meet their personalised assessed needs, so they will allegedly control their services. This level of control will mean a real rather than quasi-market in which they will become 'powerful users' (DH, 2006). There are problems with this claim, however. Firstly, eligibility criteria determine who will be a service user, so 'service users' are not the sum of all people in need. Service users who do not meet the criteria will not count as 'powerful users', unless they are wealthy enough to purchase care within the private market. Secondly, it is unlikely that service users with the levels of need required to trigger the eligibility criteria will have the information required to make choices in 'the market'. Thirdly, it is not service users but commissioners who commission services. They may consult service users, but they retain the power to make decisions.

Clarke argues that choice as a form of consumerism undermines social solidarity (Clarke, 2006). He also notes that *Modernising social services* (DH, 1998) was more concerned with independence as the empowerment theme. He sees the move of Alan Milburn to the Department of Health in place of Frank Dobson as the key turning point. Clarke argues that this is when *New* Labour took charge of social care policy.

Concerns about user empowerment are reflected in the regulatory body's annual report. The CSCI (2006) notes that, despite improvements in user involvement, it is not 'systematic or effective across the country' (DH, 2006, p 12). One of the symbolic tools of user empowerment – direct payments – is also criticised. The report notes that direct payments are 'still used by only a small minority of people' (DH, 2006, p 13). By its own analysis, it seems the regulatory body is not impressed with developments in this key policy area.

There is a divergence of opinion about direct payments, with those committed to an empowerment ethos seeing them as welcome attempts to give control to service users (Glasby and Littlechild, 2002; Leece and Bornat, 2006). Others have a negative view, evaluating them as reflecting individualism and consumerism, with users being constructed as consumers in the welfare market (Spandler, 2004).

In the policy literature on children, the rhetoric on user control is less obvious. There is choice for parents in schooling and childcare, but there is a different ethos for social care services. The White Paper *Every Child Matters* (DfES, 2003) makes reference to young people who have been listened to for the purpose of defining objectives, but there is also a 'social threat discourse' (Churchill, 2007, p 95), similar to the mental health field, where 'mainstream mental health policy has ... been characterised by an emphasis on risk and dangerousness' (Warner, 2007, p 215). This is not universal across the four countries of the UK, however, with the Welsh Assembly having created a commissioner for children who has the job of hearing the voice of young people (Butler, 2007).

Central standard setting and inspection

These themes of policy modernisation (6 and Peck, 2004) are reflected in social care through regulation, inspection and the maintenance of quality centrally and guidance on commissioning in local authority areas. Like other areas of public policy, social care is now heavily regulated (Humphrey, 2003) with a central system, separated from local authorities, implementing a national quality framework. This shift from local to central regulation has been a feature of New Labour social care policy since the first White Paper (DH, 1998). The tightening of regulation has continued, with the latest White Paper (DH, 2006) arguing for 'robust systems of independent regulation' (2006, p 20) and linking the regulatory system to 'guaranteeing quality' (p 182).

Modernising social services (DH, 1998) recognised a number of problems with the regulation system, notably its lack of independence, coherence and consistency. The answer was to create an independent, national Commission for Care Standards (subsequently the CSCI). Although the CSCI has claimed year-on-year improvement, there has been a problem of local interpretation of regulation that has maintained inconsistencies referred to as the 'postcode lottery'. It should be noted that there is little luck involved in this lottery – inequality is more the result of poverty, class and racism than a coincidence of random numbers.

The other aspect of regulation that is new is the regulation of the workforce. The General Social Care Council has the task of registering all social care workers in the country. Codes of practice that social workers must adhere to include codes for their employers, so the expectation is that, in time, this form of regulation will improve standards.

A different aspect of regulation is eligibility for services. Systems for regulating access to services by those in need has been a consistent theme since the Conservatives' White Paper *Caring for people* (DH, 1989), which introduced the policy of targeting those in most need. This policy has the unintended consequence of creating dependency and undermining choice (Baldwin, 2000). Targeting those in most need means that an individual has to wait until preferred informal support networks have fallen apart and more dependency-creating resources (for example, residential care) become necessary. In Scotland this concern has been partly eradicated by the introduction of free personal care by the Scottish Assembly (Bowes and Bell, 2007). The final Wanless report (2004) looked at the cost of long-term care and the Sutherland report argued that government should meet those costs (Royal Commission on Long-term Care, 1999). Others, however, have claimed that to pay for such care would increase dependency and the likelihood of older people ending up in residential settings (Keen et al, 2007).

In 2002 New Labour introduced a new scheme for eligibility, designed to ensure consistency across the country. This is known as FACS (fair access to care services). The criteria are graded in four bands – critical, substantial, moderate and low – with phrases defining each one (Charles and Manthorpe, 2007). There are two types of problem with these criteria. Firstly, the phrases are interpreted differently at organisational and individual levels, and, secondly, it is up to each local authority to decide which levels they will meet. Some authorities meet needs at both critical and substantial levels, whereas others will only meet critical levels. If an authority will only pay for people whose needs are critical, what are they preventing?

Prevention or targeting those in most need?

Prevention is not one of the 6 and Peck (2004) themes of modern policy, but has been mentioned by 6 (1998) as a theme of modernisation. Prevention was established, in the first White Paper (DH, 1998), as an indication of modern social care services, although the priority remained targeting those in most need. Since then further policy developments in the third term of the New Labour government have been necessary to establish prevention with more serious opportunities for implementation. The White Paper *Our health, our care, our say* has this as one of its four main themes – 'Health and social care services will provide better prevention services with earlier intervention' (DH, 2006, p 7).

Our health, our care, our say is not exclusively focused on services for adults, and children and young people are subsumed in its policy relating to prevention. In addition the Green Paper specific to children and families – *Every Child Matters* (DfES, 2003) – argues for prevention, with the Common Assessment Framework argued as promoting 'earlier intervention and a focus on prevention' (DfES, 2004, p 6).

New Labour and social justice

It is hard to pass by the swathe of legislation and policy guidance on social justice, which, as argued in an earlier evaluation of New Labour's social care policy (Baldwin, 2002), has major implications for social care services. The duty on public bodies to promote 'racial' and disability equality in the 2001 Race Relations (Amendment) Act and the 2005 Disability Discrimination Act, and additional measures to combat discrimination in relation to age, religion and sexuality in the 2006 Equality Act, have come partly as a response to examples of inequality in social care.

It should be noted (Butler, 2007) that the Welsh Assembly has adopted its own approach to protecting the rights of children under the United Nations Convention on the Rights of the Child. This, along with more general approaches of 'progressive universalism', and an 'ethic of participation' (Drakeford, 2007) in Welsh governance of social work policy, indicate areas where English policy has lagged behind Wales.

While nobody defines equality policies as 'modern', we can see the social justice theme as an antidote to empowerment within the consumerist model. The oppressive nature of other policy, such as that on asylum seekers, has undermined the social justice agenda. Social workers are increasingly worried by the requirements placed on them to act with asylum seeker families in ways that are within the immigration law but outside of the children's legislation (Mynott, 2005).

Table 5.2: Modernisation themes in social care

Extended role for private capital	This theme is present, but little more than an extension of Conservative policies – so not modern in the sense of new
Empowerment, choice and user involvement	This New Labour theme is similar to the Conservatives' – individual users seeking choice in a care market. So not modern in the sense of new
Central standards and regulation	New Labour regulatory systems are different to the Conservatives' – centralised and independent from local authorities. This fits the definition of modern
Area-based implementation	Social care services are commissioned locally as with Conservative policy, although the inclusion of other themes such as user involvement is new
Coordination and integration	This is a policy development that is a change from Conservative organisational policy and warrants the label of modern
Prevention	The focus on prevention is new and, if implemented, could lead to improvements in outcomes. Prevention, if fully implemented, could be argued as modern
Devolution but limited decentralisation	Social care services are still commissioned at local authority level. Decentralisation is limited by centrally established quality regimes and financial control. In Scotland the decision to provide free personal care is a divergence from traditional means testing
Increase in citizen obligations	There is a balance between policies – user control in social services for (for example) people with disabilities, but an expectation of 'work for those who can' in the social inclusion policy stream from the Department for Work and Pensions
Access	There have been developments in the provision of services through Care Direct in some areas. It is too early to say whether this is welcomed by service users
E-government	Information technology (IT) is used for assessment and databases. Methods may change but this is continuation, not modern in the sense of technologically new

Orders of change

So if these are the changes that have taken place during the Blair era, what is the degree of change? Hall's (1993) model suggests three central variables that are the goals that guide policy in social care, the techniques or instruments for achieving those goals and the precise settings for the use of these instruments (see Table 5.3). First order change occurs when the levels of these instruments of change are altered, for instance by changes in the criteria for regulation of social care services. Second order change occurs when the instruments and the setting are altered

Table 5.3: Orders of change in policy themes

Coordination and integration	The shift from joint commissioning to partnership to integration indicates first order change in the instruments of policy and, in some cases, change in the settings for these instruments. This is first and possibly second order change
Prevention	The policy rhetoric is now prevention but unless the instruments of change are resourced, the agenda will not be realised. This is a potential paradigm shift
Choice and empowerment	Policy rhetoric has increased and there are new instruments (individual budgets). This is not a change from Conservative policy either in the purchaser–provider split or in the creation of a market in care. These are first order changes
Regulation, quality and inspection	There are new instruments in place and the setting has shifted from local authority to independent. Regulation policy remains the same, so this is second order change
Eligibility and prioritisation	New Labour has changed the instruments but not their underlying ethos. This is first order change
Social justice	Despite the additions to social justice instruments such as the duty to promote racial and disability equality imposed on public bodies, this is more a response to new understanding than paradigm shift. This constitutes second order change

in response to prior experience (but the fundamental policy paradigm remains the same). This could, for instance, entail a shift in the level and process of regulating social care services. Third order change occurs when the instrument, settings and goals all change, constituting a paradigm shift (Kuhn, 1996). This could entail a shift to a different paradigm for regulation of outcomes, such as a shift to a prevention strategy. So how do the key policy changes listed above look in the context of this model for ranking change?

New Labour's commitment to greater coordination and integration is new. Virginia Bottomley as Secretary of State at the Department of Health in the Conservative government (1990–97) threatened local authorities that the community care changes were their last chance, with the implied threat of integration if they failed. This, however, did not happen as it has under Blair. The shift from joint commissioning to partnership to integration indicates first order change in the instruments of policy and, in some cases, change in the settings for these instruments. At the most this is second order change.

The personalisation agenda, the phrase used to define policy instruments such as direct payments and individual budgets, is claimed as a major innovation by New Labour. They are argued as a means of putting control into the hands of service users. These developments, however, are located within the Conservative community care policy paradigm. Choice and voice is designed, even with these new policy instruments, for individual consumers within a welfare market. The ethos of empowerment is only reflected in the actions of service users, or their advocates, who have the wherewithal to act as entrepreneurs in the welfare market (Scourfield, 2007). Those reliant on their own devices or on hard-pressed social workers are unlikely to have their choices met. There is no change in the structure of power relationships and so these are first order changes.

The regulatory framework has shifted in successive policy documents – mainly to achieve greater clarity – but it is not a new system; rather they mirror the performance assessment criteria of Conservative quality schemes. So, even though the instruments have changed from local to national and from local authority to independent status, this is no more than second order change. The paradigm remains the same.

Prevention as a policy stream holds the greatest claim of modern (new and improved) social care and for evidence of a paradigm shift in policy. While previous governments have talked prevention rhetoric, the most recent New Labour policy initiatives actually suggest activity. The initial evidence of policy outcomes seems tantalisingly positive, but we cannot make longer-term judgements on this theme until we see whether New Labour is prepared to put its money where its rhetorical mouth is. This area holds out the possibility for third order change in social care policy.

Conclusion

New Labour's activity in the social care sector should not be seen as either modern, in the sense of new and improved, or as constituting a paradigmatic shift in policy values. The changes are within the broad framework defined by the Conservatives' community care revolution, and maintain the fundamental aspects of that revolution. I would argue, with Kirstein Rummery, that New Labour has 'never strayed too far' from the themes of Conservative community care changes (Rummery, 2007, p 67).

Local authorities have maintained the central role in commissioning services, even though the old social services departments have largely dissolved into adult and children's departments. The introduction of a market in care, characterised as a quasi-market by Bartlett and Le Grand (1993), has been maintained. Claims that the personalisation agenda will remove the 'quasi' nature of this market are too early and probably over-optimistic. Rhetorical arguments that service users as consumers in this mixed economy of care will have more power and choice are not new, even if they are trumpeted more consistently in New Labour policy. Individualism as the overriding ideology for the development, organisation and management of services is another theme that has not changed. Service users are constructed as individuals in this market in policy documents. The safety net of collective systems of service is rapidly disappearing under New Labour. This is a continuation of Conservative community care intentions.

The paradigm shift for social care occurred in the 1980s and 1990s. New Labour has shown hints of interest in other directions such as prevention, and the social justice model of anti-discrimination legislation, but has continued to walk the Thatcherite path. The social justice policy on the promotion of equality in the provision of public services reflects a different approach to services, one which could overturn the legacy of marginalising people because of their ethnicity, their disability, their sexuality, their age or the accident of birth that left them poor and working class. Humphrey's (2003) evaluation of social services is telling: 'the concrete problem for social services is that it is difficult for them to prove their worth in terms of the value they add to the economy.... It should not be forgotten that the capitalist economy has been less than welcoming towards people who find themselves on the margins of society' (p 19).

The *Valuing people* White Paper (2001b), for people with learning difficulties, is a beacon of light in an otherwise dark world of markets and consumerism. Much could be learnt by services for other service user groups from the values expressed there. The prevention agenda being piloted now across the country holds out substantial hope for a new and very different approach to the delivery of social care services. This new vision would see people receiving services that retain them in their own homes by early, limited and largely informal intervention. If modern services are defined by being responsive to expressed needs, as claimed in the White Paper (DH, 2006), then this is one area where New Labour could make a difference. My breathing remains regular and I keep watch.

References

6, P. (1998) 'Problem-solving government', in I. Hargreaves and I. Christie (eds) *Tomorrow's politics*, London: Demos.

6, P. and Peck, E. (2004) 'Modernisation: the ten commandments of New Labour's approach to public management?', *International Public Management Journal*, vol 7, no 1, pp 1-18.

Baldwin, M. (2000) *Care management and community care: Social work discretion and the construction of policy*, Aldershot: Ashgate.

Baldwin, M. (2002) 'New Labour and social care: continuity or change?', in M. Powell (ed) *Evaluating New Labour's welfare reforms*, Bristol: The Policy Press.

Barrett, G., Sellman, D. and Thomas, J. (2005) *Inter-professional working in health and social care: Professional perspectives*, Basingstoke: Palgrave Macmillan.

Bartlett, W. and Le Grand, J. (eds) (1993) *Quasi-markets and social policy*, Basingstoke: Palgrave Macmillan.

Beresford, P., Adshead, L. and Croft, S. (2007) *Palliative care, social work and service users: Making life possible*, London: Jessica Kingsley.

Bowes, A. and Bell, D. (2007) 'Free personal care for older people in Scotland: issues and implications', *Social Policy & Society*, vol 6, no 3, pp 435-45.

Brown, L., Tucker, C. and Domokos, T. (2003) 'Evaluating the impact of integrated health and social care teams on older people living in the community', *Health & Social Care in the Community*, vol 11, no 2, pp 85-94.

Butler, I. (2007) 'Children's policy in Wales', in C. Williams (ed) *Social policy for social welfare practice in a devolved Wales*, Birmingham: BASW/Venture Press.

Charles, N. and Manthorpe, J. (2007) 'FACS or fiction? The impact of the policy fair access to care services on social care assessments of older visually impaired people', *Practice*, vol 19, no 2, pp 143-57.

Churchill, H. (2007) 'Children's services in 2006', in K. Clarke, T. Maltby and P. Kennett (eds) *Social Policy Review 19: Analysis and debate in social policy, 2007*, Bristol: The Policy Press.

Clarke, J. (2006) 'Consumers, clients or citizens? Politics, policy and practice in the reform of social care', *European Societies*, vol 8, no 3, pp 423-42.

Cowden, S. and Singh, G. (2007) 'The "user": friend, foe or fetish? A critical exploration of user involvement in health and social care', *Critical Social Policy*, vol 27, no 1, pp 5-23.

CSCI (Commission for Social Care Inspection) (2006) *The state of social care in England 2005-06: Executive summary*, Norwich: The Stationery Office.

DfES (Department for Education and Skills) (2003) *Every Child Matters*, Norwich: The Stationery Office.

DfES (2004) *Every Child Matters: Change for children in social care*, Nottingham: DfES.

DH (Department of Health) (1989) *Caring for people: Community care into the next decade and beyond*, Cmd 849, London: HMSO.

DH (1998) *Modernising social services; Promoting independence, improving protection, raising standards*, Cm 4169, Norwich: The Stationery Office.

DH (2001a) *The mental health policy implementation guide*, Norwich: The Stationery Office.

DH (2001b) *Valuing people: A new strategy for learning disability for the 21st century*, A White Paper, Norwich: The Stationery Office.

DH (2006) *Our health, our care, our say: A new direction for community services*, Norwich: The Stationery Office.

DH (2007) *Modernising adult social care: What's working*, Norwich: The Stationery Office.

Drakeford, M. (2006) 'Ownership, regulation and the public interest: the case of residential care for older people', *Critical Social Policy*, vol 26, no 4, pp 932-44.

Drakeford, M. (2007) 'Governance and social policy', in C. Williams (ed) *Social policy for social welfare practice in a devolved Wales*, Birmingham: BASW/Venture Press.

Edwards, M. and Miller, C. (2003) *Integrating health and social care and making it work*, London: Office for Public Management.

Farnsworth, K. (2006) 'Capital to the rescue? New Labour's business solutions to old welfare problems', *Critical Social Policy*, vol 26, no 4, pp 817-42.

Glasby, J and Littlechild, R. (2002) *Social work and direct payments*, Bristol: The Policy Press.

Glendinning, C. and Means, R. (2006) 'Personal social services: developments in adult social care', in L. Bauld, K. Clarke and T. Maltby (eds) *Social Policy Review 18: Analysis and debate in social policy, 2006*, Bristol: The Policy Press.

Glendinning, C., Dowling, B. and Powell, M. (2005) 'Partnerships between health and social care under "New Labour": smoke without fire? A review of policy and evidence', *Evidence & Policy*, vol 1, no 3, pp 365-81.

Hall, P.A. (1993) 'Policy paradigms, social learning and the state: the case of economic policy making in Britain', *Comparative Politics*, vol 25, no 3, pp 275-96.

Humphrey, J. (2003) 'New Labour and the regulatory reform of social care', *Critical Social Policy*, vol 23, pp 5-24.

Keen, J., Deeming, C., Moore, J. and Weatherly, H. (2007) 'New Labour, equity and public services: a Rawlsian perspective', *Policy & Politics*, vol 35, no 2, pp 197-214.

Kuhn, T. (1996) *The structure of scientific revolutions*, Chicago, IL: University of Chicago Press.

Laming, Lord (2003) *The Victoria Climbié Inquiry: Report of an inquiry*, Norwich: The Stationery Office.

Leece, J. and Bornat, J. (2006) *Developments in direct payments*, Bristol: The Policy Press.

Mynott, E. (2005) 'Compromise, collaboration and collective resistance: different strategies in the face of the war on asylum seekers', in I. Ferguson, M. Lavalette and E. Whitmore (eds) *Globalisation, global justice and social work*, Abingdon: Routledge.

Newbigging, K. (2004) 'Multidisciplinary teamworking and the roles of members', in T. Ryan and J. Pritchard (eds), *Good practice in adult mental health*, London: Jessica Kingsley.

Onyett, S. (2003) *Teamworking in mental health*, Basingstoke: Palgrave.

Ovretveit, J., Mathias, P. and Thompson, T. (eds) (1997) *Inter-professional working for health and social care*, Basingstoke: Macmillan.

Page, R. (2007) *Revisiting the welfare state*, Maidenhead: Open University Press, McGraw-Hill.

Powell, M. (ed) (2002) *Evaluating New Labour's welfare reforms*, Bristol: The Policy Press.

Quinney, A. (2006) *Collaborative social work practice*, Exeter: Learning Matters.

Rummery, K. (2006) 'Partnerships and collaborative governance in welfare: the citizenship challenge', *Social Policy and Society*, vol 5, no 2, pp 293-303.

Rummery, K. (2007) 'Modernising services, empowering users? Adult social care in 2006', in K. Clarke, T. Maltby and P. Kennett (eds) *Social Policy Review 19: Analysis and debate in social policy, 2007*, Bristol: The Policy Press.

Royal Commission on Long-term Care (1999) *With respect to old age: Long-term care – rights and responsibilities*, chaired by Sir Stewart Sutherland, Cm 4192-I, London: The Stationery Office.

Sadd, J. and Baldwin, M. (2006) 'Allies with attitude. Service users, academics and social service agency staff learning how to share power in running social work education courses', *Social Work Education*, vol 25, no 4, pp 348-59.

Scourfield, P. (2007) 'Social care and the modern citizen: client, consumer, service user, manager and entrepreneur', *British Journal of Social Work*, vol 37, no 1, pp 107-22.

Spandler, H. (2004) 'Friend or foe? Towards a critical assessment of direct payments', *Critical Social Policy*, vol 24, no 2, pp 187-209.

Wanless, D. (2004) *Securing good health for the whole population: Final report*, Norwich: The Stationery Office.

Warin, J. (2007) 'Joined-up services for young children and their families: papering over the cracks or re-constructing the foundations?', *Children & Society*, vol 21, pp 87-97.

Warner, J. (2007) 'Structural stigma, institutional trust and the risk agenda in mental health policy', in K. Clarke, T. Maltby and P. Kennett (eds) *Social Policy Review 19: Analysis and debate in social policy, 2007*, Bristol: The Policy Press.

SIX

Education: from the comprehensive to the individual

Susan Martin and Yolande Muschamp

Introduction

A radical programme of reform of education institutions had started before the election of 1997 but was adopted and became the dominating characteristic of Labour's education policy during the three terms of Tony Blair's government. However, the programme was not merely a continuation of the previous government's agenda but an attempt to further transform and modernise the state school system and make it fit for the 21st century (Paterson, 2003). Blair's commitment to 'education, education, education' was unrelenting. Every level of pupil and student engagement in schooling, from the early years to post-16, became the target for proposed reform and was subjected to an unprecedented period of change. Most of the changes were of Hall's first or second order as policy instruments altered and settings changed but one area gradually emerged as a paradigm shift and would meet Hall's criterion for a third order change (Hall, 1993). A commitment to comprehensive education, a central feature of the earlier labour manifesto and an aspect of education policy that marked a clear divide between Labour and Conservative policies, was quietly reduced and then abandoned. The debate over selection and the suitability of comprehensive education for all raged through the 1970s and 1980s. By the 1990s and the first decade of the new millennium it became clear that the debate had ended and the comprehensive school as a single type of institution within state provision was to be left behind by the process of modernisation. By the end of the three terms the debate over the comprehensive school model has all but disappeared and the change embedded to the extent that even the Conservative Party has declared 'no return' to selection and the grammar school.

The diversification of school types that followed was central to the process of the modernisation of education. Using 6 and Peck's (2004) definition of modernisation as a framework for our analysis of education reforms we can show that perhaps the process of modernisation is more visible in education than in any of the other welfare services. Table 6.1 shows only the key features of this process. The gradual abandonment of the pursuit of the single template for the state school, whatever the phase, which opened the door to a diversification of provision has resulted in an earned autonomy as a settlement between strong centralisation and the financial devolution that started with the local management of schools. The attempts to tailor reforms of institutions to local needs which followed financial devolution continued to change the relationship between the state and its citizens, casting them in the roles of consumer and client, and bringing with it more responsibility for children and their parents and carers. This new professional autonomy was only possible within the shadow of a rigorous Ofsted inspection framework. Professional autonomy became sector-wide when inspection was extended to nursery and pre-school education where a centralised early years curriculum was introduced to match that of schools and teacher training departments. The acceptance of the diverse formats of early years provision from private nurseries to local authority classrooms reflected the growing commitment to local initiatives across all phases and extended the role for private capital.

These reforms are too complex and too numerous to detail in one chapter. We have therefore focused on the consequences of this third order change and show how they led to the resolution of problems which had defeated earlier governments and may well turn out to be the central achievements of Blair's legacy. The first of these problems was the cost of providing early years education and childcare of high quality with sufficient coverage to support parental employment opportunities and to provide a secure start to schooling: an early years education which would become the 'foundation' for lifelong learning. The second was the problem of failing schools, where communities which arguably needed the best schools available were being served by underachieving secondary schools. These institutions were 'comprehensive' in name alone as a result of the abandonment of local education authority (LEA) enrolment catchment areas and because of the already established patterns of the move of middle-class families who could afford to relocate to the outlying leafier suburbs. The solution was the diversification of schools as institutions that had begun with the local management of schools in 1989. Diversification has continued with generations of school types including grant-maintained, beacon schools, schools with links to Education Action Zones, city technology colleges and now the trust schools and academies. Diversification is

Table 6.1: Education modernisation

Inspection	Full inspection by Ofsted of pre-school provision schooling and teacher training
Central standard setting	The early years curriculum complements the National Curriculum that remains, albeit in the reduced format. Centralised standards introduced for teacher performance and teacher training curricula continue; national testing and league tables remain
Area-based initiatives	Local provision that began with a focus on special education and areas of poverty (such as Education Action Zones) extended to specialist schools, and a range of school structures
Coordination and integration	The *Every Child Matters* agenda introduces comprehensive integration of services that had begun with the introduction of out-of-school care and the concept of the extended school
Devolution but limited decentralisation	Diversification allows specialist schools with control of the curriculum and enrolment supported by financial devolution
Earned autonomy as a settlement between centralism and decentralisation	Reduced inspection for successful schools and control over a greater proportion of the curriculum and enrolment regulations
An extended role for private capital	Private nurseries remain and become a large part of early years settings; schools are encouraged to find private sponsors as academies appear
A modest increase in citizen obligations	Attempts to introduce parental contracts and increase the responsibilities of parents and carers for school attendance and support for homework and school governance
Access (eg call centres, drop-in centres)	Education is now seen as lifelong and the school extended into the community
E-government	Schools become the vehicle for preparing all for the electronic age. The technical revolution is both the driver and support for education through the classroom computer and laptops for teachers and trainees

a clear example of 6 and Peck's autonomy as a settlement between centralism and decentralisation. For the school system it helped finally to put an end to the debate over the comprehensive schools and the myths that surrounded them, which included the perceived lack of direction in child-centred education and the underachievement of the gifted and talented held back by mixed ability teaching. With such decentralisation came the need for local accountability that materialised in the strengthening of the system of school inspection and with this the re-examination of the work of teachers. Teachers, already de-skilled with the introduction of an onerous and unworkable National Curriculum, were to be named and shamed by a government armed with Ofsted evaluations. By the end of the three terms the climate had changed so significantly that it is difficult to believe that this could have been tolerated by the earlier Labour government. A re-professionalisation of teachers is almost complete and the programme of reform has moved on to include related professions such as workers within the National Health Service (NHS). Local accountability supported the introduction of the concept of 'personalisation' at all levels of provision that has further indicated the demise of the comprehensive education and selection debates. Such personalisation has increased access to education for many and thus is a further example of modernisation.

These are the three strands (early years education, diversification of school types and re-professionalisation of the teaching profession) which we examine and evaluate in this chapter and which we argue are central to the modernisation programme of the Blair government and represent the major achievements of the three terms. Nine of 6 and Peck's 10 criteria are met time and time again throughout our analysis. The tenth criterion, coordination and integration, is an aspect of modernisation that has been introduced but not yet achieved. An examination of the *Every Child Matters* agenda, which, although introduced during Blair's premiership, has not yet been sufficiently established within education institutions, shows, however, that the legislation is in place to meet this tenth criterion. The *Every Child Matters* agenda is the logical and direct development of the concept of personalisation that has resulted from decentralisation, and because of the scale and force of its introduction may turn out to be a major aspect of Blair's legacy.

Early years education

At the start of the first term of the Labour government early years education as state provision was relatively unregulated and disorganised. Although an established system of family centres existed for the very poorest of children living in many towns and inner cities, beyond this, a patchwork of mixed-level provision existed. Nursery education was unstructured with provision by the voluntary sector existing side by side with private provision. The early years curriculum ranged from specialist programmes such as Steiner and Montessori to unstructured play settings run by mothers themselves. The childcare provision for working parents added to this a miscellany of both informal and more regulated networks of family arrangements, child minders and crèche facilities.

The previous Conservative government had recognised the failings of this system, identifying the difficulties faced for single mothers, working couples and the impact of family breakdown, and resolved to increase access to childcare for all with a complex voucher system, the abolition of which was one of the first tasks of the New Labour government. What followed was a radical process of modernisation. The Inspection system still feared and derided by school teachers was to be established for all early years provision. The recruitment of 200 inspectors and the extension of the National Curriculum to the early years with the early years foundation stage began to bring these centres into line with primary schools, and the early years were declared to be the foundation for lifelong learning. To complement and to justify such a radical reform, an unprecedented research programme was established (Sammons et al, 2007) to gauge the impact of the reform on the achievement of this cohort of children over the following seven years. Ironically research findings from Sylva's original Michigan study (2000) had already shown the benefits to young adults of an early years experience within a structured play environment where children's independence was nurtured with child-negotiated activities. The new early years curriculum being introduced, however, worked against this approach. The backlash from the early years networks introduced waves of reform and counter-reform that paralleled the introduction of the first version of the National Curriculum. Play was reintroduced as central to the curriculum and the findings of the Michigan study (Sylva, 2000) were promoted. The Sammons and Sylva studies have begun to reveal the impact of the early provision. Despite being challenged by Tymms et al (2007) with headlines suggesting that money had been wasted, the findings suggest that the provision is providing benefits for young children.

The early years curriculum not only specified an appropriate range of activities for the young pupils aimed at equipping them for an unknown future, it also specified an assessment regime which led to headlines of 'SATs for babies' in the tabloid press. The school entry profile was the introduction of the personalisation agenda that now continues through the *Every Child Matters* agenda and was hoping to replicate the programme introduced by the No Child Left Behind Act of 2001 in the US. In that the entry profile assessed a child's readiness for school, it also revealed the standard of parenting required and achieved and introduced a moral panic about the social skills and behaviour of English children. The social and economic situation of children could not be ignored and now social welfare programmes including Sure Start and the Early Excellence Centres have introduced the coordination and integration that *Every Child Matters* should continue with the roll-out of Children's Centres.

Diversification of school types

Within the institutions that provided for children of compulsory school age (5-16 years) the Labour Party inherited an education system that was essentially centralised, particularly for secondary schools. The National Curriculum, introduced by the preceding Conservative government, had established a traditional and core curriculum. During the Labour governments the National Curriculum was extended within primary schools in the form of National Literacy and Numeracy Strategies, which incorporated teaching methods as well as content. Selection was a further dimension that the Labour Party inherited, the driver for which had been a continuation and endorsement of diversity in school provision. Aiming for equality of provision, the Conservatives had worked towards a tailoring of provision that promoted the need for grammar schools and continuation of the 11+ examination. Within the same theme, however, the Labour Party focused on education opportunity and achievement for all (Labour Party, 2004) in a different light of believing in every child and expecting excellence from all rather than tolerating the failure of some children because of, and at the expense of, the achievement of a few. Selecting children at the age of five, 11 or 16 for failure was not to be the way forward. The emphasis was on raising standards and equalising opportunities.

Specialism, rather than selection, as a means of encouraging diversity in schools has marked the reform in school provision. While the structure of schools and schooling might not appear very different to the outside observer, there has been significant change in terms of initiatives and reform aimed at transforming the environment of teachers and learners. It is also the case that the nature of the change process has evolved. It is not clear that this was by design or whether it was more as a consequence or by-product of other initiatives. The Labour Party inherited and continued an unprecedented scale of reform with the teaching workforce in receipt of new resources at an unremitting rate. This has been perceived as unhelpful and reform perceived as change for change's sake. Although 'joined-up' government was part of New Labour's lexicon in the initial term this was subsequently lost, somewhat ironically, as schools have been able to join up more recent initiatives for themselves. The teaching workforce had grown tired with the number and the evolutionary nature of reforms and changes. For example, the National Curriculum had undergone several reviews and revisions, was generally received as a 'handed down' reform and one that was bolted on to their workload. While the profession had been consulted there was little ownership of this by teachers.

The Blair government has worked towards a programme of reform to target areas of disadvantage and to seek to ensure that all pupils, regardless of their socioeconomic background, have access to a high-quality education. This is most explicit in the academies programme, 'evolving from' the city technology programmes. Rejecting quite explicitly the principle of selection at 11 and subsequent school pathways which are distinguished by the degree to which they could be termed academic (or in reality the extent to which they could set filters to select their entry), New Labour has worked towards establishing schools which are distinguished by how they have the potential to take account of children's differing abilities. Intra- rather than inter-school differences have been seen to be the key to maximising pupil progress. The party claims to have modernised the comprehensive principle, learning from the experience of its 30 years of application. This has been driven by the dual aspect of pursuing this as a valued principle in its own right as well as an economic necessity for the nation: 'quality comes from developing the potential of all our people' (Labour Party, 2004). Thus, while schools are still in competition in the sense that they are compared, this is secondary to the principle of establishing schools which play to their individual strengths and ethos.

New Labour has been little less than radical in its approach to tackling the long neglected area of underachievement. Through the funding and targeting of underachieving areas, standards have been driven up. In parallel to the focus on underachieving areas there has been a focus on promoting improvement in standards at all levels. A series of related reforms concerning school specialisms or types started with specialist schools, originally launched as the technology colleges programme in 1993, with the opportunity to offer distinctive specialisms but still meeting National Curriculum requirements. All specialisms attract additional funding allowing for the development of centres of expertise in the respective schools that will be a common resource for all schools in partnership with them. Specialist schools have become the single most dynamic force for change and higher standards in our secondary schools (Blair, 2004).

Excellence in Cities, launched in 1999, following on from Education Action Zones, aimed at driving up standards and equalising opportunities and focused on leadership, behaviour and teaching and learning. Initially focused on secondary schools the initiative was extended to include primary schools and linked to the Primary National Strategy. There is some evidence that the rate of increase in GCSE performance for Excellence in Cities areas is approximately twice that of non-Excellence in Cities areas (in 2005). The programme became the Leading Edge Partnership programme in 2006.

The Beacon Schools programme was established in 1998. Its aims were to identify good practice and to share good practice, using partner Beacon Schools, in order to raise standards. It was inclusive of all school types and phases. Its success built on the Leading Edge Partnership programme for secondary schools, which was focused on collaborative practice in groups and Primary Strategy Learning Networks for primary schools where schools work together to target and raise performance in literacy and mathematics and to increase their capacity to deliver a broad and rich curriculum. Funding is channelled through local authorities.

Diversification continued with the creation of academies that seek sponsorship from private agencies and aim to raise standards by effecting a teaching and learning environment that will impact on pupil learning. An additional focus on aspects of schools such as behaviour, attendance, pastoral care and support are also standard aims and expectations of academies. Academies also have specialisms. They target inequality of provision by introducing diversity, breadth and opportunity in a 'holistic' approach. Innovation is also seen to have a major role to play in improvement. Academies are in part targeted at breaking the cycle and cumulative effect of underachievement. Thus, academies, in some cases, as with Fresh Start schools, have become the new institution for failing and underachieving schools. In a move which recognises a more recent introduction and emphasis on personalised learning, the outcomes expected for academies are not simply good examination results but young people who are equipped for active citizenship, committed to lifelong learning and ready for progression beyond compulsory education.

The academies programme ostensibly encapsulates Labour's current themes towards its goals of raising standards, regeneration, local flexibility and breaking the cycle of underachievement through lifelong learning. While evaluations of academies are generally positive, it is too early for meaningful results from those academies that have taken on failing schools. It is too early to tell whether academies are successful: their histories are relatively short and they have different bases for their establishment. Some have replaced previously closed or failing schools, some have reopened an existing school with a new building, and some are newly established faith schools, so preventing an osmosis of pupils to adjacent boroughs. Concerns exist about the degree of control that might be taken by a private sponsor with little or no education expertise on governance and the curriculum and in some cases, where academies are 'through' schools, there has been parental concern about the consequential closure of extant and good primary schools. Academies are viewed by some as being based on a flawed premise that standards will be raised and disadvantage tackled by passing to private sponsors the ownership of a school building, its grounds and facilities, taking these assets from the local community. There are also concerns about whether such 'tinkering', rather than a radical approach, is best placed to turn around schools with major problems. It seems clear that where academies have replaced or taken on failing schools results are less favourable, suggesting that transitions need to be managed carefully and that value added is never going to, nor should, disappear.

Thus, while diversity and collaboration are the two main vehicles for raising standards and driving improvement in teaching and learning in transforming the secondary agenda, it is clear that there are different perceptions of whether the result is complementary diversification or selection by a different name, and whether competition rather than collaboration is the ultimate outcome. That is, perceptions vary on whether diversity is seen to be primarily within as opposed to between schools, with the consequence that there is divided opinion on whether academies and specialist schools, for example, will exacerbate rather than address underachievement including that related to social disadvantage. Early analysis by the Institute for Public Policy Research showed that the admissions policy continued to cause segregation by class and ability and argued for a more balanced intake (Tough and Brooks, 2007). Research into the impact of specialist schools by Taylor (2007) showed only marginal improvement within examination results of the academies.

Re-professionalisation of the teaching profession

High standards of education rely on a well-paid, highly motivated workforce. Modernisation here comprised a programme of workforce reform which has produced real improvements to teachers' and headteachers' working conditions in the context of raising standards of education to ensure that every young person can reach their full educational potential. Teachers' pay and conditions have markedly improved in recent years and have themselves increased the professional status of teachers. Professional development has been significant in the Blair reform years, moving from a necessary but rather irrelevant dimension of a teacher's job to one viewed as complementary and useful. Reforms have increasingly been accompanied and underpinned by appropriate professional development. Changes that give greater recognition to a teacher's role in teaching and learning and a reduction in unnecessary bureaucracy have, in acknowledging them as professionals, increased teachers' sense of professionalisation. Although this is not uniform across school phases and subjects there are clear examples of moves to promote teachers as professionals in ways that befit their reasons for entering the profession. For example, teachers have a greater opportunity to take responsibility for their own development and for input into their students' learning. Also professional development that recognises teachers as ongoing learners has enabled teachers to realise such benefits both for their own career development and for their students'. This increase in autonomy has been matched through central control of career pathways by criteria and financial rewards for those able to demonstrate a contribution to improving pupil attainment.

The Key Stage 3 Strategy, designed to develop and provide continuity and progression from the National Numeracy and Literacy Strategies introduced in primary schools, was huge and radical. It focused on the transition to secondary school where generally schools saw a loss in learning and momentum on the part of pupils, and the Strategy, focusing on the basics and extending to other curriculum areas, targeted the 'slump' or Year 8 dip. Whole-school and LEA approaches implemented the Strategy, which was based on centrally driven mechanisms and a cascade model of training and development. The role and input of teachers was a radical and generally welcomed change. Consultants, working for LEAs and with teachers to implement the Strategy, were a factor in its success. Consultants were appointed for each subject strand in each LEA to the extent that this deprived some schools and smaller authorities of their best teachers, but their input working alongside teachers focusing on enhancing their teaching, in line with the Strategy themes, was a milestone in both recognising the value and quality of teachers-as-consultants' ability to mentor teachers. Teachers were able to extend their teaching and learning repertoires and 'raise their game' and had an opportunity for greater reflection on teaching and learning (Stoll et al, 2003). The Strategy provided an opportunity for schools to work on a whole-school basis across the strands to connect the Strategy with other initiatives in which the school was involved in tailoring initiatives to the needs and existing foci of the school. For example, the focus on teaching and learning was used as the basis for whole-school improvement in both Beacon Schools and in schools facing challenging circumstances. Such opportunities were not universally taken or appreciated but where schools were able to take on a whole-school approach successfully this appeared to stem from a sense of collective professionalism for staff involved.

The *Every Child Matters* agenda

This needs-based approach that incorporates integration suggests that the tenth criterion from 6 and Peck (2004), coordination and integration, has been met by the Blair reforms. However, the last major initiative from the Blair government in the form of the *Every Child Matters* agenda has not yet reached its aim of a fully coordinated and integrated approach within children's services. The introduction of trusts to local authorities to bring together education, welfare and health services to share responsibility for children and young people took place only in the last few years of Blair's term of office. The key aspects of this initiative for schools include a national system of children's centres and extended schools that will bring together specialist services and facilities to create an infrastructure to support professional collaboration. Professionals from the different services will work together to diagnose problems, assess needs and implement personalised strategies to support children and their families. The basic principles in relation to English schoolchildren are to be healthy, to stay safe, to enjoy and achieve, to make a positive contribution and to have economic well-being (Kirk and Broadhead, 2007, p 9).

It remains too early to tell how teachers will respond to this initiative. In earlier reforms teachers have responded more positively to initiatives impacting on teaching and learning, having more opportunities to use and try a wider range of teaching activities with opportunities for exchanging ideas with colleagues. The diversification of schools has supported the greater flexibility in the work of teachers, and the quality of teachers' working life and their professional development have both improved as a result. A heightened degree of professionalism, evident from within and without the profession, now reaches down to the pre-school and early years. The ways in which the profession has taken on the ownership and tailoring of initiatives that have been determined centrally has been a characteristic of developments during the Blair years. That is, while there continues to be a central drive to reform, schools now have the flexibility to interpret initiatives; and there exists a more sensible balance between centralism and decentralisation with a degree of earned autonomy in some areas. This also augurs well for a platform on which to secure sustainable change. Currently the morale, motivation and retention of teachers is much improved and needs to continue.

Conclusion

Blair's commitment to education has resulted in three dimensions or strands which have contributed to the modernisation of education – an early years curriculum, a diversification of schools and a re-professionalisation of teaching. Introduced to widen state provision in respect of age and to meet the wider needs of its pupils, the first two dimensions of an early years curriculum and the introduction of more specialist schools was also accompanied by policies which sought to give schools greater autonomy in managing their affairs as well as increasing the accountability of all schools. The specialism strand saw a move away from selection to diversification that has sought to introduce differences in emphasis of provision both in respect of curricula and the environments in which teaching and learning take place. Concerns are still expressed over the impact of specialisation and the extent to which the impact in terms of addressing underachievement has justified the expenditure (Taylor, 2007; Toynbee, 2007). There remain concerns that a diverse range of different types of schools are not as effective as the system where the diversity is provided within each school (Bangs, 2008). The third theme of this chapter, the re-professionalisation of the teaching profession, has most clearly emerged in the conditions in which teachers are engaged and in national policies which have necessitated the widespread consultation with, training and engagement of teachers. As the national agenda of *Every Child Matters* is embedded, teachers will have further opportunities for professional collaboration with specialist services and agencies that support pupils while in mainstream education.

References

6, P. and Peck, E. (2004) 'Modernisation: the ten commitments of New Labour's approach to public management', *International Public Management Journal*, vol 7, no 1, pp 1-18.

Bangs, J. (2008) 'World class?', *The Teacher*, March, pp 27-8.

Blair, A. (2004) Fabian Lecture on education at the Institute of Education sponsored by the Sutton Trust, 7 July.

Hall, P.A. (1993) 'Policy paradigms, social learning and the state: the case of economic policy making in Britain', *Comparative Politics*, vol 25, no 3, pp 275-96.

Kirk, G. and Broadhead, P. (2007) *Every Child Matters: A UCET position paper*, London: UCET.

Labour Party (2004) Manifesto, London: Labour Party.

Paterson, L. (2003) 'The three educational ideologies of the British Labour Party 1997-2001', *Oxford Review of Education*, vol 29, no 2, pp 165-87.

Sammons, P., Sylva, K., Melhuish, E., Siraj-Blatchford, I., Taggart, B., Grabbe, Y. and Barreau, S. (2007) *Investigating the continuing effects of pre-school children's outcomes at age 6 and 10 years: Emerging results from EPPE 3–11, a longitudinal study of children's progress and development in England*, EARLI Annual Conference, Budapest, September.

Sylva, K. (2000) 'School influences on children's development', in P.K. Smith and A.D. Pellegrini (eds) *Psychology of education: Main themes*, London: Taylor and Francis, pp 51-95.

Taylor, J. (2007) 'Estimating the impact of specialist schools programme on secondary school examination results in England', *Oxford Bulletin of Economics and Statistics*, vol 69, no 4, pp 445-71.

Tough, S. and Brooks, R. (2007) *School admissions: Fair choice for parents and pupils*, Report, June, London: Institute for Public Policy Research.

Toynbee, P. (2007) 'If Balls wants better schools, he must scrap faith selection', *The Guardian*, Tuesday 6 November.

Tymms, P., Merrell, C. and Jones, P. (2007) 'Changes in the attainment of children on entry to school in England 2000–2006', Paper presented at EARLI Annual Conference, Budapest, September.

SEVEN

Controlling crime and disorder: the Labour legacy

Sarah Charman and Stephen P. Savage

Introduction

When New Labour took office in 1997 few could have guessed that criminal justice policy would become a site of such frenetic activity. Of course Labour's slogan, 'tough on crime, tough on the causes of crime', was one of the most prominent features of Labour's election campaign when in opposition, signalling as it did a sea change in the approach taken by the Labour Party to the law and order question – the strategy being that no longer could Labour be labelled as 'soft on crime', something which, in the febrile political atmosphere of Britain in the mid-1990s, could spell electoral disaster. However, not even the sternest critics of New Labour could have predicted that what was to follow in policy terms would include attempts to provide the police with the power to detain suspects for 90 days without charge (in cases of suspected terrorism), that a Labour Prime Minister would be talking about 'rebalancing' the criminal justice system in favour of the 'law-abiding majority', that the prison population would reach record heights, or that Labour would create over 3,000 new criminal offences within 10 years. Accounting for such a scenario consequently presents interesting challenges.

As in other areas of policy, criminal justice policy operates according to a range of policy drivers. Political imperatives, particularly given the steady rise of crime as an electoral issue in public sentiment, is perhaps the most obvious, as will shortly become apparent. Policy transfer, most notably in relation to North American influences over British crime policy in areas such as policing and sentencing, has also played a part (Jones and Newburn, 2007). System failure, a constant driver for change in areas such as policing (Savage, 2007a, pp 23-45), has also left its mark. Most significantly this was found in response to the murder of Stephen Lawrence in 1993, which ultimately became the subject of the Lawrence Inquiry, which reported in 1999. This was an inquiry that

Labour pledged to the Lawrence family while in opposition and which generated far-reaching reforms in the police and other public services. Finally, the rise and rise of the performance culture, so evident across the public sector, was to continue to shape criminal justice policy in a range of ways. These policy drivers are a reaction to previous failures, societal pressure and the influence of the 'public voice'. Policy making as 'social learning' (Hall, 1993) or learning from past practice is clearly apparent within criminal justice policy but without the state autonomy which is often associated with it.

In addition to these wider policy drivers, there are two sets of issues more specific to crime policy which have played key roles in shaping Labour's criminal justice agenda that we can refer to as 'high crime' and 'low crime' concerns. 'High crime' concerns relate primarily to the threat of terrorism, fired by the terrorist attacks in New York in September 2001, and, more directly, the London bombings in July 2005. These exceptional events were to generate demands for 'exceptional measures' in response, most evidently in the area of police powers and by means of anti-terrorist legislation. In addition to these specific measures, concerns over the terrorist threat led to a growing climate of 'public protectionism', which challenged existing presuppositions about the value to be placed on suspects' rights and where the balance between those rights and the 'rights of the public to be protected' should rest – pushing the agenda firmly in the direction of the latter. 'Low crime' concerns have generated a very different set of policy initiatives, because they relate to 'quality of life' issues and people's – or some people's – everyday life experiences. In opposition New Labour had nailed its colours to the mast in favour of tackling 'low-level disorders', such as 'noisy neighbours', rowdy youth on the streets and general 'anti-social behaviour', which seemed to indicate at one point that Labour was in support of 'zero tolerance' policing along the New York Police Department model. Soon after taking office, Labour was to act on this concern for 'low crime', although not, it must be emphasised, along zero tolerance lines (Jones and Newburn, 2007, pp 130-42), with measures such as 'crime and disorder partnerships'. 'Low crime' problems were to continue to be the focus of Labour's criminal justice policy throughout the decade that followed. With the frenetic pace of criminal justice policy making and the 3,000-plus new criminal offences already referred to, this chapter can only focus on the *themes* that have emerged during Blair's period as Prime Minister, and, in particular, his last term in office. The chapter will also consider whether criminal justice policy adheres, firstly, to Hall's notions of 'third order change' (1993) and, secondly, it will consider the very thorough modernisation of some public services which 6 and Peck (2004) refer to.

Politics and populism

Having placed law and order firmly on the agenda in the run-up to the 1997 General Election (see Charman and Savage, 1999), New Labour and Tony Blair battled to keep it there, knowing only too well the limitations of the state's influence over crime rates. Blair struggled with the state's inability to directly control and govern social life and became almost 'hyperactive' in terms of policy 'initiatives'. Tonry (2004) notes 33 major 'initiatives' which emerged from within Blunkett's two-year period of office as Home Secretary, including crackdowns on anti-social tenants, children using fireworks, 'sex tourists', fine defaulters and parents of unruly children. The use of crime 'summits' (on issues as diverse as 'gangsta rap' and police reform) also became a staple of the Blair government. Reductions in crime rates could then be attributed to tough-sounding policy (even where the policy had little impact; see below). In doing this, Labour could point to its determination to make 'thug[s] think twice' (Blair, 2000, cited in BBC, 2000a), and the positive results of its many initiatives and interventions. However, even the Prime Minister's Strategy Unit acknowledged that 80% of the drop in crime in recent years was due to economic factors (although Solomon et al, 2007, note that this admission curiously disappears from the version posted on the Cabinet website). Sound bites, 'initiatives' and hasty policy decisions are often the hallmark of a government under pressure (Michael Howard's infamous 'prison works' speech in 1993 is a clear example of this, see Savage and Nash, 1994). However, for the first two periods in office at least, Labour was riding on a large Commons majority, a broadly supportive public and an opposition in various states of disarray, with the additional advantage of falling crime rates. The platform for legislative restraint was set. But Labour's decision was to choose a very different path.

The term 'populist punitiveness' (now generally referred to as 'penal populism') was first coined by Bottoms (1995) in an attempt to describe a situation in the early 1990s where politicians were manipulating public concerns about law and order to justify more punitive legislation. However, penal populism refers also to a more fundamental political momentum that embraces the notion of representing 'the people' (Pratt, 2007). This strategy was by no means the brainchild of New Labour but has been utilised by successive predecessors of Blair. Margaret Thatcher (a clear influence over Blair; see Jenkins, 2006) made many claims to speak on behalf of 'the people' (Ryan, 2004). Jack Straw made his intentions as Home Secretary clear to pressure groups when, on taking office, he informed the public that New Labour's policy was going to be informed not by 'a vanguard of single issue groups' but by 'the people' (Straw, 1998). According to these principles, more punitive legislation is the representation of public opinion and therefore truly 'democratic' policy making (Johnstone, 2005). Hall (1993) refers to Thatcher's policy of surrounding herself and her government with those supportive of her changing economic policy paradigm. In a similar vein, Blair, while seeking to fundamentally change the direction and goals of the criminal justice system, sought out supportive actors in the form of senior police officers and the tabloid press. This was largely at the expense of Labour's 'traditional' allies of civil liberties and lawyers' groups. Blair launched 'The Big Conversation' in 2003 with the intention of listening to the public about their 'big' concerns. Much like the 'People's Question Times' and the 'Welfare Reform Roadshows' before it, the intentions were public engagement and a justification for policy decisions. However, there was a new breed of sub-politics at work, where ostensibly the public desire to be more involved in policy decisions is evident. Direct action, whether via marches against the war in Iraq or Fathers 4 Justice dressing up as superheroes, exposes the fallacies of Britain becoming a politically apathetic nation. The response of governments is often quick, ill-informed policy (marching 'thugs' to cashpoints, 'baby' ASBOs [Anti-Social Behaviour Orders] for children under the age of 10), designed to appease a culture that demands criminal justice policies at the speed of phone-in votes on reality television. Loader refers to a 'culture of impatience' (2006, p 581) among politicians who maintain a preoccupation with immediate action.

Nowhere does the grip of populism extend its reach more firmly than within the penological context. Sentencing and prisons appear more vulnerable to political expediency than other sectors of the criminal justice system. Successive administrations under Blair's premiership enacted legislation which confirmed a steady progress towards a crime control model of criminal justice and an erosion of significant areas of both civil and human rights. The most pronounced of these pieces of legislation was the 2003 Criminal Justice Act, which saw the removal of the double jeopardy principle, the introduction of public protection sentences, further attempts at restricting the right of trial by jury plus erosions to the laws surrounding oral hearsay and bad character in court. Mandatory minimum sentences were introduced in 1997, followed by further additions to the list of eligible crimes in the 2003 Criminal

Justice Act. The number of people in prison serving indeterminate life sentences has spiralled since this piece of legislation. Padfield (2007a) notes that in the year from December 2005, the number of prisoners serving indeterminate sentences (a sentence known for its damage in terms of adaptation to imprisonment; see Padfield, 2007b) rose by 31%. This is but one contributory factor in the significant growth that has been witnessed in the prison population.

The burgeoning prison population and the increasing reliance of sentencers on custodial punishment has in many ways been the thorn in the side of New Labour's criminal justice policies. There has been widespread criticism from a range of different directions of this unswerving allegiance to a policy that fares badly on all measures of efficiency and effectiveness. A 25% increase in the prison population since 1997, and the increasing use of police cells for convicted prisoners as a regular and not an emergency measure, has not been met with any serious considerations of the proper use of imprisonment, but rather with plans to create 10,000 more places. The former chief inspector of prisons, Lord Ramsbotham, has described current prison policy as 'the Government's headlong and self-induced race to absurdity', branding it a 'shambles' (2006, p 1). If you add to this the provisions within the 2005 Mental Capacity Act that allow the detention of those with 'severe personality disorders' for as long as is required on the basis of perceived risk, we can begin to see the long shadow that is cast from accommodating an ever present 'obsession' (Faulkner, 2006) with the avoidance of risk. A further outcome of this preoccupation with managing risk is that the Parole Board are becoming more and more reluctant to release prisoners on licence given the impossibility of offering any guarantees about future behaviour. The implications of embracing this 'new penology' (Feely and Simon, 1992), with its emphasis on limiting risk and actuarial management, will inevitably lead to the widening of the criminal justice state, despite an awareness of its limitations.

However, what must be carefully considered is how far the political rhetoric of 'toughness' and 'illiberality', utilised so widely by Jack Straw and his followers into the Home Office, has been transformed into the reality of policy decisions. Toynbee recalls the 'wink and the nod' from Jack Straw in opposition indicating that the rhetoric and the reality would be markedly different (Toynbee, 2007). While, for many, election success did not bring the return of the promised liberal ideals there are clear examples of punitive *pronouncements* not according with like-minded *policy*. While the headlines of the 2007 Home Office consultation document on clearer sentencing were about the rebalancing of the system towards the victims of crime, much of the substance was about the types of people that should be considered as *not* suitable for prison sentences, for example, vulnerable women, non-violent offenders and those with mental ill health (Home Office, 2007). Whether this is a typical Labour predicament of the implementation gap (6 and Peck, 2004) or a deliberate policy of appealing to the tabloid press is debatable. Jones and Newburn (2007) refer to the case of the 1997 Crime (Sentences) Act, which, to a fanfare of punitive sentiment, was launched as the infamous 'two strikes and you're out' legislation, begun by a Conservative but enacted by a Labour government. The reality of the legislation and the impact of the policy has been limited, however, with very small numbers of offenders being affected. Garland (2001) discusses the ways in which governments adapt to the reality of high crime rates and the understanding of the limits of the criminal justice state. One such reaction is referred to as 'acting out' (Garland, 2001, p 110) and stresses the importance of the public denouncement of certain types of behaviour. What is important is an immediate public display of sentiment; what is less important is the controlling of crime. What this suggests is that, as Garland (2001) has argued, the legislation has achieved the goal of expressing moral condemnation of offenders but with little policy impact. This is exemplified in a leaked memo from Tony Blair in 2000, who outlines a plan to counter the criticism of impending rises in street crime by stressing the need 'to think now of an initiative eg locking up street muggers. Something tough, with immediate bite, which sends a message through the system' (Blair, 2000, cited in BBC, 2000b).

The insatiable desire to appeal to 'the people' marks a change in political culture and in many ways places a responsibility on the public to show restraint and rationality in their thinking and on the politicians to accurately reflect what the public think. The analysis of policy making as state-centric, with its emphasis on the autonomous role of the state, is wide of the mark with reference to criminal justice policy making. A state-structural approach to policy making, with its emphasis on politicians, the media, other 'experts' and actors, is more a feature of this sector. Perhaps the difficulty with crime is that as such a large proportion of the population have some form of experience of it, the role of 'experts' can be assigned to virtually everyone and the public feel more of a right to a 'voice'. This happens in a way that would not be experienced by, for example, foreign policy. The media play a significant role in informing the public about crime so it will come as no surprise to learn that many members of the public remain preoccupied and concerned with crime (Jansson et al, 2007), with 65%

believing (falsely) that crime is increasing (Nicholas et al, 2007). Fear of crime is something that the Labour government has been unable to control (an issue considered later), and while tackling this issue is now a key concern, as shall be argued later, some responsibility must lie with government itself. A rising prison population and an aggressive and illiberal tone through the media on crime and offenders has, in many ways, shifted the focus permanently away from the laudable drop in overall crime and created a fearful society. While referring to the media as a 'feral beast' (Blair, 2007, cited in Jones, 2007) there is no doubt that Labour's obsession with 'image' and sounding 'tough' on law and order issues has meant that the public remain largely ignorant of the trends in crime rates. While claiming to wish to represent the views of 'the people', Blair paid very little heed to the numerous reports which provided evidence of the public's growing dissatisfaction with prison and a wish for an emphasis on rehabilitation within punishment (Roberts and Hough, 2005; Glover, 2007). If populism has constantly coloured Labour's rhetoric on crime, other themes have coloured policy itself, two of which we now address here: 'modernisation' and 'partnership'.

'Modernising' criminal justice

As was the case in other areas of the public services, change in law enforcement and criminal justice has reflected the wider commitment to 'modernising government' (HMSO, 1999). The modernising government project focused on change in a range of areas, including:

- 'joined up' public services, such as better inter-agency working;
- the removal of 'unnecessary regulation' hindering front-line working;
- a strengthened focus on 'delivery' and a more 'flexible' workforce to deliver 'results';
- encouraging public services to be more responsive to citizens' needs;
- closer monitoring of public services and greater use of performance management.

These concerns very much reflect the themes of modernisation that were felt across the public services (6 and Peck, 2004). However, government intentions to force through change in criminal justice are faced with specific difficulties. The police service, for example, which consumes by far the biggest slice of public expenditure on criminal justice, had, in comparative terms, been remarkably *resistant* to change in the past (Savage, 2007a, pp 169-71), particularly during the Thatcher governments. A number of commentators have commented on the 'privileged' status of the police as a public service during the 'Thatcher revolution' of the 1980s (Jenkins, 2006, p 181; Patten, 2006, p 69). Furthermore, all governments must tread carefully around the judiciary, which, as well as being notoriously steeped in tradition, can always employ the trump card of 'judicial independence' when governments are deemed to be trespassing too closely onto its territory. While all public sectors have their 'unique' circumstances which governments committed to change must confront at some point, criminal justice presents minefields of its own which make change notoriously difficult to achieve. Nevertheless, the longer Labour was in government, the more determined it has appeared to be to 'modernise' criminal justice (see Table 7.1).

If some of the modernising measures adopted by the Labour governments to criminal justice are associated with 'first order' objectives (Hall, 1993, p 282; see also Table 7.2), such as the reduction in crime rates in particular crime areas, it is also clear that Labour has been pushing for something more akin to a 'paradigm shift' in justice policy, or 'third order change' (Hall, 1993, pp 283-4). The form this has taken is captured nicely, if bluntly, by the title of the document which spells out its core features, *Rebalancing the criminal justice system in favour of the law-abiding majority* (Home Office, 2006). In his Foreword to the document, Blair summarises the essence of this 'rebalancing' act, very much in 'modernising' terms:

> ... we must ensure that in a modern world stripped of the bonds of the past, with new opportunities for crime, the criminal justice organisations live up to their duty of protecting the rights of victims and communities. We must build a criminal justice system which puts protection of the law-abiding majority at its heart. (Home Office, 2006, p 2)

The fact that any such 'rebalancing' would seek to reverse not just the policies of previous Conservative governments but also *Labour's* earlier policies on justice should not be lost in this respect. This was not change to policy instruments or instrument settings that Hall refers to as 'first order change' (1993). This refers, rather, to fundamental changes to the goals that guide policy. Significantly, one potential target of 'rebalancing' was the human rights legislation that Labour had

Table 7.1: Criminal justice modernisation

Area	Criminal justice reform
Inspection	Cross-agency inspectorates
Central standard setting	More explicit setting of standards for the police, linked to driving up performance
Area-based initiatives	As part of the 'Reassurance Agenda', elements of policing and anti-social behaviour controls left to local variation (neighbourhood policing teams). Some local schemes strongly influenced by restorative justice principles
Coordination and integration	'Joined-up' public protection linked to multi-agency public protection arrangements (MAPPAs). Youth offending teams (YOTs) act as forms of inter-agency coordinating bodies. The National Offender Management Service (NOMS) has as one aim better coordination between prisons and probation
Devolution but limited decentralisation	A degree of tension between centralisation of policing, eg national policing plans, and 'localism' in policing at the neighbourhood level
Earned autonomy as a settlement between centralism and decentralisation	A 'lighter touch' inspection for better performing police forces
An extended role for private capital	Continuing expansion of private prisons, attempts to enhance the role of private security/policing through licensing arrangements
A modest increase in citizen obligations	Continuing the ethos of citizens' responsibility to protect themselves and their property with regard to crime prevention initiatives. Enhanced role for reparation to victims from offenders (eg community service)
Access (eg call centres, drop-in centres, web-enabled services)	Neighbourhood policing associated with drop-in surgeries at local level. Growing role for victims' information networks
E-government	Significant expansion of technological surveillance under crime prevention initiatives (CCTV). Use of technology in the administration of punishment eg electronic tagging. Detailed information on police performance at force level, divisional level and micro-local level. Online 'victims' walkthrough' available

,introduced in the 1998 Human Rights Act, which incorporated the European Convention on Human Rights into British law (Wadham and Mountfield, 1999). Although repeal of the Act was not to be one outcome of the 'rebalancing' process – the focus was to be on how the Act was interpreted in the European Courts (Home Office, 2006, pp 4-5) – a significant change in tone over human rights from that which was attached to Labour's earlier legislation was difficult to ignore.

Table 7.2: Assessment of criminal justice policy against Hall's orders of change

First order change Levels or setting changed	Second order change Policy instrument altered, goals unchanged	Third order change 'Paradigm shift'
National targets for rates of crime reduction	Local authority crime and disorder partnerships	*Rebalancing the criminal justice system in favour of the law-abiding majority* (Home Office, 2006)
Indeterminate sentences	Creation of regulatory/ standards agencies eg Policing Standards Unit	Public protection
Police community support officers	Anti-Social Behaviour Orders	

With it came the persistent and erroneous tendency to assume that the 'rights of the law-abiding majority' do not *include* the rights of those suspected of crime.

'Rebalancing' criminal justice would embrace a range of reforms (Home Office, 2006), including:

- 'swifter' justice: building on earlier attempts to 'speed up justice' in areas such as youth justice (Youth Justice Board, 1999);
- better treatment of victims and witnesses: such as giving more scope for 'victims' voices' to figure in decisions in criminal justice;
- 'fairer sentencing': for example, by ending the sentencing 'discount' for guilty pleas in certain areas;
- more *summary* justice: including 'next day justice', particularly in relation to 'quality of life' offences, such as criminal damage;
- tackling 'police bureaucracy': where 'paperwork' gets in the way of fighting crime and disorder.

The inclusion of police reforms in the menu of 'rebalancing' criminal justice is significant, not least because, as mentioned earlier, the police sector had not felt the full blast of public sector reform in the way other areas of the public sector had from the Thatcher governments onwards. For that reason alone it is useful to take the 'modernisation' of policing under Labour as a case study of the impact of the modernisation agenda on criminal justice more generally. It is also useful because the programme of reform of policing launched by Labour in the early years of the new century was quite staggering in its scope and intensity, perhaps a reflection of the relative neglect of reform in this sector in previous years.

During Labour's first term of office the change agenda, in so far as there was one for policing, focused around two sets of processes: on the one hand the 'best value' programme, according to which 'best value reviews' were undertaken across a range of police 'business areas' (Savage, 2007a, pp 108–9); on the other hand the fallout of the Stephen Lawrence Inquiry (Macpherson, 1999) regarding the police handling of the death of Stephen Lawrence in 1993. It was not until the turn of the century and Labour's second administration that the gloves for police reform came off and 'modernisation' gathered pace and was well and truly applied to the police sector. The police modernisation agenda reflected the wider rationale of 'modernising government' considered earlier, but also a number of sector-specific concerns (see Home Office, 2001a, 2001b). Firstly, despite the continued fall in crime that had been a staple of the crime scene since the mid-1990s, crime in certain areas, such as violent crime, remained 'too high'. Secondly, the *fear* of crime remained high, and the gap between 'actual' and perceived levels of crime remained too great – this is otherwise known as the 'reassurance gap' (Savage, 2007a, pp 198–9). Thirdly, police detection rates are unacceptably 'low' and police performance generally varied too greatly between the 43 police forces of England and Wales. In the context of the latter point, one measure of the *lack* of change in policing over the years has been the fact that the '43 force' structure has remained intact since the early 1970s. Fourthly, concerns were raised about the management of police resources and the declining public confidence in the police among some communities, particularly minority ethnic communities. The government's case for modernisation and reform was subsequently strengthened by a report by Her Majesty's Inspectorate of Constabulary (HMIC, 2004), which added other challenges such as global developments in terms of terrorism, migration of peoples and organised crime, as well as the growth of the 'night-time economy', as evidence of the need for change.

The package of reforms directed at such challenges by any standards justified the government's claim that it was to be 'radical'. Although 'driving up performance' was the overarching aim of the reforms, it can be argued that a form of 'bifurcation' had taken place (Savage, 2007b), pulling reform in two directions. One set of reforms focused on *centralising* police policy making, strengthening the regulatory regime responsible for monitoring police performance and police conduct across the 43 forces and, in that sense, *standardising* or seeking to standardise performance throughout England and Wales. The

2002 Police Reform Act created a new power for government to set out a 'National Policing Plan' for the police service – prior to that the government could only set out national 'priorities' – and established a new body, the Police Standards Unit, to profile the performance of forces and command units within forces against nationally determined performance targets, to identify 'poorly performing' forces and even to intervene where forces have been deemed to be 'failing'. All of these features of a new style of managing policing emphasise the very themes of modernisation referred to by 6 and Peck (2004). Standards, targets and inspectorates all contributed to a growing sense of central control while those police forces deemed to be 'successful' avoided the full glare of intervention – an 'earned autonomy' of sorts.

A different form of regulatory authority was also created by the Act in the form of the Independent Police Complaints Commission, which for the first time in England and Wales (a similar body had already been in place in Northern Ireland since 2000) allowed for the fully independent investigation of complaints against the police. The formation of such a body was recommended by the Lawrence Inquiry, as has been made clear earlier. Another creation of the Police Reform Act was the police community support officer, a police 'auxiliary' officer whose role was to provide a more visible presence of uniformed personnel on the streets. This leads to the second set of reforms, which were in many ways oriented not to centralising policy but rather to forms of *localism* in policing (McLaughlin, 2005).

While 'driving up performance' had been the core rationale for the Labour government's police reform agenda, it was the issue of the so-called 'reassurance gap' which also taxed Home Office ministers. Without really examining the reasons *why* the public sense of safety and security appears out of kilter with the 'reality' of falling crime – perhaps the predominance of crime within political discourse might just have contributed something to public anxieties about crime! – the government clearly felt that the *solutions* to the reassurance gap rested with the forces of law and order. Two interweaving strategies were subsequently pursued. Firstly, the (continued) policy of tackling *low-level disorder and anti-social behaviour*. This built upon earlier schemes to tackle anti-social behaviour, such as ASBOs, created by the 1998 Crime and Disorder Act, a piece of legislation discussed later in the context of 'partnerships' in criminal justice. The government sought to strengthen the police role in confronting anti-social behaviour by creating a framework of 'Penalty Notices for Disorder', fixed penalties which could be issued by police officers and, in some cases, police community support officers for conduct ranging from 'sending hoax messages' to throwing fireworks (Home Office, 2003, p 76). The rationale for targeting low-level disorder in these ways was to reduce the public insecurities which anti-social behaviour appears to generate. Secondly, the government sought to extend the scope of *visible and accessible policing* as a means of improving people's sense of security, through the combined efforts of the roll-out of the police community support officer scheme and the wider adoption of 'neighbourhood policing', also known as 'safer neighbourhoods'. A key part of neighbourhood policing has been the government's concern to enhance *community engagement* in localised policing. This is one reflection of the role of *partnerships* in criminal justice, the third theme of this chapter.

'Partnership' and criminal justice policy

Crime policy in the UK has tended to be oriented towards responses to crimes rather than towards processes that might *prevent* crime. Attention and resources have been concentrated on the processes of detection, trial, conviction and punishment of offenders. Crime prevention and crime reduction based on preventative strategies remained for a long time the 'Cinderella' of policing and criminal justice policy (Byrne and Pease, 2003, p 287). It is to Labour's credit that, from its earliest years in office, it sought to remedy that neglect; it did so very much under the rubric of *partnership*. It has already been noted that the pursuit of 'joined-up' government has been a key feature of Labour's programme of modernisation of the public services. Indeed, as noted by 6 and Peck, it is an area in which the Labour government was very proud (2004) Crime is a good example of a 'cross-cutting' issue that had previously been felt to be the domain only of the criminal justice agencies. Improved working between agencies responsible, among other things in some cases, for crime control and reduction, has been a recurrent theme of Labour thinking on crime. Crime prevention was the site of Labour's earliest policy initiatives in this respect.

The 1998 Crime and Disorder Act heralded the first statutory framework for partnerships between the police, local authorities, health and education authorities and other bodies aimed at reducing crime at the local level (see Charman and Savage, 1999, 2002). This framework created by the Crime and Disorder Act had many ramifications (Crawford, 1998), but three in particular are worthy of mention. Firstly, it sent out a signal that the police were to be seen increasingly as only *one* 'crime-fighting' agency among others, no longer as necessarily the 'front line' in the crime reduction process. In a very real sense it questioned the police 'monopoly' over crime control and in a sense 'decentred' the police as a crime-fighting agency. Secondly, it enabled active consideration of the extent to which *alternative providers* of 'policing services' other than the 'public police' might be employed to deliver some, at least, of those services. For example, if a local authority, having conducted a 'crime audit' in their area, identifies a particular locality as requiring intensive and visible street patrols, it may, as the body with the statutory responsibility for crime in that area, decide that 'municipal' (local authority-employed) patrol officers might be used, or even *private security* patrols, rather than (or as well as) regular police officers. The new forms of governance of the 'crime problem' inaugurated by the crime and disorder agenda opened up avenues that later developments, such as the establishment of police community support officers, would exploit. Thirdly, relating to points made earlier, the Act symbolised the inclusion of *low-level disorder* within discourses and policies on crime and insecurity. In this context low-level disorders, if not challenged at an early stage, were viewed as potential generators of more serious crimes, a thesis which was known in the US as the 'broken windows theory' (Kelling and Coles, 1996).

If crime and disorder partnerships remain the most visible embodiment of 'joined-up' government in crime policy, another form of partnership emerged under Labour targeted not at the prevention of crime but the reduction of the 'risks' associated with those convicted of crime. The 2001 Criminal Justice and Court Services Act sought to further collaborative working between the probation and police services by requiring them to undertake *joint* assessment and management of violent offenders and sex offenders, particularly those offenders living in the community who pose risks to the community. This framework subsequently developed into 'MAPPAs' (multi-agency public protection arrangements). MAPPAs are framed around three categories of offenders (Wood, 2006): category one – all registered sex offenders; category two – violent and other sex offenders not on the sex offender register; and category three – other offenders not falling into the two other categories with a conviction which indicates they are capable of causing harm to the public. The MAPPA scheme aims to deliver rigorous risk assessment through the formation of such things as 'risk management plans' based on the determination of 'risk of harm levels', ranging from 'low' to 'very high'.

The make-up and mix of the multi-agency arrangements varies according to the category of offender concerned, but at the core are the three services which constitute the 'responsible authorities' that hold the statutory responsibility for managing offenders and public protection – the police, probation and prison services. Working alongside the responsible authorities are the other agencies that might have responsibility for other aspects of the offenders' circumstances, including social services, health services (particularly mental health services), youth justice, schools and the housing authorities. The multi-agency working under MAPPA is at its most acute when overseen by multi-agency public protection panels, which sit to deal mainly with those cases deemed as the 'critical few', offenders who have been assessed as the highest risk. The panels consist of senior officers from each of the responsible authorities and of other agencies as appropriate, who are required to draw up plans which involve close cooperation at a senior level due to the complexity of the case and/or because it will require unusual resource commitments. The rationale for the whole MAPPA scheme is to avoid the system failures of the past where serious crimes have been committed by offenders living in the community who have been 'allowed' to reoffend because they have fallen through the net of agency working, as a result of poor communication and disjointed decision making by the agencies concerned. The fact that the framework operates under the umbrella of risk assessment and risk management is also evidence of the managerialist culture that increasingly permeates the work of criminal justice agencies such as the probation service.

If the MAPPA scheme involves tightly defined partnership working between identifiable statutory and non-statutory agencies, the third example of the expansion of partnerships within criminal justice under Labour is more ephemeral and relates to the 'neighbourhood policing' initiative considered earlier. One feature of neighbourhood policing, according to government plans, is its capacity to actively engage local communities in the process of identifying local problems, deciding on priorities for action and determining ways in which those priorities can be addressed. The model of policing attached to this vision is one based on *citizen participation* and *community engagement* in tackling problems of crime and disorder, in other words a *partnership* between the police and the local community. The role of the neighbourhood policing teams at the heart of this strategy was to be one which:

> ... will take an intelligence-led, proactive, problem-solving approach to enable them to focus on and tackle local issues. They will involve their local community in establishing and negotiating priorities for action and identifying and implementing solutions. (Home Office, 2004, p 7)

It is clear from such a statement that Labour has fully signed up to certain policing models which had been appearing on the police scene – often under US influence in terms of policy transfer (Savage, 2007a, pp 50-67) – in terms of 'problem-oriented policing' and the like. However, neighbourhood policing entails a shift to *localism* in service delivery which, rather than seek to simply standardise policing in the way encouraged in the police performance regime, actually furthers the *differentiation* of policing in the sense that policing priorities are to reflect local conditions and local community preferences. Almost by definition, the vision of neighbourhood policing is one which culminates in varied approaches to tackle crime and disorder across communities which are themselves variable in nature. In turn, the vision embodies other principles found elsewhere in Labour's 'modernisation' of the public sector: *consumerism* – the community as active consumer of policing services; *choice* – the community's preferences for policing are to be reflected in local policing plans; *empowerment* and the *enabling state* – communities are to be encouraged to engage actively in shaping local policing policies. In these ways Labour's partnership approach brings policy on crime and disorder in line with wider visions associated with the New Labour project.

Conclusion

As stated earlier, while Labour kept extremely busy with 'first order change' (Hall, 1993) in the shape of concentrations on reducing crime, the punishment of offenders and reoffending rates, the Labour government, under Tony Blair, also concerned itself with more fundamental 'third order change' or 'paradigm shifts' (Hall, 1993). From the first utterance of the 'tough on crime, tough on the causes of crime' mantra, Labour made it very clear that crime and law and order would be headline priorities. These 'paradigm shifts' which Blair presided over were dominated by politicians in an effort to respond to what they felt to be the concerns of the public. A rebalancing of the criminal justice system away from the offender and increasing (and some would say belated) efforts focused on the victims of crime has been a fundamental shift in emphasis. We have also witnessed a distinct change of focus in terms of the aims of the criminal justice system. The protection of the public is now the overriding concern of a system where in the past offenders and their treatment have always taken centre-stage. However, the dangers inherent within current criminal justice policy are that in listening to what it *believes* the public wants and being so heavily influenced by the media and opinion polls, political expediency may also be a dominant influence on Labour. A strong and coherent policy paradigm will be all the stronger for a convincing theoretical underpinning (Hall, 1993). With numerous new laws, a penal system effectively facing bankruptcy and an apparent concern to appeal to the people, the dangers in maintaining that vision may become apparent.

References

6, P. and Peck, E. (2004) 'Modernisation: the ten commitments of New Labour's approach to public management?', *International Public Management Journal*, vol 7, no 1, pp 1-18.

BBC (2000a) 'Police concern at yob fines' (http://news.bbc.co.uk/1/hi/uk_politics/813953.stm, 6/12/07).

BBC (2000b) 'Full text of Blair memo' (http://news.bbc.co.uk/1/hi/uk_politics/836822.stm, 6/12/07).

Bottoms, A. (1995) 'The philosophy of punishment and sentencing', in C. Clarkson and R. Morgan (eds) *The politics of sentencing reform*, Oxford: Clarendon Press.

Byrne, S. and Pease, K. (2003) 'Crime reduction and community safety', in T. Newburn (ed) *Handbook of policing*, Uffculme: Willan Publishing.

Charman, S. and Savage, S.P. (1999) 'The new politics of law and order: Labour, crime and justice', in M. Powell (ed) *New Labour, new welfare state? The 'third way' in British social policy*, Bristol: The Policy Press.

Charman, S. and Savage, S.P. (2002) 'Labour, crime and justice', in M. Powell (ed) *Evaluating New Labour's welfare reforms*, Bristol: The Policy Press.

Crawford, A. (1998) *Crime prevention and community safety*, Harlow: Longman.

Faulkner, D. (2006) *Crime, state and citizen* (2nd edn), Winchester: Waterside Press.

Feely, M. and Simon, J. (1992) 'The new penology: notes on the emerging strategy of corrections and its implications', *Criminology*, vol 30, pp 449-74.

Garland, D. (2001) *The culture of control*, Oxford: Oxford University Press.

Glover, J. (2007) 'More prisons are not the answer to punishing criminals, says poll', *The Guardian* (www.guardian.co.uk/prisons/story/0,,2157364,00.html), 28 August.

Hall, P.A. (1993) 'Policy paradigms, social learning, and the state: the case of economic policy making in Britain', *Comparative Politics*, vol 25, no 3, pp 275-96.

HMIC (Her Majesty's Inspectorate of Constabulary) (2004) *Modernising the police service*, London: The Stationery Office.

HMSO (Her Majesty's Stationery Office) (1999) *Modernising government*, London: The Stationery Office.

Home Office (2001a) *Criminal justice: The way ahead*, London: Home Office.

Home Office (2001b) *Policing a new century: A blueprint for reform*, London: Home Office.

Home Office (2003) *Respect and responsibility: Taking a stand against anti-social behaviour*, London: Home Office.

Home Office (2004) *Building communities, beating crime*, London: Home Office.

Home Office (2006) *Rebalancing the criminal justice system in favour of the law-abiding majority*, London: Home Office.

Home Office (2007) *Making sentencing clearer: A consultation and report of a review by the Home Secretary, Lord Chancellor and Attorney General*, London: Home Office.

Jansson, K., Budd, S., Lovbakke, J., Moley, S. and Thorpe, K. (2007) *Attitudes, perceptions and risks of crime: Supplementary volume 1 to Crime in England and Wales 2006–7* (www.homeoffice.gov.uk/rds/pdfs07/hosb1907.pdf, 7/12/07).

Jenkins, S. (2006) *Thatcher and sons: A revolution in three acts*, London: Allen Lane.

Johnstone, G. (2005) 'Democratising crime policy', *Safer Society*, Spring, pp 19-21.

Jones, G. (2007) 'Blair launches attack on UK media beast' www.telegraph.co.uk/news/main.jhtml?xml=/news/2007/06/12/nmedia112.xml, 7/12/07), 13 June.

Jones, T. and Newburn, T. (2007) *Policy transfer and criminal justice*, Maidenhead: Open University Press.

Kelling, G. and Coles, C. (1996) *Fixing broken windows: Restoring order and reducing crime in our communities*, New York: Simon and Schuster.

Loader, I. (2006) 'Fall of the "platonic guardians": liberalism, criminology and political responses to crime in England and Wales', *British Journal of Criminology*, vol 46, no 4, pp 561-86.

Macpherson, W. (1999) *The Stephen Lawrence Inquiry*, London: The Stationery Office.

McLaughlin, E. (2005) 'Forcing the issue: New Labour, new localism and the democratic renewal of police accountability', *Howard Journal*, vol 44, no 5, pp 473-89.

Nicholas, S., Kershaw, C. and Walker, A. (2007) *Crime in England and Wales 2006–7* (www.homeoffice.gov.uk/rds/pdfs07/hosb1107.pdf, 7/12/07).

Padfield, N. (2007a) 'Ten years of sentencing reform', *Criminal Justice Matters*, vol 67, Spring, pp 36–7.

Padfield, N. (2007b) (ed) *Who to release? Parole, fairness and criminal justice*, Uffculme: Willan Publishing.

Patten, C. (2006) *Not quite the diplomat*, London: Penguin.

Pratt, J. (2007) *Penal populism*, Abingdon: Routledge.

Ramsbotham, D. (2006) 'Justice system is absurd. Chaotic. Broken', *Independent*, 30 November, p 1.

Roberts, J. and Hough, M. (2005) *Understanding public attitudes to criminal justice*, Maidenhead: Open University Press.

Ryan, M. (2004) 'Red tops, populists and the irresistible rise of the public voice(s)', *Journal for Crime, Conflict and the Media*, vol 1, no 3, pp 1–14.

Savage, S. (2007a) *Police reform: Forces for change*, Oxford: Oxford University Press.

Savage, S. (2007b) 'Neighbourhood policing and the reinvention of the constable', *Policing: A Journal of Policy and Practice*, vol 1, no 2, pp 203–13.

Savage, S. and Nash, M. (1994) 'Yet another agenda for law and order', *International Criminal Justice Review*, vol 4, pp 37–51.

Solomon, E., Eades, C., Garside, R. and Rutherford, M. (2007) *Ten years of criminal justice under Labour: An independent audit*, London: Centre for Crime and Justice Studies.

Straw, J. (1998) 'Crime and old Labour's punishment', *The Times*, 8 April.

Tonry, M. (2004) *Punishment and politics*, Uffculme: Willan Publishing.

Toynbee, P. (2007) 'Posturing and peddling myths, these prison enthusiasts are blind to history' (www.guardian.co.uk/commentisfree/story/0,,2223693,00.html), 7 December.

Wadham, J. and Mountfield, H. (1999) *Human Rights Act 1998*, London: Blackstone Press.

Wood, J. (2006) 'Profiling high–risk offenders: a review of 136 cases', *Howard Journal*, vol 45, no 3, pp 307–20.

Youth Justice Board (1999) *Speeding up youth justice*, London: Youth Justice Board.

EIGHT

Social investment: the discourse and the dimensions of change

Alexandra Dobrowolsky and Ruth Lister

Introduction

This chapter assesses the nature and scope of changes to the welfare state in relation to the 'social investment' turn. We argue that Tony Blair's New Labour governments recalibrated welfare state priorities, programmes and expenditures, both as a response to social risk and to promote economic competitiveness, through an embrace of social investment discourses and practices. While social investment, at its core, is all about activation (that is, labour market policy 'concerned with helping people successfully master transitions across the life-course'; see Giddens, 2007, p xi), it has nevertheless 'activated' far wider realms and actors than initially anticipated, having an impact on policy ideas and instruments, as well as institutions, interests and identities (Dobrowolsky and Saint-Martin, 2005), with implications beyond the conditional welfare state (see Chapter Twelve, this volume).

6 and Peck suggest that modernisation represented more than 'some general slogan' (2004, p 4). Similarly, social investment was not just about words (Dobrowolsky, 2002; Dobrowolsky and Jenson, 2005). It required 'coordination and integration' and involved various processes of 'standard setting', targeting and benchmarking (for example, reducing child poverty by 2020). Social investment policies reflected 'devolution but limited decentralisation' and typically played out in terms of 'area-based initiatives' (for example, Sure Start). At the same time, we see both an 'extended role for private capital' (for example, public–private partnerships, or PPPs) as well as an 'increase in citizen obligations'. Consequently, social investment, like modernisation, produced an 'organisational settlement'.[1]

The actual term 'social investment' was coined by Anthony Giddens (1998, p 117). His view that states should manage risk (1994), his advocacy of partnerships between states, markets, families and communities with respect to welfare provision, as well as his conceptualisation of social investment, intended as a term that would foreground human capital (1998), encapsulate the principles of a Blair government that would describe itself as 'maximising opportunities and minimising risks'. Giddens recently offered the following concise definition for the social investment state: 'State-provided or regulated investments in human or social capital' (2007, p xiii).

In brief, under the rubric of social investment, social policy reforms were geared towards excelling in the competitive global marketplace. Investing in human capital – increasing the capacity of everyone to engage in the productive economy – became a core preoccupation. The Blair governments were bent on increasing 'opportunities' by promoting employability, as well as a range of training/education initiatives. Additionally, New Labour encouraged the accumulation of assets, that is, investment in financial capital, particularly among lower-income groups and in social capital to counter social exclusion. A significant proportion of these investments paid unprecedented attention to the young, and the very young.

Blair's shorter-term social investment goals consisted of promoting opportunity, choice and fairness, and longer-term objectives included creating prosperity and producing a more inclusive society filled with independent, self-improving adult citizens, especially good 'citizen-workers' (Lister, 2003). The lines between social and economic policy became increasingly blurred as 'social spending' today was abandoned in favour of 'investing' in the future for tomorrow.

Given their payback potential, New Labour increasingly identified children and youth as valuable 'investments'. Along with education reforms, the Blair governments' social investment mandate extended to reducing child poverty and providing for quality childcare (Dobrowolsky, 2002; Lister, 2003; Dobrowolsky and Jenson, 2005; Dobrowolsky and Saint-Martin, 2005). There was also a coercive side to social investment that involved compulsion and control directed towards some young people. The view here was that 'social risks' needed to be taken in hand, early on, with authoritarian control measures geared towards perpetuating security and 'social cohesion' in the longer run. Notably, other 'security risk' children, such as asylum seekers, were not factored into 'social exclusion' efforts at all. They were not seen as future citizens and thus not part of the social investment agenda (Dobrowolsky with Lister, 2006; Lister, 2006).

The social investment project required a new role for the state, distinct from that of the New Right, laissez-faire, purchaser, or Old Labour, paternalistic, provider, state. The new 'enabling' state was active, both facilitative and directive, albeit pitched as 'empowering' (Labour, 2003, p 6) in that it found 'new ways to enable citizens to share in decision-making' (Blair, quoted in Finlayson, 2003, p 103). Duties and obligations fell equally to individuals, families and communities, as well as to voluntary organisations and firms. The enabling state perpetuated a different conception of equality: a future-oriented distribution of opportunities and life chances; instead of equality/inequality in the here-and-now. It also initially spoke the language of social exclusion in place of poverty (Lister, 1998), with the former seen as stemming from a shortfall in education and employment opportunities. Therefore, New Labour invested in opportunities to gain skills and enter paid work, but calls for improvements in social security benefits were dismissed as Old Labour.

Why and how social investment played out (the idea and its goals, its targets and settings) will be explored in the first part of this chapter. We will examine its content (the policy instruments, mechanisms and techniques) in the second part, with reference to policies that epitomise: (a) investment in human capital; (b) investment in financial capital; and, finally, (c) investment in social capital, as they offer the clearest illustration of social investment and its conflation of economic and social realms. Cumulatively, this will demonstrate that social investment represents, in the words of Peter Hall, 'the kind of "punctuated equilibrium" that often applies more generally to political change' (Hall, 1993, p 277). And, although we trace shifts, as a result of divergent influences across the three Blair administrations, social investment's fundamental parameters remain intact, thereby providing ample evidence for the emergence and evolution of a paradigm that has had an impact on the nature, forms and future of the welfare state.

The logic

Here we examine the logic of social investment, and the goals that underpin the policies detailed in the second part of this chapter. By pointing to various internal and external influences, we show that more was at stake than the conventional 'social learning' typical of 'first order' change, given that the latter is 'relatively insulated from the kind of pluralist pressures we often associate with the broader political system' (Hall, 1993, p 281). We also discuss consequences, mostly in terms of shifts in both policy targets and settings, suggesting that beyond second order changes, more of a 'third order' 'paradigm shift' (Hall, 1993) took place.

Ideas and influences

Tony Blair and New Labour pointedly rejected radical ideas at both ends of the political spectrum. The avid adoption of Clintonian 'Third Way' speak in the early days was followed by frenetic policy experimentation that seemed to be guided by the pragmatic rationale of what matters is what works, and what works is what counts. However, in hindsight, and over time, it becomes apparent that the government's priorities dovetailed with notions of social investment in a response to a mixture of endogenous and exogenous influences.

While Giddens' writings on the 'Third Way' and 'social investment' provided much of the intellectual spark and discursive spring (1998), many of the ideas that 'worked' could be found in the 1994 Commission on Social Justice (CSJ). It advocated a middle way through creation of an 'investor's Britain'. The CSJ spoke of social justice, but also economic efficiency and the promotion of equality of opportunity through 'lifelong learning'. It also saw the potential in children: 'they are 100% of the nation's future ... the best indicator of the capacity of our economy tomorrow is the quality of our children today' (1994, p 311). Giddens' writing continued in this vein. In recent work he remarks that we live in 'the era of the "prized child" ... [where] parents and prospective parents recognize (or should do) that responsibilities for children stretch for twenty years or more, with corresponding implications for income security.... Policies for transitional labour markets, with a life span perspective, should play a fundamental role here' (2007, p 92).

At the same time, the social investment agenda corresponded to developments in the wider European context (and to a lesser extent in North America, but with some significant Canadian resonances), where there had been movements afoot to construct a new social architecture (Vandenbrouke, 2001; Saint-Martin, 2007, p 281). Gøsta Esping-Andersen identified and endorsed the foundational building blocks of a new European social model in terms of:

> ... a strong family and child centred strategy for welfare state reconstruction. A revised social model requires a future-oriented perspective, and must therefore focus on those who will become tomorrow's adults. When goals for the future are defined in terms of maximizing Europe's competitive position in the world economy, the need to invest in today's children becomes obvious. (2000, p 31)

In contrast to the postwar welfare state's mandate of social spending in the here-and-now, the social investment discourse either downplayed or defended present-day expenditures with the promise that they would reap rewards later on. Investing in children, in education and training, in health and healthy populations, would pay off not only in terms of higher labour force participation rates down the road, but also in terms of fewer future demands on the state with respect to school failure, crime, health crises and so on. This explains Giddens' assertion that the 'future of the European social model is bound up with successful investment in children – for economic reasons and reasons of social justice' (2007, p 95).

Whereas children did not register on the radar screen initially, it was not long before the figure of the child appeared in numerous Blair government pronouncements, pledges and policies (Dobrowolsky, 2002). Blair proclaimed: 'We have to ensure all our children get a decent start in life…. Provide more ladders of opportunity through better education and assets for all' (2003, p 2). In Blair's and Brown's eyes, there was 'good' and 'bad' spending: spending on education, 'on pensions, child benefit, and people with disabilities: good, we like that … spending on unemployment and people on benefit when they should be at work: bad, we want to decrease that' (Blair, cited in Powell, 1999, p 21). Expenditures on children and youth were 'ideal' investments in the future.

Social investment cleared a path between New Right and Old Left interests and identities. It can be seen to be an indirect reaction against Thatcherite extremism, and a direct response to the radicalism of 'loony left' factions. The child, in other words, was strategically deployed to fashion the new, New Labour identity.

Beyond the party, interactions between state officials and think-tanks, as well as prominent children's organisations, help to explain the expanding child focus. Labour women ministers, with feminist academic and activist contacts, and roots in institutes outside of the state, seized on the figure of the child, using it as a lever for policies like the National Childcare Strategy. Numerous children's charities and advocacy groups also left their mark on social investment policies. They lobbied, provided policy inputs and monitored outputs. The activism of children's organisations prompted the Labour government to announce, belatedly in February 2005, the creation of a Children's Commissioner for England (following the lead of Scotland and Wales). Children's advocates added more nuance to various child-centred welfare reform initiatives, and children's groups became vigorous service providers.

Social investment relied on multiple partnerships, including 'an enhanced role for local agencies' as well as 'greater use ... made of independent organisations, both voluntary and commercial' (Johnson, 2001, pp 184-5). Because the voluntary sector was viewed as 'an essential element of a civil society encouraging active citizenship' (Johnson, 2001, pp 184-5), it was prompted to take a much larger and more formal role in social services, in partnership with business and the state. The private sector continued to be a highly influential 'partner', with business leaders even asked to give advice on policy and join project teams. But partnerships extended well beyond business encompassing relationships with and between the 'central government, the new national assemblies, local government ... the "third sector" of voluntary organisations, academic research and education, and so forth' (Fairclough, 2000, p 124). Partnerships thus became part and parcel of social investment, and how the Blair government 'delivered'. Yet, as we shall see, social investment still required a directive state.

Goals and consequences

Chancellor Brown's first term spending freeze soon gave way to strategic expenditures on programmes considered to be 'good' investments such as the financing of welfare-to-work, education and health. These policies will be discussed in the second part to this chapter, but here the intent is to underscore that social policy that generated an educated/employed, healthy and responsible citizenry, primed for a new flexible, competitive labour market, became a clearly defined social investment goal.

In addition, while the Blair government promised to be tough on crime – a familiar Tory refrain – it was also aware of the fact that high crime rates occurred in the most deprived neighbourhoods. Therefore, state investments were often site-specific, with government schemes focused on large-scale social rental estates and policies that encouraged more of a mix of tenure in them (Hawtin and Kettle, 2000, pp 113-15). The intent was to strengthen social capital through regeneration and neighbourhood renewal (Tiesdell and Almendinger, 2001), and thereby attenuate future, costly societal transgressions.

'Community' became emblematic as the source of 'shared moral values which [were] seen as a means of social cohesion' (Johnson, 2001, pp 184-5). The rediscovery of 'the social' distinguished New Labour from its Conservative predecessors. Still, the modernisers' particular version of communitarianism helped to distance the party from its historic labour-oriented and welfare state commitments.

While the days of 'tax and spend' Old Labour were long gone, the austerity and downsizing of the neoliberal state were also deemed passé: 'under-investment would turn the tide of opinion. In 1997 public services looked worn and shabby, private affluence, public squalor indeed. It was Labour's mission to prove that money could bind the welfare state into the twenty first century' (Toynbee and Walker, 2005, p 6). The new state was to be 'streamlined' and efficient, but its role was by no means passive. However, unlike the welfare state that 'rowed', the social investment state was more prone to 'steer', and in the direction of future dividends. This meant some benefit retrenchment (for example, lone parents), but also targeted expansion and strategic new spending on children and family policy, tax credits, education and health (Lewis, 2006), all viewed as ways to combat social exclusion and save money in the long run.

Although New Labour initially spoke the language of social exclusion in place of poverty, within a couple of years of taking office, the 'P' word was officially rehabilitated, most prominently with Blair's pledge to eradicate child poverty by 2020. This core social investment concern reflected more redistributive, 'European' tendencies. By acknowledging poverty, New Labour set itself apart from Thatcher under whom there was 'no official concession that poverty existed' (Piachaud and Sutherland, 2001, p 5). By focusing on *child* poverty, the Blair government also introduced a different focal point from that of Old Labour. In other words, class and other collective identities were out, and children and youth were in, for they were marketable, productive investments, now and for the future.

Here Blair and Brown would not simply talk the talk, but would walk the walk. Although the government's first interim target was not met, by 2005/06 there were 600,000 fewer children living in poverty. This came in part by moving social security recipients 'from welfare to work', but it was also effected through targeted benefit increases, including financial support for children in out-of-work families. Yet, these increases were largely unsung.

Social justice aspirations remained obscured as the Blair government was loathe to refer to 'redistribution', and initially engaged in 'redistribution by stealth' (Lister, 2001). Over time, however, it became clearer that this was an objective in the Chancellor's budgets. Alongside substantial increases in public spending on public services such as health and education and previously neglected areas such as childcare, Brown devoted considerable sums (without the wholehearted support of Blair) to the new tax credit scheme, with its twin aims of tackling child poverty and 'making work pay'.

The European social model became much more prominent in the safety of the second term. Here income growth was greatest at the bottom of the income distribution, particularly among families with children, largely as a result of tax credits (Brewer et al, 2007). An intensification of social investment became apparent in the third term. For instance, in 2007, as part of the Comprehensive Spending Review, £4 billion would be injected over three years into Sure Start children's centres, early years education and childcare. The aim was to have a Sure Start children's centre in every community by 2010 (DCSF, 2007). Also part of the Review was a policy appraisal of children and young people resulting in three major reports setting out programmes to improve services for children and families, children with disabilities and young people. The third term also saw moves to 'refresh' the poverty strategy.

In sum, social investment ideas and goals were present prior to coming to power, as seen in the CSJ, but they were then fleshed out as the first term progressed, and appeared more fully formed in Blair's second and third terms. Children and youth constituted an excellent rhetorical device to mark investments in the future and to mask the scale of redistributive efforts. Let us now highlight policies that 'delivered' on social investment promises. This combination of goals, settings and techniques is indicative of Hall's third order of change (1993).

Policies, programmes and techniques

Beyond aims and aspirations, social investment translated into concrete policy mechanisms with specific outcomes, monitored through progress reports and benchmarks. We see many of the features outlined by 6 and Peck, from 'common standard setting' and 'area-based policies', to the incorporation of both the private sector and an increasingly responsibility-laden citizenry (2004). We will review these features more systematically by turning to policies and programmes representing investment in human, financial and social capital. While social policy was accorded high priority in Blair's modernised state, this terminology still highlights the fact that the 'social' was the 'handmaiden' of economic policy (Lister, 2003).

In effect, what took place through social investment discourses, mechanisms and techniques was the amalgamation of social and economic policy. This constitutes quite a contrast to social democracy where 'certain areas of social life were meant to be separated or protected from the influence of economic relations. Education and health, for example, were understood to be something other than tradable goods or commodities' (Finlayson, 2003, p 155). The Blair government, conversely, 'reject[ed] this separation. Indeed, it embrace[d] the conjoining of all areas of life with economic productivity' (Finlayson, 2003, p 155).

Investing in human capital

Enhancing human capital over the life course lay at the heart of Blair's social policy agenda. Lifelong learning and employability, in particular, were seen as the best bets for future security and prosperity. Education became a 'national and global commodity' and, with it, all members of society were deemed to 'have a duty to develop their own human capital' (Tomlinson, 2004, p 75). This was a 'supply-side vision of education as integral to human capital formation and economic efficiency' (Brehony and Deem, 2003, p 180). For adults, Blair concentrated on improving skills and competitiveness; for young people, schooling and training were critical; and for children, we see new, interrelated efforts with respect to early childhood education, the eradication of child poverty and more equitable childcare arrangements. For adults and youth, then, the main emphasis was on redistributing opportunity, whereas for children, we see both opportunity and even some redistribution of income.

Blair was particularly keen on lifelong learning as a social investment, stressing not only education, but training, skills development, technology and invention (MacGregor, 1998, p 264). A post-Fordist, globalised world meant that the days of secure jobs were over. Increased investment in education was linked to a more flexible workforce, the 'welfare-to-work' strategy, as well as the promotion of both social inclusion and social mobility. Labour's 1998 welfare Green Paper emphasised that: 'A skilled workforce is essential to a modern economy, and high educational standards offer people their best chance of a secure and prosperous life' (cited in Finlayson, 2003, p 163).

Augmenting human capital via labour attachment was reflected in the early roll-out of the Labour government's New Deals (see Chapters Four and Twelve, this volume). In addition to representing a cornerstone of Blair's 'conditional welfare state' (see Chapter Twelve), the New Deal schemes are readily viewed through the lens of social investment. Indeed, the first New Deal was oriented to young people in order to deal with long-term youth unemployment, and to avoid long-term adult unemployment in future. Social investment also explains why concessions were subsequently made to other objectives beyond 'work first', such as the need for skills acquisition, and for support, once in work, to keep people employed and to move them into better jobs, goals that emerged more clearly in the third term.

Investing in human capital was the common denominator in programmes geared towards children and youth such as the National Childcare Strategy, Sure Start and Connexions. Serving the dual social investment aims of promoting early childhood education and freeing up those who are primarily responsible for care, that is, mothers, to engage in paid work, the National Childcare Strategy was originally launched in 1998, but then a 10-year strategy was announced in Blair's second term. Advances in childcare included: greater entitlement to free nursery education for three- and four-year-olds; extended provision for out-of-school facilities including childcare between 8am and 6pm throughout the year; and, by 2008, a new statutory duty on local authorities to improve child outcomes, and ensure an adequate supply of childcare with mechanisms to regulate and inspect early education and childcare facilities.

New Labour's childcare policy was mostly delivered through designated tax credits. Childcare campaigners criticised this as insufficient public investment in supply. Moreover, this 'taxification' of social policy (Bashevkin, 2002, p 136) reflects the shift in policy instruments that took place over the Blair years. Nevertheless, childcare advocates did acknowledge that the Childcare Strategy signalled that caring for children was not purely a private responsibility. Recent steps to fold the Childcare Strategy into the Sure Start initiative, with the advent of Sure Start children's centres, also aim to make childcare 'more universally available'; however, here the concern is that the centres may be 'spreading resources too thinly to sustain impact' (Williams, 2005, p 293).

Sure Start was pitched as 'pioneering a co-ordinated approach to services for families with children aged under four, tackling the causes of poverty – lack of educational opportunity, lack of parental support, lack of health advice – by adopting an integrated approach to childcare, early education and play, health services and family support' (Brown, 1999, p 4). It was fully costed and modelled on the 'successes' of the American Head Start policy, which claimed that for each $1 invested in a pre-school child, the return to a taxpayer was $7 saved. In spite of this shrewd calculus, this location-based programme was generally well regarded, although there were fears about meeting the needs of children who fell outside the targeted zones.

Various spin-offs followed. Whereas Sure Start covered 0- to 3-year-olds, a more recently announced Action Plan on Social Exclusion involves a number of parenting support health service demonstration projects for pre-birth to two-year-olds aimed at tackling social exclusion and preventing future anti-social behaviour (Social Exclusion Task Force, 2006). Moreover, one of Brown's last Budget announcements as Chancellor was that, from April 2009, all pregnant women would become eligible for the universal child benefit from week 29 of their pregnancy, in recognition of the fact that enhancing the health and outcomes of future children required support in pregnancy (for example, promoting a healthy diet for mothers-to-be).

Before turning to financial capital investments, it is important to underscore the Treasury's new prominence in social policy, as it illustrates the interweaving of social and economic policy and centrality of social investment. The Brown Treasury played a pivotal role in the direct management of domestic policy and moved from providing a 'limited although important role of directing economic policy to assuming broad responsibility for shaping, delivering and monitoring social policy across the field', with a range of new tools adopted, among them Comprehensive Spending Reviews, cross-cutting reviews and public service agreements (Cohen et al, 2004, p 82). It was none other than the Chancellor who rallied to meet child poverty reduction deadlines and who championed childcare, early childhood education and Sure Start, as well as the Child Trust Fund.

Investing in financial capital

The Child Trust Fund epitomises social and financial capital investment priorities through its targeting of the very young and its objectives of asset acquisition and acceleration. This 'baby bond' provides a fixed state endowment for every child at birth, topped up at age seven, with higher payments for children in low-income families. Contributions from friends and family are also encouraged with money deposited into a special savings account to be held tax free until the age of 18. When the final version of the Fund was announced in the 2003 Budget, it was depicted as a long-term savings and investment account, clearly an asset-based welfare policy and investment primed for the future.

Similarly, the new Savings Gateway was piloted to encourage low-income adults to build up shorter-term savings by providing matching savings (Sodha and Lister, 2006) and is scheduled to be introduced in 2010. Saving and 'financial literacy' were not only touted as individual assets, but as a social good: that is, growth in savings and assets was good for individuals, good for business and good for the country as a whole. In the Blair years, saving became 'elevated from a private aspiration of the prudent individual' to a 'core duty' of the 'good' citizen (Hewitt,

2002, cited in Kemp, 2005, p 26). New Labour's long-term pension strategy is yet another example of asset-based welfare. To respond to the retirement needs of low-paid and insecure workers, new incentives combine individual savings with a longer working life, in order to obtain more generous pensions.

Investments in human capital and financial capital were both considered to be a future-oriented public good. Economic productivity and asset management should not only be actively pursued by individuals, young and old, but also by families and communities. The pivotal role for the latter is highly apparent in initiatives that were meant to boost social capital.

Investing in social capital

Blair's new communitarianism was evident in the government's promotion of social capital, namely those 'features of social organization such as networks, norms, and social trust that facilitate co-ordination and co-operation for mutual benefit' (Putnam, 1995, p 67). One of the top priorities of the Blair government, tackling social exclusion, is illustrative. Unlike the unbridled individualism of Thatcher, New Labour concerned itself with the impact of social exclusion on wider society, encouraging individuals, families and firms, as well as the voluntary sector, to take part in promoting social inclusion and cohesion. Thus, the Social Exclusion Unit (SEU) was one of the first new institutions established (the unit was up and running by December of 1997), and its aims and design (for example, to tackle social exclusion, to work across departments, to build partnerships in and outside the state, and to concentrate on children and youth), became a model for other governance initiatives.

Many of the Blair governments' social capital drives worked to forge partnerships and networks that involved families and children. For instance, early in its first mandate, New Labour set up the charity/ advice bureau the National Family and Parenting Institute (NFPI) and piloted family and advice networks. It then went on to fund a child advocacy umbrella group and later developed the £450 million Children's Fund aimed at encouraging voluntary organisations to develop diverse programmes for children. By Blair's third term, the SEU was replaced by a Social Exclusion Task Force with a new action plan. Its first progress report noted that large investments were being made to promote positive outcomes for children and young people, including a major expansion in parenting provision and capacity (Social Exclusion Task Force, 2006, p 11).

Neighbourhoods were also part of social capital investment. New Labour identified perceived 'problem' areas, such as housing estates and poor neighbourhoods, as prime places to tackle social exclusion and, in turn, boost social capital. Children were part of the equation as well. For instance, the Neighbourhood Nurseries initiative launched in early 2001 pinpointed children and families in disadvantaged areas 'by helping to fund well-designed premises in communities with little or no provision.... These nurseries were mainly to be provided by the private sector, but with direct government funding' (Cohen et al, 2004, p 74).

The Blair governments' efforts at investing in social capital were distinctive. Nevertheless, here, as elsewhere, the premise of investment perpetuates the not unproblematic 'interpretation of social phenomena and problems in the language of economics' (Finlayson, 2003, p 159). Finlayson cautions:

> Erosion of social bonds and resources is not understood as an effect of economic activity, which clashes with it, but as a result of imperfect or improperly understood economic activity. The correct response is to begin accounting for social capital and auditing it. Consequently, social relations can once again become an object of government activity in a way they – formally – were not within neoliberal frameworks of thought. However, in the process social relations undergo a relocation in the conceptual structure. (2003, p 160)

Conclusion

The foregoing analysis of social investment attests to the fact that not only the aims but the mechanisms and outcomes of the state shifted under Tony Blair's tenure, involving first, second and third order change. Growth, security and prosperity, the goals of the Blair governments, depended on creative investment. As a result, aspects of social investment rhetoric would have to become a reality. Consequently, the Blair governments' policy priorities, instruments and mechanisms were operationalised in ways that served to institutionalise the social investment perspective (Dobrowolsky and Jenson, 2005).

Gordon Brown, as Chancellor, was a pivotal player in this project and thus it can be expected that social investment will continue under his premiership. Brown was instrumental in promoting a discourse of social investment and was a prime mover in investments aimed at reducing child poverty, which he depicted as 'a scar on the soul of

Britain' (Brown, 1999, p 1). Then, in his first speech to Conference as leader of the Labour Party, Brown reiterated his resolve to end child poverty and called for expansion in education opportunity (2007). One of his first actions as Prime Minister was to create a new Department for Children, Schools and Families under his close ally Ed Balls. When at the Treasury, Balls had demonstrated his commitment to tackling child poverty, and to improving the position of children with disabilities in particular. In his first statement to the House of Commons, Balls explained that the new Department 'brings together for the first time ever in one place responsibility for all policy across Government to promote the well-being of children and young people' (House of Commons, 2007, col 1319). The reference to children's 'well-being' and other statements made by the new Secretary of State, including acknowledgement of the importance of play, suggests that the future orientation of social investment might be somewhat tempered under Brown's watch by greater attention to children's well-being in the present (Lister, 2008). An important signal here is Balls' Children's Plan, a 170-page document published at the end of 2007, 'that aims to make Britain the "best place in the world for our children to grow up in"' (Montgomery, 2007, p 16). There are also signs of a greater focus on the needs of young people and the lack of adequate youth facilities, partly in response to several incidents that fanned the flames of public concern about violence among this age group.

Despite initial faltering, and in response to both internal and external pressure, the new Brown government committed additional resources to tackling child poverty in its first Budget. However, Brown still speaks the Blairite future-oriented language of opportunity and aspiration, rather than that of equality and redistribution. Moreover, without increased tax revenue, the scope for greater social investment is likely to be constrained by the limits on public expenditure growth set by Brown when he was still Chancellor.

Mirroring New Labour, the Conservative Party, under David Cameron, has pledged initially to maintain existing public spending levels, even though in the longer term the Conservatives are still committed to tax cuts. This also suggests that the resources available for social investment will likely diminish. Nevertheless, the Conservative Party has, to some extent, bought into a number of New Labour's social investment goals, in particular, the commitment to eradicate child poverty and the importance of investment in the early years and education. However, the means they would promote to meet these goals would probably be very different. Most notably, the Conservatives would take 'the state' out of the 'social investment state' as far as possible, relying even more on the voluntary and private sectors, and emphasising the 'social responsibility' of society as a whole. As the Conservative leader enunciated in his Scarman Lecture, his government would stress: 'more professional ... personal ... corporate.... And more civic responsibility' in tackling poverty rather than relying so heavily 'on the large, clunking mechanisms of the state' (Cameron, 2006).

Whoever wins the next election, many of the priorities established under Tony Blair's (and Gordon Brown's) social investment agenda will continue to shape social policy. The main dividing lines are likely to be around the role of the state in, and the resources available for, social investment.

Note

[1] The foregoing quotations from 6 and Peck (2004) denote markers of modernisation.

References

6, P. and Peck, F. (2004) 'Modernisation: the ten commitments of New Labour's approach to public management?', *International Public Management Journal*, vol 7, no 1, pp 1-18.

Bashevkin, S. (2002) *Welfare hot buttons: Women, work and social policy reform*, Toronto: University of Toronto Press.

Blair, T. (2003) 'Big conversation', Foreword in *A future fair for all: Big issues need a big conversation*, printed and promoted by David Triesman, General Secretary of the Labour Party on behalf of the Labour Party, London: Labour Party.

Brehony, K.J. and Deem, R. (2003) 'Education policy', in N. Ellison and C. Pierson (eds) *Developments in social policy 2*, Houndmills: Palgrave MacMillan, pp 177-93.

Brewer, M., Goodman, A., Muriel, A. and Sibieta, L. (2007) *Poverty and inequality in the UK: 2007*, IFS Briefing Note No 73, London: Institute for Fiscal Studies.

Brown, G. (1999) Speech by Chancellor of the Exchequer Gordon Brown MP at the Sure Start Conference, 7 July (www.hmtreasury. gov.uk./newsroom_and_speeches/speeches/chancellorexchequer/ speech_chex_70799.cfm).

Brown, G. (2007) First speech to Conference as leader of the Labour Party (www.labour.org.uk/conference/brown_speech).

Cameron, D. (2006) *From state welfare to social enterprise*, The Scarman Lecture, London: Institute of Education, 24 November (www. thescarmantrust.org/lecture/David%20Cameron.pdf).

Cohen, B., Moss, P., Petrie, P. and Wallace, J. (2004) *A New Deal for Children? Re-forming education and care in England, Scotland and Sweden*, Bristol: The Policy Press.

CSJ (Commission on Social Justice) (1994) *Social justice: Strategies for national renewal. Report of the Commission on Social Justice*, London: Vintage.

DCSF (Department for Children, Schools and Families) (2007) 'Government announces £4bn for Sure Start, Early Years and childcare' (www.dfes.gov.uk/pns/DisplayPN.cgi?pn_id=2007_0144).

Dobrowolsky, A. (2002) 'Rhetoric versus reality: the figure of the child and New Labour's strategic "social investment state"', *Studies in Political Economy*, vol 69, pp 43-73.

Dobrowolsky, A. and Jenson, J. (2005) 'Social investment perspectives and practices: a decade in British politics', in M. Powell, L. Bauld and K. Clarke (eds) *Social Policy Review 17: Analysis and debate in social policy*, Bristol: The Policy Press, pp 203-30.

Dobrowolsky, A. and Saint-Martin, D. (2005) 'Agency, actors and change in a child-focused future: "path dependency" problematised', *Commonwealth and Comparative Politics*, vol 42, no 1, pp 1-33.

Dobrowolsky, A. with Lister, R. (2006) 'Social exclusion and changes to citizenship: women and children, minorities and migrants in Britain', in E. Tastsoglou and A. Dobrowolsky (eds) *Gender, migration and citizenship: Making local, national and transnational connections*, Aldershot: Ashgate, pp 149-81.

Esping-Andersen, G. (2000) *A welfare state for the 21st century*, Report to the Portuguese Presidency of the European Union, prepared for the Lisbon Summit (www.nnn.se/seminar/pdf/report.pdf).

Fairclough, N. (2000) *New Labour, new language?*, London: Routledge.

Finlayson, A. (2003) *Making sense of New Labour*, London: Lawrence and Wishart.

Giddens, A. (1994) *Beyond Left and Right: The future of radical politics*, Cambridge: Polity Press.

Giddens, A. (1998) *The Third Way: The renewal of social democracy*, Cambridge: Polity Press.

Giddens, A. (2007) *Europe in the global age*, Cambridge: Polity Press.

Hall, P.A. (1993) 'Policy paradigms, social learning and the state: the case of economic policy making in Britain', *Comparative Politics*, vol 25, no 3, pp 275-96.

Hawtin, M. and Kettle, J. (2000) 'Housing and social exclusion', in J. Percy-Smith (ed) *Policy responses to social exclusion towards inclusion?*, Buckingham: Open University Press, pp 107-29.

Hewitt, M. (2002) 'New Labour and the redefinition of social security', in M. Powell (ed) *Evaltuating New Labour's welfare reforms*, Bristol: The Policy Press.

House of Commons (2007) *Hansard*, 10 July, para 1319 (www. publications.parliament.uk/pa/cm200607/cmhansrd/cm070710/debtext/70710-0003.htm).

Johnson, N. (2001) 'The personal social services', in S.P. Savage and R. Atkinson (eds) *Public policy under Blair*, Houndmills: Palgrave Macmillan.

Kemp, P.A. (2005) 'Social security and welfare reform under New Labour', in M. Powell, L. Bauld and K. Clarke (eds) *Social Policy Review 17: Analysis and debate in social policy*, Bristol: The Policy Press.

Labour Party (2003) *A future fair for all: Big issues need a big conversation*, printed and promoted by David Triesman, General Secretary of the Labour Party on behalf of the Labour Party, London: Labour Party.

Lewis, J. (2006) 'Employment and care: the policy problem, gender equality and the issue of choice', *Journal of Comparative Policy Analysis*, vol 8, no 2, pp 103-14.

Lister, R. (1998) 'Fighting social exclusion … with one hand tied behind our back', *New Economy*, vol 4, no 1, pp 14-18.

Lister, R. (2001) 'From equality to social inclusion: new Labour and the welfare state', *Critical Social Policy*, vol 18, no 2, pp 215-26.

Lister, R. (2003) 'Investing in the citizen-workers of the future: transformations in citizenship and the state under New Labour', *Social Policy and Administration*, vol 37, no 5, pp 427-43.

Lister, R. (2006) 'Children (but not women) first: New Labour, child welfare and gender', *Critical Social Policy*, vol 26, no 2, pp 315-35.

Lister, R. (2008) 'Investing in children and childhood: a new welfare policy paradigm and its implications', *Comparative Social Research*, vol 25, pp 387-413.

MacGregor, S. (1998) 'A new deal for Britain', in H. Jones and S. MacGregor (eds) *Social issues and party politics*, London: Routledge, pp 248-72.

Montgomery, I. (2007) 'A happy childhood on government's agenda', *The Guardian Weekly*, 12 December, p 16.

Piachaud, D. and Sutherland, H. (2001) 'Child poverty and the New Labour government', *Journal of Social Policy*, vol 30, no 1, pp 95-118.

Powell, M. (1999) *New Labour, new welfare state? The 'third way' in British social policy*, Bristol: The Policy Press.

Putnam, R. (1995) 'Bowling alone: America's declining social capital', *Journal of Democracy*, vol 6, pp 65-78.

Saint-Martin, D. (2007) 'From the welfare state to the social investment state: a new paradigm for Canadian social policy?', in M. Orsini and M. Smith (eds) *Critical policy studies*, Vancouver: University of British Columbia Press, pp 279-98.

Social Exclusion Task Force (2006) (www.cabinetoffice.gov.uk/social_ exclusion_task_force/publications/reaching _out.aspx).

Sodha, S. and Lister, R. (2006) *The Saving Gateway: From principles to practice*, London: Institute for Public Policy Research.

Tiesdell, S. and Almendinger, P. (2001) 'Neighbourhood regeneration and New Labour's third way', *Environment and Planning: Government and Policy*, vol 19, pp 903-26.

Tomlinson, S. (2004) 'The rise of the meritocracy? New Labour and education in the second term', in N. Ellison, L. Bauld and M. Powell (eds) *Social Policy Review 16: Analysis and debate in social policy, 2004*, Bristol: The Policy Press, pp 61-80.

Toynbee, P. and Walker, R. (2005) *Better or worse? Has New Labour delivered?*, Harmondsworth: Penguin.

Vandenbrouke, F. (2001) 'European social democracy and the third way: convergence, divisions and shared questions', in S. White (ed) *New Labour: The progressive future?*, Houndmills: Palgrave Macmillan.

Williams, F. (2005) 'New Labour's family policy', in M. Powell, L. Bauld and K. Clarke (eds) *Social Policy Review 17: Analysis and debate in social policy*, Bristol: The Policy Press, pp 289-302.

NINE

Risk and the Blair legacy

David Denney

Introduction

This chapter examines risk scenarios that have been structured into New Labour policy discourses since 1997. I will argue that the approach taken to risk by New Labour, although complex and sometimes contradictory, can be understood as a feature of late modernity. New Labour, like all governments in advanced capitalist societies, is experiencing and responding to processes of 'reflexive modernisation' (Beck, 1992). The work of 6 and Peck will be utilised to identify emergent themes of change associated with New Labour (6 and Peck, 2004a). Central policy variables discussed by Hall will also be used to discuss the extent of changes introduced by New Labour with regard to risk (Hall, 1993).

New Labour reflexive modernisation and risk

For Beck (1992), calculating risk is part of a modern narrative in which the welfare state no longer gains its legitimacy through its capacity to protect citizens against dangers with the provision of state-funded assistance. Risk has become a 'Systematic way of dealing with hazards and insecurities induced and introduced by modernisation itself' (Beck, 1992, p 21).

Individuals in what Beck has called the 'risk society' are required to make major decisions about employment, education and self-identity in a world in which beliefs about class, gender and the family are being overturned (Beck, 1992; Mythen, 2004).

New Labour guru Anthony Giddens, in a similar vein, has argued that late modernity can be characterised by uncertainty about claims to truth that has led to mass insecurity (Giddens, 1998). This has been accompanied by a growing scepticism about the ability of experts to predict risk and a blurring of distinctions between lay and professional knowledge (Foster and Wilding, 2000). For Giddens, the present age is no riskier or dangerous than previous periods of history, although risks are more likely to be manufactured. Active risk taking is a core element in the creation of a dynamic economy and an essential prerequisite to participation in a technologically based global era (Giddens, 1998).

One of the problems with this position, however, is that risks are not experienced in an undifferentiated manner across groups in society. The impact of risks associated with flexible working patterns and the maintenance of family life have a disproportionate reflexive impact on the lives of poorer people (Taylor-Gooby, 2000).

New Labour risk and positive welfare

Beveridge identified the 'giant' risks to living a healthy and fulfilled life as: idleness, ignorance, squalor, want and disease. The risk of suffering as a result of one of these risks was partly ameliorated by social insurance, a combination of individual contribution and state intervention (Beveridge, 1942).

New Labour's 'joined-up' approach was also intended to attack all the 'giants' as Beveridge had intended (Powell and Hewitt, 2002). Just as the Attlee government had brought about a paradigmatic change in the provision of state welfare, another major change began in 1976 and was consolidated into a break with classic welfare with the election of Margaret Thatcher in 1979. Monetarism provided a coherent challenge to Old Labour and represented a rare simultaneous paradigmatic shift in the goals, techniques and settings of welfare instruments (Hall, 1993). Blair argued that the old labour welfare infrastructure is irrelevant:

> Beveridge's stated ambition was care from the cradle to the grave. In fact the welfare state more or less disappeared after childbirth until it was time for primary school. We have begun the process of filling the gap. (Blair, 2006, p 2)

For New Labour the risk of personal hardship cannot be reduced by direct state intervention, but through paid employment and flexible labour markets. This was a three-way contract between central government, local agencies and individuals in which all parties recognised their rights and responsibilities (Powell and Hewitt, 2002). 'Positive welfare' aimed to create macro-economic stability, promote investment in education and health, releasing individual potential and reducing dependency on the state (Giddens, 2000; Kemshall, 2002).

Discourses of risk: New Labour and the risk society

Three dominant New Labour risk discourses marked a change from 'needs-led' to 'risk-led' welfare (Kemshall, 2002). Firstly, the discourse of mass affluence reduced the need for universal welfare and state-sponsored risk protection. According to Giddens (2000, p 13), 10% of the population were long term chronically poor. The central dilemma confronting New Labour was how to include the truly disadvantaged minority without alienating the contented majority (Stenson, 2001).

Secondly, New Labour emphasised the precautionary principle that attempts to identify risks and act on them before they occur. New Labour's construction of 'risk environments' in both foreign and domestic policy has been based on the selective generation of possible scenarios that emphasise risk. Just as the invasion of Iraq had been presented by Bush and Blair as a pre-emptive act of self-defence, similar discourses can be seen with respect to social policy (Denney, 2005). Some New Labour risk-led precautionary measures appear to mark a radical shift with the past. The introduction of control orders in 2005 extended the executive power of the Home Secretary to impose curfews and house arrest (*The Guardian*, 2005). The current 28-day time limit for detention without charge is far longer than in any other comparable democracy (*The Guardian*, 2007). The elimination of the double jeopardy rule in 2005 resulted in the possibility of individuals facing a new trial after being acquitted if new and compelling evidence emerged.

Thirdly, New Labour restated the relationship between risk, responsibility and regulation as a rapidly emerging theme in policy development. The Better Regulation Commission, set up by Blair, promoted risk, emphasising 'resilience, self reliance, freedom, innovation and a spirit of adventure' (Better Regulation Commission, 2006, p 3). Although New Labour regarded regulatory mechanisms as being necessary to offer protection against risks, in areas such as health and safety, the implementation of the Hampton Review signalled a reduction in the number of regulatory bodies (Blair, 2006).

New Labour's approach to risk appears to mark a distinctive break with the Old Left and the New Right. 6 and Peck (2004a) have provided the most detailed analysis of the central commitments that characterise New Labour public management. These are: inspection, central standard setting, area-based initiatives, coordination and integration, devolution but limited decentralisation, earned autonomy, an extended role for private capital, a modest increase in citizen obligations, access and e-government. Hall (1993) has argued that 'first' and 'second order' change are part of normal policy making. These forms of change preserve broad continuities usually found in patterns of policy, but signify a change in the settings and instruments of policy. Third order change is for Hall a more 'disjunctive process', marking radical changes in policy discourse (Hall, 1993, p 279). The ideas of 6 and Peck and Hall will be used to evaluate the nature of the changes introduced by New Labour and the extent of policy shift in relation to risk.

Inspection and central standard setting

In keeping with Giddens' enthusiasm for positive risk, New Labour have attempted to make inspection appear to be a form of risk assessment (CSCI, 2007). Inspections are carried out in accordance with standards laid out in government directives, although risk is the foundation on which inspections are based (HM Treasury, 2005). The Commission for Health Improvement developed audit quality control procedures that were administered by hospital and primary care groups. Scheduled and unscheduled inspections were also a feature of this inspectorial operation. The creation of the National Institute for Clinical Excellence (NICE) provided a regulatory function with respect to treatment protocols (6 and Peck, 2004b). Ofsted gained new powers to inspect local authorities as well as schools. The Care Standards Act of 2000 established a new regulatory body, the National Care Standards Commission. This created a regulatory system for residential homes, nursing homes, children's homes, domiciliary and care agencies and fostering and adoption agencies, including private hospitals, clinics and private primary care premises (www.opsi.gov.uk). The Commission for Social Care Inspection now claims to provide 'risk-based regulation' for 28,000 services in England and Wales (Snell, 2007). National Service Frameworks set service standards drawing on meta-analyses of service evaluations, providing an 'evidence-based' approach to risk management.

The proliferation of risk management through inspection and audit has yet to be justified.

Area-based initiatives

Area-based initiatives target residual welfare at 'high-risk' populations. New Labour's attempts to regenerate local communities are similar but distinct from the social engineering of postwar slum clearance, and the construction of 'rational' communities which were subject to more centralised control (Hope, 1995; Young, 2001). New Labour claimed that risks associated with social exclusion and youth crime could be tackled through early intervention, identifying what works, better coordination of the many separate agencies, balancing personal rights and responsibilities and intolerance of poor performance (6 and Peck, 2004a; Blair, 2006).

These principles have been applied selectively to specific localities designated by New Labour as being high risk, inhabited by vulnerable dysfunctional people (Furedi, 2007). Fear, social malaise, loss of community, urban decline and the break up of the traditional family were risk factors that needed to be tackled (Blair, 2006).

Such New Labour thinking gave rise to the Sure Start and *Every Child Matters* initiatives that were heavily influenced by research on childhood risk factors and risk-focused intervention (Farrington and Welsh, 2007). In 1998 Sure Start was designed to provide coordinated projects in early intervention and play, child health and family support for the under-fours and 'difficult-to-reach' families. There was a flaw here. Since all disadvantaged children do not live in deprived areas, each small Sure Start programme could only serve a minority of disadvantaged children. Those living in adjacent areas could not participate. As Glass comments, although 'what works' is important, 'how it works' is equally if not more significant (Glass, 2003, p 12).

Another risk-led policy can be seen in the movement from 'crime prevention' to localised 'community safety'. Community safety targeted high-risk areas prone to crime for increasing surveillance and control, while barriers between agencies working in these localities would be broken down (Van Swaaningen, 2002). Voluntary and statutory agencies would work together flexibly while professional rivalries would be set aside (Blair, 2006, p 4).

Risk assessment formed the basis for providing increased levels of intense supervision to individuals in the community Statutory community partnerships and safer schools partnerships were created on the assumption that non-attendance greatly increases the risk of crime. More coercive measures were also introduced to manage risks crated by children. The abolition of doli incapax now makes children under the age of 10 criminally responsible (Morgan and Newburn, 2007). This form of risk management reflected 'instrument' change with consistent goals of crime risk reduction, rather than a paradigm shift (Hall, 1993).

Risks posed by terrorism were used to justify a more aggressive New Labour approach to security in all areas of life. Attention was focused on risks attributed to young men living in materially deprived Muslim communities throughout Britain (Macey, 2002). An unknown number of prisoners were held without trial under the provisions of the 2001 Anti-terrorism, Crime and Security Act, and the House of Lords ruled that indefinite detention without trial for foreign subjects suspected of terrorism contravened the European Convention of Human Rights (*The Guardian*, 2005).

Coordination and integration

A powerful policy discourse within New Labour rhetoric has been the commitment to 'joined-up' and coordinated government. This has been seen with the development of local partnerships as mentioned above in relation to communities, funding for multi-disciplinary intervention and mergers across services (6 and Peck, 2004a).

In the delivery of social care, New Labour moved beyond the internal market introduced by the Conservatives in the 1990 NHS and Community Care Act. The 1990s saw an increasing preoccupation with risk assessment in social services practices (Kemshall, 2002). Blair further enhanced this by introducing 'pooled budgets from council social services, cash from the Independent Living Fund, Disabilities Facilities Grant and access to work grant' (Blair, 2006, p 6). This, he argued, would provide more flexible and integrated services, filling the risky gaps left by previous bureaucratised welfare arrangements (Blair, 2006).

Klein (2006) has suggested that, faced with the requirement to perform on a number of policy fronts simultaneously, NHS managers put the achievement of measurable targets over reducing inequalities. This could have placed those in most need of long-term community care, characteristically those who have long-term mental health problems or older people, at greater risk. An integrated approach to the delivery of services can also diminish the ability of local agencies to provide community safety, dividing groups who are trying to provide services (Bradley and Walters, 2002). Agencies can often be self-protective and inadequately resourced which can result in infighting, with some agencies having dominance over others. The New Labour Connexions project, which was meant to coordinate all services for 13- to 19-year-olds, failed, partly due to the tension between being both a targeted and universal service. This is not to say that integrated and co-coordinated working is in some instances essential when addressing risk. Numerous inquiries into the murders of children while in the care of social services departments indicate the urgent need for a more coordinated approach to child protection (Laming, 2003). Even in the delivery of cancer services, where coordinated risk management is also essential, evidence indicating the effectiveness of multi-disciplinary teams is scarce (Fleissig et al, 2006). New Labour has taken up considerable time with the discussion of partnerships and monitoring schemes while less attention has been paid to the analysis of the origins of the risks services are meant to be addressing.

Devolution but limited decentralisation

The devolving of healthcare budgets to primary care trusts, the introduction of foundation hospitals and lighter touch inspection for the best performing hospitals do appear to show significant decentralisation, which continued a trend towards devolved power, begun under the Conservative government. However, the focus of primary care is rarely on people with long-term physical or mental illness (6 and Peck, 2004b). Those often at greatest risk in society benefit little from this development. The machinations of decentralisation do not appear to be congruent with the polemic of robust risk assessment and public safety.

Earned autonomy as a settlement between centralism and decentralisation

New Labour's modernisation agenda incorporated the:

> continued separation of planning and provision in the context of collaboration and decentralised responsibility for operational management. (6 and Peck, 2004a, p 5)

Earned autonomy can be seen when successful institutions are subjected to lighter touch inspections (Blair, 2005). However, the New Labour approach has been described as reflecting an 'arm's-length but hands-on' policy approach (Crawford, 2001, p 63) The ambiguity is illustrated well with respect to the *Guidance on statutory crime and disorder partnerships* (Home Office, 1998). Although New Labour advocated flexibility at local level, ruling nothing out or in, the same document identified a number of risks which local partnerships are asked by central government to consider.

An extended role for private capital

Under New Labour state-funded provision is becoming more individualist, privatised and dependent on the private sector (Jordan,

1998). Those who are at most risk from social change may be more inclined to see greater flexibility as constituting a series of threats rather than new opportunities (Taylor-Gooby, 2000). 6 and Peck (2004b) argue that in the mental health sector many managers see the private sector as the provider of last resort. Given the high risks involved in the provision of mental health services the private sector has shown limited interest in mainstream mental health provision.

Some Conservative initiatives to promote private welfare such as the assisted places scheme, nursery vouchers and tax relief on private medicine for those aged 60 or above were abandoned. New Labour has supported the development of the private finance initiative (PFI). This has been criticised as potentially creating more risk for patients and heralding the possible demise of the NHS and movement of patient risk towards the private sector. PFI enables private companies to make financial decisions about healthcare in situations in which there is inadequate accountability. This leaves scope for corruption and could see rising costs of healthcare when compared with traditional funding of NHS capital developments (Smith, 1999). In 1990 the Conservatives froze student grants and offered top-up loans. New Labour went further than this, replacing student grants with loans and means-tested tuition fees. This adds a further dimension of risk when young people are considering higher education, while student loans differentially affect lower-income groups (Cappannari, 2002).

In the Green Paper *Partnership in pensions* (DSS, 1998), New Labour made it clear that individual citizens were expected to secure their own financial security in old age. This is despite the fact that older people are vulnerable to the risk of suffering a major bereavement, disability, social exclusion, lack of work, unsuitable accommodation and inadequate income (Heywood et al, 2002).

Offenders are also more likely to have experienced risk factors associated with large families, poor child-rearing methods, low parental involvement, neglect and disrupted families (Farrington and Welsh, 2007). In 2004 New Labour advocated the merging of prison and probation services and the creation of a market to deliver more effective and efficient probation services (NAPO, 2006). All these examples indicate 'second order' changes whereby the needs of high-risk groups who may be at risk are seen by New Labour as being best served through partnerships with the private sector (Hall, 1993).

A modest increase in citizen obligations

In describing New Labour's modernisation, 6 and Peck (2004a) describe a modest increase in citizen obligations. New Labour's emphasis on personal responsibility reflects changes in settings and policy instruments (Hall, 1993). Blair argued that:

> In place of an atomised, individualised, selfish society, people yearn for a society that heals itself, a politics that reduces division, intolerance and inequality ... individuals realise their potential best through a strong community based on rights and responsibilities. (Blair, 1999, quoted in Franklin, 2006, p 157)

Such active citizenship was premised on a balance between rights and obligations, engagement in, for instance, voluntary work, becoming a magistrate or involvement in governing local schools (Powell and Hewitt, 2002). Active citizenship was also reflected in an individual's ability to provide their own housing, which represented an amalgam of individualisation, independence and risk. New Labour extended the Thatcherite government's 'Right to Buy' policy of the 1980s. As the dynamic of home ownership has increased, many individuals have underestimated the potential risks involved and easy borrowing has propelled some borrowers into unsustainable home ownership (Munro, 2000)

Old age brings a greater risk of homelessness. In his first party conference speech on coming to power, Blair emphatically stated that he did not want children to be brought up in a country:

> Where the only way pensioners can get long term care is by selling their home, where people who fought to keep the country free are now faced every winter with a struggle for survival, skimping and saving, cold and alone, waiting for death to take them. (Blair, 1997, p 5)

The Royal Commission on Long-term Care, chaired by Sir Stewart Sutherland, was set up by New Labour in 1997 and recommended free nursing and personal care according to assessed need (Royal Commission on Long-term Care, 1999). New Labour ruled out acceptance of these proposals on the basis of cost (*The Guardian*, 2001). In the Green Paper *Partnership in pensions*, the government made it clear that individual citizens were expected to provide for their own financial security in old age (DSS, 1998; Ring, 2003). It is difficult for older people to be enthusiastic about 'positive' welfare when pensions based on a defined flat rate percentage of theit final salary are abandoned in favour of a private system dependent on the vicissitudes of international finance. Modest increases in obligation underplay the major responsibility for risk placed on citizens by New Labour.

Access to services

New Labour initiatives to reduce risk by increasing access to services such as NHS Direct and walk-in primary care centres have changed levels of previous policy, signifying 'first order' change. In mental health the National Service Framework sets out standards for access to primary care and for 24-hour access to crisis services. Evidence suggests that early intervention and crisis response teams have had some success in creating speedier access to successful interventions thereby reducing public risk (6 and Peck, 2004b).

E-government and technology

The knowledge economy is based on the proposition that e-commerce provides unique opportunities and challenges. Failure to grasp the technological nettle created the risk of uncompetitiveness. Blair implored the nation to embrace the challenges of e-commerce and the internet, just as Wilson had argued that Britain would be forged in the white heat of the scientific revolution in the 1960s (Allender, 2001; Blair, 2005).

New Labour set up agencies such as the Performance and Innovation Unit (PIU) in 2000 to promote new ways of working with technology (Blair, 2000). However, events have shown that an over-reliance on technology, combined with human error, can create risks. The uncontrollable costs of the ineffective Child Support Agency set up by the Conservative government in 1993 were mainly due to the ineffectiveness of its information technology (IT) systems. New Labour failed to change these inappropriate and costly arrangements for child support until 2004 (Silicon.com, 2006). The loss by Her Majesty's Revenue & Customs of two CDs on 18 October 2007 containing names, addresses and in some cases including banking details of 7.25 million families claiming child benefit created a major embarrassment for the Brown government in November 2007, and security risks to the public.

Risk and the impact of change

Some measures designed to reduce the risk of offending, including the electronic surveillance of offenders and intensive supervision of young offenders, were 'first order' extensions of ideas introduced by previous administrations.

Area-based initiatives and community safety can best be described as 'second order' change in that only the settings and instruments of policy delivery have been altered. Blair argued that children at risk of

Table 9.1: Assessment of risk and New Labour policies against Hall's orders of change

First order change Levels or settings changed	Second order change Policy instrument altered; goals unchanged	Third order change 'Paradigm shift'
Risk assessment for the disruptive and vulnerable, eg intensive probation supervision for high-risk offenders, youth curfews, safer schools project	Community safety and pooled budgets to combat risk in area-based projects	Increased responsibility for personal risk, eg older people required to provide for their own financial security
Providing access to services for those at risk, eg emergency access to mental health services, NHS Direct	Interdisciplinary efforts to control risks to the public and the vulnerable	The precautionary principle – pre-emptive action to minimise risk takes precedence over human rights and previous due process, eg imposition of control orders, indefinite detention, abolition of doli incapax, removal of double jeopardy rule
	Risk management through social inclusion, early intervention, targeted precautionary programmes, eg Sure Start	
	Partnership with private sector to provide high risk services, eg PFI	
	'Positive citizenship' linked individual responsibility to risk promotion (Better Regulation Task Force), eg more home ownership, student loans	
	From needs-led to risk-led residual targeted welfare, eg housing of older people	

being brought up in 'dysfunctional homes' should be targeted for early intervention. There was no point in:

> Waiting until the child goes off the rails, we should act early enough, with the right help, support and disciplined framework for the family to prevent it. (Blair, 2006, p 6)

New Labour was not the first to identify self-reliance and greater responsibility of citizens as policy goals. However, New Labour added the precautionary principle as a form of risk management. Dysfunctional individuals would be assisted by coordinated, area-based instruments that would lead to independence, thereby reducing risk of state dependence. State-targeted early preventative help to support

Table 9.2: Risk, New Labour and modernisation

Area	Risk-based policy
Inspection and central standard setting	Precautionary principle, central standard setting as a technique of avoiding risk. Inspection central feature of risk management
Area-based initiatives	Early intervention to avoid risk, eg Sure Start. From crime prevention to community safety. Risk of crime linked to clean, safe environment. Active citizenship to prevent risk
Coordination and integration	Local partnerships in communities. Multi-disciplinary teams and pooled budgets. More effective services to control risk
Devolution but limited decentralisation	Incongruity between polemic of risk assessment and policy implementation
Earned autonomy	'Arm's-length but hands-on.' Retreat from stated aim of autonomy particularly in the area of creating community safety
Extended role for private capital	Increased insecurity and risk for some groups, eg pensioners, students. Use of private capital to promote positive risk. Private sector used to finance and manage public services associated with risk, eg health, criminal justice, education, social care
Modest increase in citizen obligations	Strong increase in obligations. Citizens are now responsible for management of risk in more aspects of personal life. Part of low state dependency culture. Obligation for citizens to make risky communities safe by voluntary effort
Access to services	Increased access to crisis services has developed. Recognition of some health problems eg mental health
E-government	Use of technology to control risky populations. Systems failures, eg Child Support Agency. Loss of child benefit data that creates a risk to the public

children in dysfunctional families took the place of Joseph's idea of 'immoral' state dependence:

> The only hope we can give to the poor is helping them to help themselves; to do the opposite, to create more dependence is to destroy their morality whilst throwing an unfair burden on society. (Keith Joseph, quoted in George and Wilding, 1995, p 33)

Despite £17 billion expenditure on Sure Start since 1998, it is not entirely clear how effectively these measures have impacted on reducing risks to children and families, and its future is unclear (Glass, 2003).

'Second order' changes made by New Labour's risk-based inspections have had a limited impact on vulnerable people. In social care the chief inspector of care standards has argued that despite gradual improvements, there are major concerns relating to the impact of the movement of welfare responsibilities from the state to individuals, families and the private sector. One third of care homes do not reach safety standards with respect to the administration of medication and recruitment. One third of children's homes are not reaching appropriate health and safety standards. There are still variations in the standards of service that could generate risk (Snell, 2007). The repayment of student loans on graduation and means-tested tuition fees moves beyond the policies of the Conservatives and represents a shift away from state-subsidised higher education. Loans also create the risk of a financial burden disproportionately falling on graduates from poorer homes.

Hall (1993) argues that the literature provides less guidance in modelling third order paradigmatic change. However, New Labour's aim to make older people responsible for their financial security challenges the overall terms of previous policy discourse. This also signifies a shift in settings, instruments and goals of policy delivery while severely underestimating the risks encountered by this group.

New Labour's adoption of the precautionary principle in relation to the due process of law has meant that pre-emptive action based on risk has occasionally overshadowed human rights, reflecting a shift from state protection to risk regulation.

Conclusion

The relationship between New Labour and risk constitutes a contradictory combination of policies. New Labour's idea of the risk society emphasises area-based coordinated efforts to reduce fear, while extending instruments of social control. Little autonomy appears to have been earned by private or public organisations ostensibly reducing risk, while citizens are expected to take significantly more responsibility for their own risks. Partnerships between private capital and the state are seen by New Labour as offering a viable form of risk management. New Labour conceptualises risk as presenting the basis for a new form of active self-sufficient citizenship while removing any expectation of 'no fault' state risk protection (Kemshall, 2002).

It is possible to overemphasise the impact of changes under New Labour given that new goals and themes are never perfectly administered or applied uniformly. It has been argued that New Labour's utilisation of risk contains contradictions that have made the application of social control through the creation of a risk discourse problematic (Garland, 2001). At the same time many consumers of welfare are aware of the need for a state-provided safety net. Individual responsibility does not automatically preclude state-centred welfare institutions (Taylor-Gooby, 2000).

New Labour's attempts to promote risk and responsibility as positive aspects of social policy have become engulfed in a wider pessimistic search for security in a battle being waged against invisible and unknowable dangers at home and abroad. This will remain an enduring feature of the Blair legacy despite modest progress in many areas of service delivery.

References

6, P. and Peck, E. (2004a) 'Modernisation: the ten commitments of New Labour's approach to public management', *International Public Management Journal*, vol 7, no 1, pp 1-18.

6, P. and Peck, E. (2004b) 'New Labour's modernisation in the public sector: a neo-Durkheimian approach and the case of mental health services', *Public Administration*, vol 82, no 1, pp 83-108.

Allender, P. (2001) 'What's new about New Labour?', *Politics*, vol 21, no 1, pp 56-62.

Beck, U. (1992) *Risk society: Towards a new modernity*, London: Sage Publications.

Better Regulation Commission (2006) *Risk, responsibility and regulation – Whose risk is it anyway?*, October (www.brc.gov.uk).

Beveridge, W. (1942) *Social insurance and allied services*, Cmd 6404, London: HMSO.

Blair, T. (1997) Speech to the Labour Party Annual Conference, Brighton, September (www.prnewswire.co.uk/cgi/news).

Blair, T. (2000) 'Foreword' in Performance and Innovation Unit, *e-commerce@its.best.uk*, in M. Raco (2002) 'Risk, fear and control: deconstructing the discourses of New Labour's economic policy', *Space and Polity*, vol 6, pp 25-47.

Blair, T. (2005) Speech on Compensation Culture to the Institute for Public Policy, 26 May, *The Guardian Unlimited* (www.politics. guardian.co.uk).

Blair, T. (2006) *Our nations future: Social exclusion*, 5 September (www. pm.gov.uk).

Bradley, T. and Waters, R. (2002) 'Prevention and community safety: the New Zealand experience', in G. Hughes, E. McLaughlin and J. Muncie (eds) *Crime prevention and community safety: New directions*, London: Sage Publications.

Cappannari, A. (2002) 'American college students graduate with record levels of debt', 22 April (www.wsws.org/articles/2002).

Crawford, A. (2001) 'Joined up but fragmented: contradiction, ambiguity and ambivalence at the heart of New Labour's Third Way', in R. Matthews and J. Pitts (eds), *Crime disorder and community safety*, London: Routledge.

CSCI (Commission for Social Care Inspection) (2007) *Annual Report 2006-7* (www.csi.org.uk).

Denney, D. (2005) *Risk and society*, London: Sage.

DH (Department of Health) (1998) *Modernising mental health services: Safe, sound and supportive*, London: DH.

DSS (Department of Social Security) (1998) *New ambitions for our country: A new contract for welfare*, Cm 3805, London: The Stationery Office.

Farrington, D.P. and Welsh, B.C. (2007) *Saving children from a life of crime: Early risk factors and effective intervention*, Oxford: Oxford University Press.

Fleissig, A., Jenkins, V., Catt, S. and Fallowfield, L. (2006) 'Multi-disciplinary teams in cancer care: are they effective in the UK?', *Lancet Oncology*, vol 7, pp 935-43.

Foster, P. and Wilding, P. (2000) 'Whither welfare professionalism?', *Social Policy and Administration*, vol 34, no 2, pp 143-60.

Franklin, J. (2006) 'Politics and risk', in G. Mythen and S. Walkgate (eds) *Beyond the risk society*, Maidenhead: Open University Press.

Furedi, F. (2007) 'The only thing we have to fear is the "culture of fear" itself', *Spiked*, 4 April (www.spiked-online.com).

Garland, D. (2001) *The culture of control: Crime and social order in contemporary society*, Oxford: Oxford University Press.

George, V. and Wilding, P. (1995) *Welfare and ideology*, Hemel Hempstead: Harvester Wheatsheaf.

Giddens, A. (1998) *The Third Way: The renewal of social democracy*, Oxford: Polity Press.

Giddens, A. (2000) *The Third Way and its critics*, Cambridge: Polity Press.

Glass, N. (2003) 'Surely some mistake?', *Education Guardian*, 5 January, p 12 (www.guardian.co.uk).

Guardian, The (2001) 'Q & A, Sutherland Report', *Guardian Unlimited*, 24 January (www.guardian.co.uk\society\2001).

Guardian, The (2005) 'Lawyers criticise house arrest plan', 27 January, p 3.

Guardian, The (2007) 'UK terror detention limit is longest of any democracy', 12 November, p 1.

Hall, P.A. (1993) 'Policy paradigms, social learning and the state: the case of economic policy making in Britain', *Comparative Politics*, vol 25, no 3, pp 275-96.

Heywood, F., Olman, C. and Means, R. (2002) *Housing and home in later life*, Buckingham: Open University Press.

HM Treasury (2005) *Reducing administrative burdens: Effective inspection and enforcement*, March (www.berr.gov.uk).

Home Office (1998) *Guidance on statutory crime and disorder partnerships*, London: Home Office.

Hope, T. (1995) 'Community crime prevention', in M. Tonry and D. Farringdon (eds) *Building a safer society: Strategic approaches to crime prevention*, Chicago, IL: University of Chicago Press.

Jordan, B. (1998) *The new politics of welfare*, London: Sage Publications.

Kemshall, H. (2002) *Risk, social policy and welfare*, Buckingham: Open University Press.

Klein, R. (2006) *The new politics of the NHS: From creation to reinvention* (5th edn), Oxford: Radcliffe Publishing.

Laming, H. (2003) *The Victoria Climbié Inquiry*, London: The Stationery Office.

Macey, M. (2002) 'Interpreting Islam: young Muslim men's involvement in criminal activity in Bradford', in B. Spalek (ed) *Islam, crime and criminal justice*, Uffculme: Willan Publishing.

Morgan, R. and Newburn, T. (2007) 'Youth justice', in M. Maguire, R. Morgan and R. Reiner (eds) *The Oxford handbook of criminology*, Oxford: Oxford University Press.

Munro, M. (2000) 'Labour market insecurity in the owner-occupied housing market', *Environment and Planning*, vol 32, no 8, pp 175-89.

Mythen, G. (2004) *Ulrich Beck – A critical introduction to the risk society*, London: Pluto Press.

NAPO (National Association of Probation Officers) (2006) *A history of NOMS –Three years of costly bureaucracy chaos* (www.napo.org.uk).

Powell, M. and Hewitt, M. (2002) *Welfare state and welfare change*, Buckingham: Open University Press.

Raco, M. (2002) 'Risk, fear and control: deconstructing the discourses of New Labour's economic policy', *Space and Polity*, vol 6, pp 25-47.

Ring, P. (2003) 'Risk and UK pension reforms', *Social Policy and Administration*, vol 37, no 1, pp 65-82.

Royal Commission on Long-term Care (1999) *With respect to old age: Long-term care – rights and responsibilities*, chaired by Sir Stewart Sutherland, Cm 4192-I, London: The Stationery Office.

Silicon.com (2006) 'Child Support Agency IT costs rise to £1.1 bn', 30 June (www.silicon.com/).

Smith, R. (1999) 'The private finance initiative is a "free lunch" that could destroy the NHS', *British Medical Journal*, vol 319, p 7201 (www.bmj.com).

Snell, P. (2007) Speech to Birmingham Council, 6 June (www.csci.org.uk).

Stenson, K. (2001) 'The new politics of crime control', in K Stenson and R. Sullivan (eds) *Crime, risk and justice*, Cullompton: Willan Publishing.

Taylor-Gooby, P. (ed) (2000) *Risk, trust and welfare*, London: Macmillan.

Van Swaaningen, R. (2002) 'Towards a replacement discourse on community safety', in G. Hughes, E. McLaughlin and J. Muncie (eds) *Crime prevention and community safety: New directions*, London: Sage Publications.

Young, J. (2001) 'Identity, community and social exclusion', in R. Matthews and J. Pitts (eds), *Crime disorder and community safety*, London: Routledge.

TEN

Going private?

Mark Drakeford

Introduction

The opening chapter to this book (Chapter One) provided a comprehensive taxonomy of the ways in which the term 'modernisation' in the Blair years was deployed by the government and understood by those who sought to analyse it in action. This chapter focuses on just one of those conceptual categories, the sense in which modernisation has been used to mean a preference for, and a replacement by, private sector means and methods for those utilised in and by the public sector. In doing so private welfare is understood in three main ways (Drakeford, 2000):

- as the *ownership of assets* and whether they lie in public or private hands;
- as the *provision* of welfare services – whether the state directly supplies such services, or whether it 'outsources' or subcontracts that responsibility to a private sector provider;
- as the *allocation of responsibilities* between the state and the individual – to find a job, for example, or to deal with the collapse of a private pension plan.

Running through all of these is the question of *zeitgeist* – whether the underlying set of fundamental attitudes and beliefs that the Blair governments brought to this question of welfare amounts to the sort of disjunctive step-change that Hall (1993) identifies.

Just three notes of caution are needed before the main discussion of the chapter begins. Firstly, as Burchardt et al (1999, p 1) point out, 'Welfare has never been the exclusive preserve of the state'. Private welfare has always been a substantial player in the lives of many citizens. Secondly, this chapter focuses on the English welfare state under New Labour. Devolution means that a chapter that focused on private welfare in Wales, Scotland or Northern Ireland would be very different.

Thirdly, the chapter organises itself around four of the 'five giants' of the Beveridge report. Social services are not discussed here because, to a degree not shared by the other four, they remained, throughout the postwar era, characterised by a wide mixture of public, voluntary and commercial providers. Discussion of private welfare in this field can be found in Jordan (2004), Netten (2005), Drakeford (2006) and Scourfield (2007).

Table 10.1: Private welfare modernisation

Area	Private welfare reform
Inspection	Substantial expansion of private sector involvement in inspection itself, especially in education, and in deployment of private sector techniques more generally
Central standard setting	Services remain subject to strongly centralised, publicly determined, standards
Area-based initiatives	In all four dimensions considered in this chapter area-based initiatives have included strong representation from private sector interests, and a dilution of local, public democratic structures
Coordination and integration	Not a relevant consideration
Devolution but limited decentralisation	Three of the four services are wholly devolved, with different developments in relation to public and private welfare in Scotland, Wales and Northern Ireland
Earned autonomy	Private sector management techniques, eg in the NHS, deploy the rhetoric, but more rarely the reality, of earned autonomy
An extended role for private capital	A key theme in private involvement in welfare services, through PFI/PPP in health and education and stock transfer in housing
A modest increase in citizen obligations	Substantial increase in obligations on welfare users, involving transfer to private individuals of responsibilities previously accepted by public services
Access (eg call centres, drop-in centres)	Growth in privately provided call-centres in social security and in private sector provision in health
E-government	New debates on private–public interface, particularly in relation to security of personal information provided to public authorities, but handled and shared via private providers

Table 10.1 identifies the contribution of private welfare reform to 6 and Peck's themes of modernisation, and Table 10.2 presents those reforms which may be considered third order changes.

Table 10.2: Third order changes in private welfare refor,m

- A shift from public ownership to private and quasi-private possession. Especially true in housing, through Right to Buy and stock transfer, but also a strong feature of health and education, with ownership of schools and hospitals retained, in PFI/PPP schemes, by private investors.

- A shift from public to private providers of services. Most controversially in health, with independent sector treatment centres at the forefront of wider 'diversification' of supply, but with substantial shifts in housing from council to third-sector providers, and in education through private sector involvement in city academies, 'super-foundation' schools and so on.

- Shifts between public and private responsibilities. A more mixed pattern in which the state accepted some new responsibilities previously regarded as primarily private matters, while at the same time divesting itself of obligations previously accepted as public duties. Examples of the former include the commitment to abolish child poverty. Examples of the latter include the substitution of loans for grants in higher education.

What did New Labour inherit?

The shifting boundary between private and public responsibility for social welfare is one of the *longue durée* stories of Western history (see Powell, 2003, Stewart, 2007) The century which preceded the Blair premiership had largely seen an extension to collective, state-guaranteed and provided social rights, as a concomitant of the judicial and democratic rights which had emerged over a longer period (Marshall, 1950). A concerted attempt to check and reverse that apparently inexorable tide came with the election of the 1979 Thatcher government. Far from being the means by which collective solutions could be applied to individual difficulties, the government was now regarded as stultifying initiative, eroding freedom, preventing private enterprise and vulnerable both to 'producer-capture' and over-consumption (Wright, 1994) The boundary between public and private was to be 'rolled back', leaving less in the hands of a sluggish, unresponsive, morally bankrupt and monopolistic state and more in the hands of private individuals and a nimble, energetic, competitive private sector.

The future was to be one of customers not clients, purchasers not providers, managers not administrators, competition not allocation, regulation not planning and equality of opportunity not equality of outcome (see Drakeford, 2000, for an elaboration of all these points). In this way, between 1979 and 1997, private provision of welfare moved from being an unfortunate necessity to an ambition to be warmly embraced. New Labour, by contrast, came to power in 1997 with a promise to 'modernise' the welfare state, not to privatise it. It is to that promise which this chapter now turns.

Housing

'In housing perhaps more than any other part of the welfare state', Malpass (1998, p 184) suggested, 'the Conservative years were characterised by the mantra of 'private good, public bad'. Yet, when the first New Labour housing Green Paper was produced in 2000, Murie (2007, p 53) suggested that it was 'more marked by continuity with the previous decades than radical change'.

In terms of ownership and assets, New Labour continued policies that transferred housing from public to private hands. Take-up of the Right to Buy increased in every year of New Labour administration until 2006 (Lloyd, 2007, p 14). A new enthusiasm for stock transfer placed substantial pressure on local authorities, after 1997, to 'outsource' the management and ownership of council housing to registered social landlords. Before the end of the second Blair term a million council houses had left public ownership by this route.

At the level of the individual, New Labour's housing record in altering the balance between private and public welfare is mixed. On the one hand, it extended the state's protection for individuals living in some of the worst private sector accommodation, by introducing a mandatory national licensing system for larger houses in multiple occupation. For homeless people, too, a second term Priority Need Order (2002) increased the range of groups eligible for priority rehousing to include young people leaving care and people fleeing from domestic violence, as well as vulnerable ex-service personnel and custody leavers. The government also took action to limit use of bed and breakfast accommodation for families with children. The important point to note here is that there were aspects of the Blair years in which the state accepted new responsibilities, extending the scope of public welfare, as well as divesting itself of them.

Nevertheless, Lund (2004, p 18) concludes that the dominant purpose of the Homelessness Directorate was 'to shift dominant notions of the causes of homelessness from the "political" to the "personal"', a characteristic which extended more generally to help for those at the bottom of the housing ladder. Kemp (2005, p 28), for example, summarises the second term introduction of local housing allowances as placing an obligation on tenants 'to make trade-offs between quality and price when looking for accommodation in the rental housing market

... becoming active and responsible consumers in the market place', a policy thrust which was pursued further in the third term.

Finally, in this brief consideration of shifting boundaries of responsibility, to note that, in housing, the Blair governments were at their most distinctive in focusing on the connection between living conditions and anti-social behaviour. 'Nuisance neighbours' had featured in a pre-election party publication, *Protecting our communities* (Labour Party, 1997). Its proposals found an immediate place in Labour's first legislative programme for almost 20 years. The Crime and Disorder Bill promoted Anti-Social Behaviour Orders (ASBOs) as a key way of dealing with unruly tenants. The consequences for those whose behaviour was identified as unacceptable were draconian. The price of social failure was to be criminalisation and eviction. In the terms of this chapter, the boundary was to be redrawn between responsibilities previously accepted by the state and their relocation in the lives of individuals themselves.

To summarise, New Labour's housing policy provides some, minor, departures from the approach inherited from the Thatcher and Major years. In essence, however, it pressed ahead with market-dominated solutions, in which private was always to be preferred to public, not simply in management techniques but in ownership of assets. The policy tools of choice in housing, through the Blair period, were summed up by Malpass (2005, p 74) as 'a commitment to market, or market-like solutions wherever possible' and by Murie (2007, p 61) as 'privatisation, demunicipalisation and residualisation'. In terms of the linking analysis of this book, New Labour's housing policies accepted and accelerated the third order change, or paradigm shifts (Hall, 1993), which had begun under Mrs Thatcher, in transferring ownership away from public authorities and in replacing the role of public planning with market mechanisms. As far as the themes of modernisation identified by 6 and Peck (2004) are concerned, three can be identified as most salient to private welfare: a substantial fondness for area-based initiatives, where these could bypass public accountabilities, a more than 'modest' increase in citizen obligations and, through stock transfer in particular, a highly extended role for private capital.

Social security

In the run-up to the 1997 General Election, New Labour placed a greater emphasis on reform and modernisation of social security than on any other aspect of social welfare. In government, there was a swift enactment of the windfall tax on privatised utilities and the establishment of New Deals for Unemployed Young People and others. The appointment of Frank Field as Minister for Welfare Reform was intended as a clear signal of the Prime Minister's intentions both to think and act radically in this area. Indeed, the new minister was soon briefing reporters that his intention was to 'pave the way for a massive expansion of private sector provision and a dwindling role for the state' (*The Times*, 1998).

All this presaged one of the major themes of the Blair years: an emphasis on the new responsibilities that citizens were to assume for their own social security. Work was the best form of welfare, and the system was radically recast in the form of both carrots and sticks designed to assist, and insist, that unemployed individuals should enter the workforce. This approach remained a constant, throughout the Blair era, with welfare reform Green Papers in the first and final years of his premiership. McKay (2007, p 112) suggested that the key tools of the 2006 version were essentially amplifications of previous techniques – 'intensive advice about work, training, childcare and the like ... accompanied by a degree of increasing conditionality of entitlement to benefits for these groups'. In pensions, too, self-provision was, as Hewitt (2003, p 189) points out, 'elevated from a private aspiration of the prudent individual to a core duty of the good citizen'.

Even here, however, the more differentiated pattern identified in housing policy was also apparent. Bennett (2004, p 51) sets out the new rights which New Labour introduced in April 2003 in which, 'for the first time ever fathers became entitled to paid paternity leave....Women could have six months' paid maternity leave, followed by six months' unpaid leave if desired'. In this way, welfare issues that had previously been a private matter between individuals and their employers became part of a new set of publicly guaranteed rights. Likewise, the 2004 Civil Partnership Act gave new social security rights to survivors' benefit and bereavement benefit to same-sex pensioner couples who had registered a civil partnership, in a further example of New Labour's willingness, in selected instances, to expand the reach of public rights into hitherto private territory.

More broadly, the commitment to abolish child poverty within a generation stands out across the whole of social policy as an example of New Labour extending public responsibility. McKay (2007, p 116) suggests that, in doing so, 'the policy emphasis strongly shifted towards child poverty as an objective, and away from the earlier focus on making people face responsibilities'. Childcare, for so long regarded as an entirely personal and private responsibility, was wholeheartedly accepted by the Blair administrations as an area for public policy and provision.

To summarise, in the field of social security, the Blair years saw the line between public and private welfare move in both directions, with the state accepting some new responsibilities, as well as divesting itself of others. The strongest policy tides, however, were in the direction of greater self-provision for individuals, and greater use of the private sector in delivery of social security services. Analytically, it can be argued that both in extending and narrowing public responsibilities New Labour's most significant policies lay at the 'paradigm shift' end of Hall's spectrum. Accepting the abolition of child poverty as a public policy goal and legislating to provide new rights for civil partners are both examples of third order change in social security policy. By contrast, the involvement of private sector providers – from the privatisation of the Benefits Agency Medical Service in 1997 to the proposals of the 2007 Freud Report to move work from the public service of Jobcentre Plus to the private and voluntary sectors – involves a scale of change that represents a paradigm shift. As to the modernisation themes of 6 and Peck (2004), the three of relevance to the field of private welfare include the more-than-modest transfer of obligation and responsibility from state to citizen. As to access, modernisation in social security has involved a progressive withdrawal from publicly provided face-to-face services in favour of a greater reliance on privately procured call centres often with spectacularly unsuccessful results.

In the related field of e-government, the original architects of the welfare state had constructed rigid lines of demarcation between information provided by the citizen for particular purposes, believing that such information ought to be accessible only for the reasons it had been provided. The Blair years saw a rapid acceleration in the destruction of this principle, in favour of the 'information sharing' that advances in electronic data storage and handling made possible. As the security with which such information was held came under question, however, a different debate took place, in which the boundary between the rights of private citizens, and the actions of public authorities (a key underlying preoccupation of this chapter) came powerfully to the surface.

Education

The Blair administration of 1997 inherited a set of reforms in education that were the product of Mrs Thatcher's third and most radical term. The policy landscape had been formed by the 1988 Education

Reform Act which aimed to create an education market by liberating the demand side – placing greater power in the hands of parents and pupils – and differentiating the supply side – creating a greater variety of schools and colleges among which newly empowered consumers could make choices. Open enrolment, devolved budgets and a national curriculum and testing regime were all innovations of the Act. A new species of grant-maintained schools was able to 'opt out' of local education authority control, becoming what Mrs Thatcher described as 'independent state schools'. In the words of the Act's author, Kenneth Baker, the Act served 'to blur the boundaries between public and private schooling and widen the scope of the process of privatisation occurring within education' (quoted in Flude and Hammer, 1990).

Asked to identify his priorities for an incoming New Labour government, Tony Blair famously replied with his mantra of 'education, education, education'. Yet, at the end of his first term, continuities with the previous Conservative reforms, rather than new directions of its own, marked the government's record. Early moves to abolish the Assisted Places Scheme soon stood out as an isolated nod in the direction of traditional Labour thinking. Rather, as Turner (2001, p 189) concluded, New Labour's education policy converged around the retention and extension of many former Conservative policies in relation to both structures and standards; the increasing deployment of managerial and prescriptive initiatives and increasing privatisation.

The second Blair term pursued this path even more strongly. 'Academy' schools were promoted as direct descendants of the Conservative city academies, and with many of the same features, including the attraction of private funding, in exchange for which investors secured the right to 'name the school and nominate a majority of the governing body' (Catalyst, 2005, p 1). While assets, as well as management freedoms in terms of hiring, firing and remunerating staff, became the property of the academies, the financial risks – capital overspends, salaries, overheads – remained with the state. By the end of the second term, the interpenetration of public and private funding of the maintained education sector in England ran at a very high level. A total of £600 million from private sector sponsors was flowing into the academy and specialist schools programme, while, in 2002/03, £1.8 billion of non-capital public money was spent on private sector providers of education services, covering issues as diverse as the outsourcing of national strategies for numeracy and literacy, to school-level purchase of private sector services, from dealing with bullying to staff recruitment. The Confederation of British Industry (2005), reviewing the impact of marketisation on the English system, described the private sector presence in education as 'broad and deep'.

In capital expenditure the involvement of the private sector in education had gone further still with the private finance initiative (PFI) in England providing half of New Labour's £45 billion investment in 457 different school building projects (House of Commons Education Select Committee, 2007). As the Committee reported, warning that the programme represented a 'risk' to local councils, bound into expensive 30-year contracts, press reports appeared of newly constructed PFI schools closing in Brighton and Essex, only three years after opening, and with millions of pounds having to be paid to private contracts in order to bring PFI arrangements to a premature close (*Daily Telegraph*, 2007a).

The second term also saw new departures in relation to outsourcing of education services. In 1999, a severely critical report from Ofsted and the Audit Commission resulted in the education services of the London Borough of Southwark being put out to tender and transferred to the private company, W.S. Atkins. The firm was widely acknowledged to have had virtually no experience in running schools and none whatsoever in delivering public services on such a large scale. In 2003 this contract collapsed but the general trend towards handing over management of 'failing' schools and authorities to private companies continued. By 2005, nine local education authorities had been taken over in this way.

In the run-up to the 2005 General Election the Prime Minister confirmed his intention to use a third term for policies of radical privatisation in education. Private sector businesses were to be allowed to bid for contracts to run state schools for profit (*The Business*, 2005), allowing them new freedoms to select pupils according to ability, expel troublemakers and exclude children with special educational needs, 'who cost more money to teach' (*Mail on Sunday*, 2004). Highest performing primary schools were to be allowed to become independent, owning their own assets and controlling their own admissions policies. Looking forward to the third Blair term, Hulme and Hulme (2005, p 47) predicted a wider 'spread of the education market', based on 'the progressive dismantling of comprehensive education and the reinvention of grammar schools as specialist schools', including the promotion of city academies, foundation specialist schools and 'ultra-free' 'super-foundation' schools as' 'independent specialist schools within the state sector'. The post-election Education and Inspections Bill, increasing the powers of private sponsors and allowing for the outsourcing of entire local education authorities, bore out these predictions. Ball (2007, p 27), reviewing the 10 years of Blair's premiership, concluded that education policy had 'taken up where the Conservatives left off and indeed had gone much further'.

To summarise, the boundary between private and public welfare in education moved very sharply during the Blair years. In Hall's terms, these had been third order changes, or paradigm shifts, in favour of private ownership of basic assets and the transfer of core education services from public to private providers. While public education remained, largely, free at the point of use the relationship between 'consumers' (parents and children) and 'providers' (schools and colleges) had been radically recast on a marketised basis. The modernisation themes of 6 and Peck (2004) were reflected in the introduction of commercial organisations and techniques into school inspection, the adoption of area-based initiatives, such as Education Action Zones, where these bypassed local authorities, a vastly extended role for private capital through PFI and, in common with housing and social security policy, a substantial increase in citizen obligations.

In the process, those with the greatest pre-existing advantages (money, access to information, academic ability) were able to use them to gain improved market position, while those with the least (special educational needs, challenging behaviour, social disadvantage) were left to deal with the consequences of market failure.

Health

The creation of the National Health Service in 1948 represented, in the words of its founding genius, Aneurin Bevan (1978, p 109), 'a triumphant example of the superiority of collective action and public initiative applied to a segment of society where commercial principles are seen at their worst'. Public affection for the NHS meant that it was only in the fourth, and final, Conservative administration that the creation of an internal market was attempted, in which 'fund-holding' GPs were freed up to 'purchase' secondary healthcare services from a wide range of autonomous, competing hospital trusts (see Ranade, 1997, for a fuller account of what she terms the 'creeping privatisation' of health services during this period).

The new-style health service proved highly controversial. In opposition it was attacked by the Blair-led Labour Party for its inefficiency and bureaucracy, as well as for creating a two-tier system in which the well-informed and the articulate could force their way to the front of the queue. In the event, and in a manner consistent with other policy areas, the first period of Blair administration appeared to draw back from previous Conservative plans. As Allsop and Baggott (2004, p 34) point out, there was no reference at all to the private sector in the first, 1997, health White Paper. This position, however, was short-lived. In 2000, the Secretary of State for Health, Alan Milburn, signed a concordat with the private sector which was widely regarded as 'crossing the Rubicon' in New Labour's thinking about private welfare. The concordat committed the NHS to use private sector facilities and to bring private sector management into the NHS. The document made it clear that the arrangements were not to be some short-term stopgap but a long-term commitment.

During the second Blair term, the interpenetration of the two sectors increased. Primary care trusts were instructed, in 2004, to spend at least 10% of their annual budgets on private sector treatments, particularly those provided in the government-sponsored independent sector treatment centres (ISTCs). As successive waves of ISTCs were announced, industry analysts concluded that, from a standing start just five years earlier, NHS spending on privately provided treatments was due to reach the £1 billion mark (Laing & Buisson, 2006). Almost the whole of the growth in an otherwise static private healthcare sector had come from government spending.

The second term also saw the introduction of foundation hospitals (for more extended accounts see, for example, House of Commons Health Select Committee, 2003; Mohan, 2003), but which were widely promoted by government ministers as providing 'choice' for patients. Further liberalisation of the market followed. In the final months of the Blair premiership Timmins (2006) reported the first ever contract to be awarded to the private sector to run an entire NHS hospital when the Partnership Health Group was named as the preferred bidder to take over the £36 million, PFI-built, Lymington Hospital in the New Forest. Existing NHS organisations also took advantage of new opportunities to transfer activity to private providers. In the week in which the Prime Minister announced his retirement the Hillingdon Primary Care Trust was widely reported as intending to use these new powers in response to having 'lost control of its spending' (*Pharmaceutical Journal*, 2007). It moved to outsource all its activities, other than those in which it was, itself, directly involved with patients and the public. The 70% of the Trust's £210 million commissioning budget devoted to purchasing hospital services was to be put out to immediate tender, with its chief executive telling the *Health Service Journal* (2007) that 'I want to get rid of everything – outsource it'.

To summarise, health policy began, in the first Blair government, with an effort to distinguish itself from the reforms of the Conservative period. That effort soon subsided and the key reforms of the early 1990s – an internal market, patient choice, outsourcing and institutional reform – were revived and reinforced. Paradigm shifts here included establishment of the private sector as an integral part of health service provision and deployment of private capital to a greater degree than in any other aspect of social welfare. While political ownership of the NHS was regularly claimed by New Labour its fondness for public ownership was far less pronounced. Modernisation themes, now familiar from other aspects of social welfare, included area-based initiatives, such as Health Action Zones, the extended role for private capital and a major increase in the use of private providers on the basis of improving access.

After Blair

In sharp contrast to the Blairite fondness for declaratory position papers which attempted to define a distinctive New Labour philosophy (see, for example, Blair, 2002), the incoming premier, Gordon Brown, took office with only the barest previous record of statements dealing with welfare matters. In 2003, in a speech to the Social Market Foundation, he had set out a set of limits to the usefulness of markets in social welfare that was widely interpreted as an attack on the grander privatising ambitions of the New Labour vanguard. Driver (2005, p 267) summarises what was known of the Brown position in this way:

> The problem Gordon Brown has with greater diversity and autonomy in public service provision – what he sees as 'marketisation' – is that they will undermine the unity, ethos and political economy of that provision – and they will not work (Brown, 2003). Brown's fear [is] that markets undermine the public service ethos of organisations such as the NHS…. Diversity and choice in health and education lead to a 'two tier system' that undermines the unity and equity of the system.

Right-wing commentators took an early opportunity to assert that the Brown premiership would be marked by a determination to 'curb NHS privatisation' and to establish his own more sceptical credentials on marketisation in social welfare (*Daily Telegraph*, 2007b). Yet, nearly a year into the post-Blair era, Kremlinologists continue to dissect each new pronouncement of the Brown premiership, quarrying for gobbets to 'prove', variously, that he is either the true fount of New Labourism, or equally determined to revert to the true path of Old Labour. The future seems likely to be less clear-cut. Gordon Brown is personally and politically identified with some of the most important themes of the New Labour era – from PFI to the creation of 'flexible' labour markets. At the same time, the limits of welfare markets are also known to be one of the more fundamental points on which he differed from Blair, from foundation hospitals to academy schools.

By contrast, the welfare policies of the Conservative Party show few such hesitations. The Cameron-led Conservatives have committed themselves to matching Labour's level of investment in public spending over the next Parliament, but the ways in which such spending would be dispersed are unambiguously linked to further liberalisation of welfare markets and a greater role for the private sector. In a rare example of public approbation for the conservatism of the 1980s, David Cameron evoked the spirit of 'Friedrich von Hayek, the intellectual guru of Thatcherism' in support of his contention that 'one of the great philosophical divides between the Conservatives and Labour in the next decade' would be between 'state welfare' and 'social welfare'. While at pains to point out that 'we are explicitly not proposing the privatisation of public services', he nonetheless concluded that private and voluntary organisations were better placed to deliver public services than ever before (Cameron, 2006).

Conclusion

The Blair years were characterised by a shifting boundary between public and private responsibility for welfare. There are important instances – creating civil partnerships, the ban on smoking in public places, for example – in which, for welfare reasons, New Labour administrations extended the reach of government into the private sphere, taking on new responsibilities, as well as refusing them.

Moreover, if 'modernisation' was the price that had to be paid for retaining the loyalty of the middle classes for the welfare state, then there is evidence that New Labour has succeeded. Boone and Timmins (2007) report that, as far as use of private welfare services is concerned, during the Blair years:

> ... the numbers covered by private medical insurance have remained virtually static for more than a decade, while the numbers prepared to pay for treatment from their own

pockets have declined as NHS waiting times have fallen.
The same applied to schools where the private sector has
barely increased in the last 10 years.

Yet, the argument of this chapter has been that the price involved has
been substantial in shifting the balance between public and private
welfare services firmly away from the former and towards the latter.
Assets that were previously in public ownership are now in private
hands. Services which were previously provided in the public sector
have been 'outsourced' to private companies, while remaining public
services have, as Jordan (2005, p 433) argues, 'been required to model
themselves on their commercial counterparts, in relation to flexibility
and consumer preferences'. In this process of commodification,
the protections and defences that the state had previously supplied
'against the rigours, vagaries, demands and inequities of the market
and the unconstrained powers of capital' (Clarke, 2005, p 452) have
been withdrawn. In their place, responsibility has been diverted to
the sphere of the private individual with the result, as Jordan (2005,
p 434) puts it, that 'better-off citizens cluster together round the best
facilities, leaving more needy, poorer and less mobile ones to endure
the lowest quality services'.

Does all this amount to an underlying, fundamental order of change?
Stuart Hall (2005, p 323) argues that in each successive instance, and
over the whole of the Blair period, commentators have obsessively
discussed whether or not the latest policy movement has represented
the point at which privatisation has *really* arrived – an endeavour which
he characterises as a form of 'trivial pursuit'. Far from proceeding in
a non-ideological, pragmatic way, Hall argues that New Labour has
been characterised by a profoundly ideological preference for 'market
fundamentalism' in which 'markets and market criteria are the true
measure of value' (Hall, 2005, p 323). In the process, 'the whole
concept of the "public interest" and the "public good" has collapsed'
(Hall, 2005, p 325), citizenship is privatised and reduced to the status
of passive consumerism (Needham, 2003, p 8), 'need' is privatised into
the lives of those least able to fend for themselves, and 'modernisation'
is a one-way street in which mimicking the market is the only future
for public services. While others take a different emphasis, the sense
that the Blair years were marked by the purposeful pursuit of welfare
pluralism is largely uncontested (see Powell, 2007).

The Thatcherite preference for privatisation, in the narrow sense of
services privately funded, purchased and provided, was halted during the

Blair years. Yet 'modernisation', in the broader sense, entailed the onward march of marketisation and privatisation across the whole welfare frontier. It amounted to a sustained, interconnected and comprehensive paradigm shift away from public services and responsibilities and in favour of private welfare.

References

6, P. and Peck, E. (2004) 'Modernisation: the ten commitments of New Labour's approach to public management', *International Public Management Journal*, vol 7, no 1, pp 1-18.

Allsop, A. and Baggott, R. (2004) 'The NHS in England: from modernisation to marketisation?', in N. Ellison, L. Bauld and M. Powell (eds) *Social Policy Review 16*, Bristol: The Policy Press/SPA, pp 29-44.

Ball, S.J. (2007) '"Going further?" Tony Blair and New Labour education policies', in K. Clarke, T. Maltby and P. Kennett (eds) *Social Policy Review 19*, Bristol: The Policy Press, pp 13-31.

Bennett, F. (2004) 'Developments in social security', in N. Ellison, L. Bauld and M. Powell (eds) *Social Policy Review 16*, Bristol: The Policy Press/SPA, pp 45-60.

Bevan, A. (1978 [first published in 1952]) *In place of fear*, London: Quarto.

Blair, T. (2002) *The courage of our convictions*, London: Fabian Society.

Boone, J. and Timmins, N. (2007) 'Running to stand still: how Labour has struggled to hold back the rising inequality', *Financial Times*, 2 May.

Brown, G. (2003) 'A modern agenda for prosperity and social reform', Speech to the Social Market Foundation, London, Cass Business School, 3 February.

Burchardt, T., Hills, J. and Propper, C. (1999) *Private welfare and public policy*, York: Joseph Rowntree Foundation.

Business, The (2005) 'Blair woos private sector to run new state schools', 6 March.

Cameron, D. (2006) 'From state welfare to social welfare', Speech to the National Council for Voluntary Organisations, 14 December (www.conservatives.com/tile.do?def=news.story.page&obj_id=134139&speeches=1, 31/12/07).

Catalyst (2005) *Academy schools: Talking point*, London: Catalyst.

CBI (Confederation of British Industry) (2005) *The business of educational improvement: Raising LEA performance through competition*, London: CBI.

Clarke, J. (2005) 'New Labour's citizens: activated, empowered, responsibilised, abandoned?', *Critical Social Policy*, vol 25, no 4, pp 447-63.

Daily Telegraph (2007a) 'School building PFIs "will cost taxpayer billions"', 9 August.

Daily Telegraph (2007b) 'Brown's first task is to curb NHS "privatisation"', 9 May.

DH (Department of Health) (1997) *The New NHS: Modern, dependable*, Cmnd 3807, London: The Stationery Office.

Drakeford, M. (2000) *Privatisation and social policy*, Harlow: Longman.

Drakeford, M. (2006) 'Ownership, regulation and the public interest: the case of residential care for older people', *Critical Social Policy*, vol 26, pp 932-44.

Driver, S. (2005) 'Welfare after Thatcherism: NL and social democratic politics', in M. Powell, L. Bauld and K. Clarke (eds) *Social Policy Review 17*, Bristol: The Policy Press, pp 255-72.

Flude, M. and Hammer, M. (1990) 'Opting for an uncertain future', in M. Flude and M. Hammer (eds) *The Education Reform Act 1988: Its origins and implications*, Basingstoke: Falmer Press, pp 51-72.

Hall, P.A. (1993) 'Policy paradigms, social learning and the state: the case of economic policy making in Britain', *Comparative Politics*, vol 25, no 3, pp 275-96.

Hall, S. (2005) 'New Labour's double-shuffle', *The Review of Education, Pedagogy and Cultural Studies*, vol 27, no 3, pp 319-35.

Hewitt, M. (2003) 'New Labour and the redefinition of social security', in M. Powell (ed) *Evaluating New Labour's welfare reforms*, Bristol: The Policy Press, pp 189-209.

House of Commons Education and Skills Select Committee (2007) *Sustainable schools: Are we building schools for the future?*, London: House of Commons.

House of Commons Health Select Committee (2003) *Foundation trusts*, London: House of Commons.

Hulme, R. and Hulme, M. (2005) 'New Labour's education policy: innovation or reinvention?', in M. Powell, L. Bauld and K. Clarke (eds) *Social Policy Review 17*, Bristol: The Policy Press, pp 13-49.

Jordan, B. (2004) 'The personal social services', in N. Ellison, L. Bauld and M. Powell (eds) *Social Policy Review 16*, Bristol: The Policy Press/SPA, pp 81-98.

Jordan, B. (2005) 'New Labour: choice and values', *Critical Social Policy*, vol 25, no 4, pp 427-46.

Kemp, P.A. (2005) 'Social security and welfare reform under New Labour', in M. Powell, L. Bauld and K. Clarke (eds) *Social Policy Review 17*, Bristol: The Policy Press, pp 15–32.

Laing & Buisson (2006) *Health and care cover: UK market report 2006*, London: Laing & Buisson.

Lloyd, T. (2007) 'Housing', in *Closer to equality? Assessing New Labour's record on equality after 10 years in government*, London: Compass, pp 11–16.

Lund, B. (2004) 'Housing policy: coming in from the cold?', in N. Ellison, L. Bauld and M. Powell (eds) *Social Policy Review 16*, Bristol: The Policy Press/SPA, pp 13–28.

Mail on Sunday (2004) 'Fury over Labour's schools for profit', 14 March.

Malpass, P. (1998) 'Housing policy', in N. Ellison and C. Pierson (eds) *Developments in British social policy*, London: Macmillan, pp 173–87.

Malpass, P. (2005) 'Housing in an "opportunity society"', in M. Powell, L. Bauld and K. Clarke (eds) *Social Policy Review 17*, Bristol: The Policy Press, pp 69–83.

Marshall, T.H. (1950) *Citizenship and social class and other essays*, Cambridge: Cambridge University Press.

McKay, S. (2007) 'Laying new foundations? Social security reform in 2006', in K. Clarke, T. Maltby and P. Kennett (eds) *Social Policy Review 19*, Bristol: The Policy Press, pp 107–24.

Mohan, J. (2003) *Reconciling equity and choice? Foundation hospitals and the future of the NHS*, London: Catalyst.

Murie, A. (2007) 'Housing policy, housing tenure and the housing market', in K. Clarke, T. Maltby and P. Kennett (eds) *Social Policy Review 19*, Bristol: The Policy Press, pp 49–65.

Needham, C. (2003) *Citizen-consumers: New Labour's marketplace democracy*, London: Catalyst.

Netten, A. (2005) 'Personal social services', in M. Powell, L. Bauld and K. Clarke (eds) *Social Policy Review 17*, Bristol: The Policy Press, pp 85–103.

Pharmaceutical Journal (2007) 'PCT considers major outsourcing', vol 278, no 7438, p 157.

Powell, M. (2003) 'Quasi-markets in British health policy: a *longue durée* perspective', *Social Policy and Administration*, vol 37, no 7, pp 725–41.

Powell, M. (ed) (2007) *Understanding the mixed economy of welfare*, Bristol: The Policy Press.

Ranade, W. (1997) *A future for the NHS? Health care for the millennium*, London: Longman.

Scourfield, P. (2007) 'Are there reasons to be worried about the "cartelisation" of residential care?', *Critical Social Policy*, vol 27, no 2, pp 155-80.

Stewart, J. (2007) 'The mixed economy of welfare in historical context', in M. Powell (ed) *Understanding the mixed economy of welfare*, Bristol: The Policy Press, pp 23-40.

Times, The (1998) 'Private schemes to fund growth in welfare bills', 19 February.

Timmins, N. (2006) 'Private sector to take on NHS hospital health service', *Financial Times*, 22 December.

Turner, M. (2001) 'School-level education policy under New Labour and New Zealand Labour: a comparative update', *British Journal of Education Studies*, vol 49, pp 187-212.

Wright, V. (ed) (1994) *Privatisation in Western Europe: Pressures, problems and paradoxes*, London: Pinter Publishers.

ELEVEN

Choice in public services: 'no choice but to choose'

Catherine Needham

Introduction

During the second half of Tony Blair's premiership, the concept of choice came to symbolise the tensions within the Labour Party over the direction of welfare reform. Although those who were resistant to Blair's reforms were keen to stress that they were not *anti*-choice, it was clear that the word had become a rallying cry for the vanguard of Blairites such as Cabinet Ministers Alan Milburn (2001), Stephen Byers (2004) and John Reid (2005). A succession of reports published during Labour's second and third terms by think-tanks, parliamentary bodies and academics framed choice as the symbolic core of the Blairite welfare state (Greener, 2003; Lent and Arend, 2004; Clarke, 2005; Farrington-Douglas and Allen, 2005; PASC, 2005; Clarke et al, 2006). Choice was seen by some as the central strand of a broader commercial agenda in public services, in which the service user was being remade as a citizen-consumer (Hall, 2003; Needham, 2003, 2007; Marquand, 2004; Clarke et al, 2007). Part of Gordon Brown's positioning to become party leader involved endorsing the pro-choice thrust of specific Blairite policies (Tempest, 2004) while signalling his wariness about certain forms of choice and consumerism (Brown, 2003).

Like modernisation, choice is characterised by 'indeterminacy', laden with political significance but essentially vague in policy terms (Clarke et al, 2006). The same social, political and economic shifts that shaped the reinvention of the Labour Party as New Labour put choice centre stage: neoliberal political movements across English-speaking countries championed the moral primacy of choice in political life (Thatcher, 1987); sociologists pointed to the centrality of choice to a new reflexive individualism (Giddens, 1994); and economic observers identified post-Fordist modes of regulation which responded to consumer choices rather than production cycles (Murray, 1989; Warde, 1994). Thus, like modernisation, choice came to be presented as part of New Labour's progressive logic, an inevitable response to a new political terrain.

However, also like modernisation, choice under New Labour has taken many forms, about which it is difficult to generalise. Drawing on Hall's (1993) orders of change, it is possible to see choice expressed in the overarching goals of public policy, in the policy instruments used to attain those goals and in the precise settings of those instruments. The '10 commitments' of modernisation developed by 6 and Peck (2004) can also be applied to the various forms of choice developed by New Labour. The implementation of choice has also varied over time, between services and between different types of user. To make sense of this complexity it is helpful to explore New Labour's approach to choice at each of Hall's three levels, and to consider how 6 and Peck's themes of modernisation are manifest in detailed policy settings. The chapter also considers changes over Blair's two-and-a-half terms as Prime Minister and between different public services. It highlights the government's growing fascination with choice, and the tendency to offer distinctive models of choice to different welfare users. The chapter finishes by considering how political leaders after Blair are interpreting and applying choice in public services, highlighting the narrowness of mainstream party agendas, which offer users 'no choice but to choose' (Giddens, 1991, p 80).

Choice as an idea

While choice was not entirely absent from the welfare state pre-Thatcher (some choice of general practitioners [GPs] has long been available, for example), it was the Conservative governments in power in the UK from 1979 to 1997 that drew explicitly and implicitly on choice as a distributional principle (Barnes and Prior, 1995). Choice was framed as the basis not only of a new governmental efficiency but also of a new ethical framework. As Thatcher (1987) said, 'Choice is the essence of morality. It is the essence of all religion' (quoted in Jordan, 1989, p 19). New choices were offered to public service users, either to leave the state sector altogether – as in 'Right to Buy' arrangements in social housing – or to access the best performing services, in the case of parental choice of schools. For Thatcher choice was conceived both as a mechanism to empower users and a tool to discipline producers – thus users were 'both an end and a means' in relation to service reform (Klein, 2001, p 116).

Under John Major, the Citizen's Charter initiative aimed to 'give the citizen a better deal through extending consumer choice and competition' (Cabinet Office, 1991, p 4). However, it could be argued that the Major reforms were more instrumental in establishing the foundations on which New Labour's choice reforms could later be built – a commitment to publishing performance data, a split between purchasers and providers in the NHS internal market, for example – rather than in creating new choices for users.

It was under Blair, and particularly in his second and third terms of office, that choice re-emerged as both a moral compass and organisational tool of government. As a Prime Minister keen to assert his party's distinctiveness from previous Labour incarnations, choice was expressive of various useful polarities: it was an alternative to the 'one size fits all' welfare state of the postwar era (Blair, 1999) and it was a corrective to the powers of producers (with their tendency to hoard resources and foster inefficiency) and to the power of professionals (and their outmoded ideas of deference and client passivity) (Blair, 2004). More broadly choice was deployed within an anti-elitist rhetoric, opening up to all service users the choices previously enjoyed only by the middle class (Blair, 2003). Confusingly, choice was also to be a tool for keeping middle-class users in the public sector, ensuring that they did not defect to private services (Blair, 2002). Choice was also the mechanism through which the welfare state could demonstrate its embrace of the wider socio-cultural strands of individualism and consumerism that were reshaping relationships between government and the individual (Blair, 2001a).

As these new dualities were repeatedly emphasised, older concerns about choice (such as its relationship to equity and voice) were robustly rejected. Indeed, one of the distinctive features of Blair's account of choice was the refusal to accept that choice was incompatible with equity in public service delivery; rather it was a way for poorer service users to put pressure on providers and to reflect diversity of needs (Blair, 2003). The New Labour conception of diversity, as Clarke et al point out, 'flattened structured difference (and its inequality producing effects) into a field of idiosyncratic and individualized wants, needs and desires' (2007, p 40). Concerns that choice was inferior to and inimical to more conventional modes of influence in civic life were also rejected (Needham, 2003, 2004; Marquand, 2004). Voice was seen as too heterogeneous, elitist and ineffective to be more than a bit part player in the efficient and populist Blairite welfare state (Le Grand, 2007). Claims that choice was synonymous with empowerment and flexibility were endorsed (Giddens, 2003), while links between choice and anxiety were disparaged (Ministers of State for Departments of

Health, Local and Regional Government and School Standards, 2004; Schwartz, 2004).

Choice as a policy instrument

Moving beyond choice as a rhetorical device, and understanding its significance to the distinctively Blairite welfare state, requires further disaggregation. There are many different types of choice (and types of chooser) available, with widely variable impacts on service provision. Le Grand calls for attention to be paid to *who* is choosing *what, where, when* and *how* (2007, p 39; emphasis added). It may be the end user who is making the choice, or it may be a professional acting on behalf of the user (a GP purchasing care from a hospital), or it may be the provider who makes the choice (as in the case of an oversubscribed school). Choices may be made by individuals and families (such as school choice, choice-based lettings or direct payments in social care) or they may be made collectively (such as decisions over community wardens or controlled parking zones) (Audit Commission, 2004, p 3; Lent and Arend, 2005, p 44). In terms of *what* is chosen, it may be a choice of provider (and/or between different types of provider – public/private/third sector) or about a choice of the form that the service will take (for example, how it will be accessed). It is also necessary to distinguish between *when* and how often choices are made – for example, between one-off, long-term choices (such as a choice of school) and short-term choices, such as the venue for a day surgery procedure (Audit Commission, 2004, p 8). The question of *how* choice is exercised brings in mechanisms such as real and virtual vouchers or co-payments by users (Lent and Arend, 2004, p 56).

It is hard to find any public service that does not involve choice in at least one of these senses (excluding, perhaps, parts of the prison service), and it would be difficult to find any historical period in which the welfare state did not offer its users some such choices. However, since 1997 there has been a deliberate effort to expand the range of choosers and the range and frequency of choices available to them within public services. It has been choice of provider by individual users that has attracted the most attention from the Blair governments and their critics (PASC, 2005, §104; Le Grand, 2007, p 40). Within education the Labour governments sought to simplify the process of parental choice and to expand the diversity of providers, through the creation of new types of secondary school (specialist schools, academies, foundation schools). Dissatisfied users were to have enhanced opportunities to access new provision (DfES, 2005). Within the NHS, the flagship policy has been the expansion of hospital choice for patients awaiting elective surgery. Since January 2006 all such patients should have been offered a choice of four or more appropriate providers – including independent sector treatment centres (ISTCs) as well as NHS hospitals. A payment-by-results arrangement ensures that hospitals are rewarded for their ability to attract patients. Like under the Conservatives before them, and unlike earlier versions of choice in the welfare state, choice of provider was explicitly designed to discipline providers, driving up standards through exposing and punishing unpopular hospitals (Timmins, 2005).

Two other areas in which user choice of provider has been expanded are choice-based letting of social housing and direct payments in social care. The 2000 housing Green Paper encouraged local authorities to move to a 'choice-based letting service' in which waiting time becomes the 'currency' of the social housing market (DETR, 2000, §9.21). The choice-based approach was said to 'enable people to balance their own "felt" need, as measured by the time they felt able to wait, against the availability of the properties they might be able to secure' (DETR, 2000, §9.20). Within social care, the direct payments scheme allocates funds away from local commissioning bodies and towards users who can choose how best to support their own needs (Ungerson, 2004). Money may be spent on employing carers and/or purchasing equipment or other support services. The scheme, originally developed by the Conservative governments before 1997 and first introduced for those with physical disabilities, is being extended to cover all adult social care services (Brindle, 2007)

These four types of choice – school choice, choice in elective surgery, choice-based lettings and direct payments in social care – dominate the debate on choice in Blair's welfare state, although there are various other ways in which choice has been expanded. The Expert Patients scheme, for example, has given those with chronic conditions more choice about treatment regimes (DH, 1999). Housing stock transfer ballots have given social housing tenants a collective choice over who manages their estates (Lent and Arend, 2004). People have been given a range of new investment choices, for example with regard to pensions and Child Trust Funds, as part of a 'social investment state' (Lister, 2003). Thus choice as a policy instrument takes diverse forms although there are some common themes in the detail of implementation, discussed below.

Choice as a setting

In the policy settings through which choice is operationalised, it is possible to find resonances with 6 and Peck's (2004) 10 'commitments' of modernisation. Table 11.1 summarises the relevance of choice to each of the commitments and categorises the relevance as high, medium or low. Looking first at inspection and central standard setting, both have been portrayed as part of a 'command' agenda that is distinct from the choice approach (PASC, 2005; Le Grand, 2007). However, it is clear that inspection and central standards support choice in two important ways. First they (in theory) provide a guarantee that all service providers meet a minimum level of service. Otherwise, as the Public Administration Select Committee point outs, a choice is being made between poor quality services, which is really no choice at all (PASC, 2005, §6). Second they offer information about differences between services, enabling users to make choices (Burgess et al, 2005, p 9). In schools, for example, it is difficult to envisage meaningful choice without the Ofsted inspection framework and the use of standardised measures of quality such as SATs and GCSE results. In relation to health, the inspection framework provides a star rating system that is one of the forms of information patients can use to make a choice between hospitals. Initiatives such as the National Student Survey have made it easier for users to exercise informed choice in relation to higher education.

As 6 and Peck (2004) note, enthusiasm for area-based initiatives and joined-up government – action zones and horizontal partnerships of various kinds – was waning by the end of Labour's first term. In their current incarnation – local strategic partnerships – the government remains committed to encouraging local agency collaboration and the development of local area agreements. It is clear that the choice agenda has the potential to promote greater inter-agency working – for example pupils could choose to take classes in a range of schools in order to facilitate access to a diverse curriculum; social care users could spend their budgets with local education and leisure facilities as well as social services. However, such collaborations have long proved elusive in the welfare state, and they are unlikely to be fostered by the competitive pressures attendant in choice, with schools and hospitals in competition for users and resources.

The devolution agenda has a clearer relevance to choice as it provides UK citizens with different welfare state packages in England, Scotland, Wales and Northern Ireland. Free prescriptions, free personal care for older people and lower university tuition fees are among the benefits available to citizens choosing to live outside England, while those in England have choices within health and education that are not available to those in other parts of the UK. Such is the degree of difference that Gill Morgan of the NHS Confederation has argued that there is no longer a *national* health service: 'We basically have four different systems, albeit with the same set of values' (Branigan and Carvel, 2008, p 13). There may be scope for further residential differentiation in the notion of 'double devolution', floated during Labour's third term, in which powers are to be passed down to town halls and out into local communities (DCLG, 2006; Miliband, 2006).

However, as 6 and Peck point out, this is limited decentralisation in which autonomy must be earned and is only ever partial. New providers may be given freedom to devise their own packages of services in order to diversify provision, but performance and inspection regimes remain in place. Effective user choice programmes may in future require more controls on providers rather than fewer (PASC, 2005). For example, if 'cherry-picking' of the most desirable pupils and patients is to be avoided without the provision of surplus capacity, mechanisms must be introduced to ensure that it is not providers who are doing the choosing (Le Grand, 2007). It is clear also that politicians remain wary of the political consequences of letting the market determine the fate of schools and hospitals, with ministers individually campaigning against closures in their own constituencies.

An extended role for private capital is evident in a range of choice schemes, most particularly health where ISTCs compete with the NHS for patients. In education, academy schools, part funded and run by private philanthropists and trusts, are part of the expanding market of schools. The 2006 Education and Inspections Act opened the way for more schools to develop partnerships with the private and voluntary sectors. Plans have been floated to bring in private companies to compete for a range of core state services such as legal aid, probation services and primary care (Labour Party, 2005). Across public services – in social housing and leisure, for example – there has been an expansion of the role of so-called 'third sector' organisations that are considered to be more responsive to the choices of users at a local level (Miliband, 2006). Pressures from the European Union (EU) and the World Trade Organization are likely in the future to lever open public services to greater competition from private companies (Rowland et al, 2004). The use of more private providers has generally been accompanied by a presumption of enhanced user choice (as, for example, in the case of ISTCs and academy schools). However, it is evident that certain forms of public–private partnership (PPP) have run counter to the choice agenda. For example, where service providers have entered into 25-year contracts with the private sector to provide facilities, contractual rigidities may inhibit responsiveness to new user choices (Pollock, 2004). This scenario emerged when the television chef Jamie Oliver created greater parental demand for fresh ingredients in school lunches, which contracted-out school catering services could not deliver (Lawrence and Quarmby, 2005).

There is evidence too of what 6 and Peck describe as 'a modest increase in citizen obligation' in relation to choice. Citizens are required to make responsible choices – and to bear the costs of those choices – in relation to services such as health, education, housing and pensions. Plans have been floated to make public service provision in general more explicitly conditional on lifestyle choices, as part of a new state–citizen contract (PMSU, 2006). There are parallels here with the 'devolution but limited decentralisation' agenda that has been evident at the institutional level. Users are told that they have more choices when it comes to provision, but that if they make the wrong lifestyle or investment choices the state will not necessarily bear the costs.

Access in general, and e-government more specifically, have been key to the development of choice. Much of the debate around choice and equity has revolved around the extent to which choice increases or decreases access to services for the least well-off (see, for example, the exchange of letters in the *Financial Times* between Appleby, 2006, Le Grand, 2006b and Blunden, 2006). Successful choice schemes, such as the London Choice Pilot, invested resources to facilitate access, providing choice advisers and covering transport costs (Le Grand, 2007, p 119). In rolling out the scheme nationally the government has recommended but not mandated that primary care trusts do the same (PASC, 2005, §218). E-government has been a key mechanism for various choice schemes, including patient choice in the NHS and choice-based lettings. However, concerns about the cost, security and effectiveness of software such as the NHS Choose and Book programme have raised doubts about its future operability. Where choice schemes rely heavily on electronic forms of access, such as choice-based lettings, consumer associations have expressed concerns about exclusion of those less able to access such technologies (Revill, 2008).

Variations of choice

Although choice has been a central theme of the Blairite welfare state it is important to note the variability of its implementation. Rhetorically, choice was a theme of Labour's second and third terms rather than

Table 11.1: The 10 commitments of choice

Area	Relevance to choice
Inspection	High. Bodies such as Ofsted and the Healthcare Commission generate service ratings, which allow users to make informed choices
Central standard setting	High. Central standards provide assurances to users that different choices meet minimum standards
Area-based initiatives	Low. Collaborative relationships may expand user choice but are undermined by competitive pressures
Joined-up government	Low, although packages such as 'Choose and Book' and 'Tell us Once' may facilitate choice for users through improving horizontal integration
Devolution but limited decentralisation	High. Devolution extends the packages of choices available within the UK, and 'double devolution' increases local diversity, although pressures on standards remain in place
Earned autonomy	Medium. Choice may expand the autonomy of individual providers but requires careful management to avoid 'cherry-picking' and facilitate user autonomy
Private capital	High. Can facilitate provider competition, although can also create new supply-side rigidities
Increase in citizen obligations	Medium. Users are being required to choose in many services and to bear the costs of choices
Enhanced access	High. One of the key mechanisms of choice, alongside choice of provider
E-government	High. The main channel through which choices are expressed in a range of services

the first (Clarke et al, 2007, p 34). After the 2001 General Election Blair made choice one of his four key principles of public service reform (Blair, 2001b), and this commitment is reflected in his speeches and in government White Papers and strategy documents. Content analysis of these texts shows that the vocabulary of targets, standards and responsibility which dominate the first term becomes matched in frequency by a discourse of choice, diversity and responsiveness in the second term (Needham, 2007, pp 101, 134-5). The word 'choice' itself is used more than twice as often in Labour's second term than in the first (Needham, 2007, pp 101, 223-5).

At the meso-level of policy instruments, the crucial time period for the establishment of choice varies across services. In housing, the choice-based letting initiative came during the first term with the 2000 Green Paper (DETR, 2000). In social care, direct payments were coming into effect in 1997 and were continued by the Labour government, although initial take-up was low (Frew, 2006). In education and health, Labour began its time in office abolishing reforms that seemed to be pro-choice: grant-maintained schools and the NHS internal market. However, both reforms were effectively neutralised almost immediately – in education by the introduction of foundation schools, and in health by the development of primary care trust-based commissioning of secondary care. Since then the pattern in education has been a gradual proliferation of school types – academies, specialist schools – to facilitate choice, reinforced by the 2006 Education and Inspections Act. In health, the shift towards competition and choice appeared to come just before the 2001 General Election, as the then Health Secretary Alan Milburn signed a concordat with the private sector to deliver services (O'Neale Roach, 2000).

The variable timing and pace of choice initiatives provides a clue to the motivations underlying the introduction of choice in the different services. In social care direct payments followed a long campaign from well-organised user groups, keen to gain greater control over their care (Independent Living Institute, 1996). The choice-based letting initiative was driven by a chronic lack of capacity and investment in housing, and a desire to draw on international lessons about how to utilise capacity more efficiently (Agnew, 2001). In health and education, the pressure for enhanced choice appeared to be not a shortage of funding or direct calls for choice from service users, but a sense that too much money had been spent during the first term without adequate service improvements (Goss, 2007). For Blairite ministers, choice offered a way to flush out and discipline poor quality providers and identify where spare capacity was most needed, enhancing user autonomy as a side benefit (Ministers of State, 2004).

Just as the rationale for choice differs across services so the way in which choice operates is distinctive. In some services, particularly those with supply-side flexibility, users can exercise a wide range of choices with a reasonable hope of them being fulfilled, whereas services with supply-side constraints (education and housing, for example) can offer users little more than the opportunity to express a preference. Here again, though, the picture is variable – urban parents are likely to have more choices than rural parents; high demand areas for housing will restrict applicant choices more than low demand areas. Users also vary in the amount of choice they want. Simmons found that some types of user are more comfortable making choices than others (2009, forthcoming). Greener argues that people may be more prepared to make choices in one service than another. Based on interviews with parents, he found that: 'Rationality appeared to be extremely contextual, with parents moving from almost passive recipients of healthcare to highly calculative, participative choosers of education within the space of a few seconds' (2005, p 238).

Some services and service users have had only limited exposure to choice. It remains of marginal relevance in policing, for example, where emphasis has been placed instead on responsiveness (Clarke et al, 2007; Needham, forthcoming). Some people have found their choices reduced rather than extended, for example lone parents, jobseekers and asylum seekers have been subject to new forms of coercion around access to benefits. There have been new limits set on freedom of choice – including smoking in public places, the purchase of cigarettes by 16- and 17-year-olds, and the provision of high fat foods in schools – leading to accusations that New Labour embodies not enhanced choice but the 'nanny state' (Sylvester, 2004). A number of authors have pointed to the way that New Labour's discourse has offered only a certain kind of sanctioned choice: people *must* choose independence and responsibility (Clarke et al, 2007, p 63).

Choice after Blair

As Brown prepared to take over as Prime Minister in spring 2007, the future of the choice agenda appeared to hang in the balance. Since then he has chosen his words carefully. His first party conference speech as leader spoke of an NHS that was 'personal to you' rather than of choice (Brown, 2007a). The autumn's Comprehensive Spending Review (HM Treasury, 2007) developed this personalisation theme, also calling for services that were 'flexible' and 'tailored' (Treasury, 2007, p 31). Immigration Minister Liam Byrne signalled a shift in emphasis when he argued, 'we have to move the debate about "choice" to a debate about personal control' (Rossiter and Byrne, 2007, p 65).

In launching Lord Darzi's interim report into the NHS in autumn 2007, Brown endorsed the importance of choice but qualified it in an important way: 'The British people want an NHS that is there for them when they need it, at the time that they want, with the doctors they want, and the choices *that they themselves want to make*' (Brown, 2007b; emphasis added). There is a sense here of moving away from what we might call the strong choice position, as expounded by some of Blair's ministers and his health adviser Julian Le Grand (2006a), that people should be given choice of provider whether they want it or not because that is the only way to drive up standards. Instead there may be greater sensitivity to identifying how and when people want to make choices. Calls from exiled Blairites such as Alan Milburn (2008) for Brown not to 'truncate' the choice agenda suggest concern about Brown's retreat from the high watermark of choice. More broadly, Brown has endorsed a 'new type of politics' that expands mechanisms associated with 'voice' rather than 'choice', such as citizens' juries (Brown, 2007c). His emphasis on the importance of deliberation appears to signal a greater interest in collective forms of choice than under his predecessor.

However, below the rhetoric, the expansion of provider choice continues. Direct payments are to be extended to elderly people, and eventually will be the basis of support for all adult social care users (Brindle, 2007). Legal aid services are to be opened up to competition from the private sector (DCA, 2005). Patient choice in the NHS will be fully rolled out from April 2008, although the purchasing of services from ISTCs has been scaled back (Timmins, 2007). Lord Darzi's interim report indicated that patient choice would 'be embedded within the full spectrum of NHS funded care, going beyond elective surgery into new areas such as primary care and long term conditions' (DH, 2007a). Rather than a reduction in choice, perhaps most evident in Brown's government is a little more honesty about the limitations of choice. For example the Schools Minister, Jim Knight, giving evidence to the education select committee admitted that school choice was limited in rural areas, later saying that the department needed to be more careful at 'managing expectations' of parents (Curtis, 2008).

The leaders of the Conservative and Liberal Democrat Parties draw on rhetoric and policy mechanisms regarding choice that are hard to separate out from those of the government. The Conservative Party's schools Green Paper, published in autumn 2007, committed the party to improving choice and control for users. It indicated that the party would encourage the broadest possible diversity of providers in order to improve choice for parents, with a commitment to increase capacity so that choice was available even in deprived and rural areas (Conservative Party, 2007). Senior party figures have shown an interest in expanding the direct payments scheme in health to give a broader range of users access to personal health budgets (Osborne, 2007). Liberal Democrat leader Nick Clegg has talked of the need to increase the diversity of providers in local services such as health and to reclaim 'freedom, innovation, diversity and choice' as 'liberal concepts' (Clegg, 2008).

Conclusion

It is possible to argue that individual user choice is one of the most distinctively Blairite strands of the welfare reform programme. In the final weeks of his premiership Blair talked about his 'big regrets' and said that he wished he had acted more quickly on public service reform, talking of 'three wasted years' after 1997 (Watt and Wintour, 2007). Thus the period after the 2001 General Election – the key period for the entrenchment of choice across public services – is arguably the most characteristically Blairite. Whereas Thatcher and Major principally promoted choice as an idea, Blair carried it into Hall's second and third order of change, developing choice as a policy instrument and setting.

Under Brown, choice has been reinvented as personalisation but remains an important rhetorical tool. As a policy mechanism the implementation of choice seems to have been injected with a dose of realism, but overall the commitment to expanding individual user choice in public services continues. In terms of policy settings there is evidence of a little more scepticism about the role of private capital (such as the reduction in funding for ISTCs) but the difference is small, perhaps no more than a nod to those on the left of the party to keep the faith a little longer. Otherwise the same tensions are evident as under Blair – standardisation alongside diversity, decentralisation alongside control.

Evaluation of the impact of the choice agenda is at an early stage. Lent and Arend argue that choice works best under the following conditions: 'enhanced user choice resolves a problem with the delivery of a service; the problem is recognised as such by users through their direct, day-to-day experience of the service; the user's choice is integral rather than incidental to the resolution of that problem' (2004, p 6). Direct payments and choice-based lettings meet these conditions more fully than other choice schemes and have high levels of user satisfaction (Audit Commission, 2004). However, broader issues are also relevant such as the extent of service rationing. Lack of capacity inhibits choice in education, as acknowledged by the government's schools commissioner (Curtis, 2008), as it does in housing. New forms of school, such as academies, are heavily oversubscribed, although there is some doubt about whether this marks the success or failure of parent choice (compare Blair, 2005, with Millar and Benn, 2006). In health, there is uncertainty about how far patients are being offered a choice by GPs, with less than half recalling being offered a choice of hospital for their first outpatient appointment (DH, 2007b), although initial evaluations of pilot schemes show high levels of patient satisfaction (Coulter et al, 2005).

The impact of choice on equity and service standards remains highly contested. Given the diverse ways in which people can exercise choice in relation to public services, generalisations are not helpful. Even if choice is narrowed down to the current political terrain of choice of provider by individual users, different schemes raise divergent issues about access and service quality. It is also difficult to disaggregate the impact of choice from the other variables (demographic and financial, for example) that shape front-line service provision. Thus it is premature to draw conclusions about the impact of choice as a policy mechanism and setting. More conclusive is the triumph of choice as an idea. There is currently no major political party leader that does not call for services to be more responsive to individual users, albeit in Brown's case with an emphasis on personalisation rather than choice per se. Although some of this positioning depends on the creation of a false opposition between choice and the 'one size fits all' traditional welfare state, it does involve new presumptions about delegated decision making. Citizens are to be empowered to make their own choices – and must take responsibility for making the right ones.

References

6, P. and Peck, E. (2004) 'Modernisation: the ten commitments of New Labour's approach to public management?', *International Public Management Journal*, vol 7, no 1, pp 1-18.

Agnew, J. (2001) 'Allocations: but not as we know it', *Advisor*, September/October, pp 6-8.

Appleby, J. (2006) 'Not convinced that greater patient choice improves equity of access', *Financial Times*, 1 March.

Audit Commission (2004) *Choice in public services*, London: Audit Commission.

Barnes, M. and Prior, D. (1995) 'Spoilt for choice? How consumerism can disempower public service users', *Public Money & Management*, vol 15, pp 51-7.

Blair, T. (1999) Speech at the opening of the Central Middlesex Ambulatory Care Centre, 2 December.

Blair, T. (2001a) Speech on the Reform of Public Services, 16 July.

Blair, T. (2001b) Speech on Public Service Reform, 16 October.

Blair, T. (2002) *The courage of our convictions: Why reform of the public services is the route to social justice*, London: Fabian Society.

Blair, T. (2003) 'Progress and justice in the 21st century', The Inaugural Fabian Society Annual Lecture, 17 June.

Blair, T. (2004) Speech on the economy, 3 December, Edinburgh.

Blair, T. (2005) Speech on education to City of London Academy, 12 September, London.

Blunden, F. (2006) 'Choice needs to be carefully managed', *Financial Times*, 24 February.

Branigan, T. and Carvel, J. (2008) 'Cameron calls for superbug hospital penalties', *The Guardian*, 3 January.

Brindle, D. (2007) 'Disabled to get cash to choose care options', *The Guardian*, 10 December.

Brown, G. (2003) 'State and market: towards a public interest test', *Political Quarterly*, vol 74, no 3 (edited version of a speech delivered to the Social Market Foundation, Cass Business School, 3 February).

Brown, G. (2007a) Speech to the Labour Party Conference, 23 September, Bournemouth.

Brown, G. (2007b) 'Gordon Brown launches NHS Review', 4 October (www.number10.gov.uk/output/Page13406.asp).

Brown, G. (2007c) 'PM pledges new type of politics', 3 September (www.pm.gov.uk/output/Page13012.asp).

Burgess, S., Propper, C. and Wilson, D. (2005) *Will more choice improve outcomes in education and health care? The evidence from economic research*, Bristol: Centre for Market and Public Organisation.

Byers, S. (2004) Speech to Social Market Foundation, 6 April, London.

Cabinet Office (1991) *The Citizen's Charter: Raising the standard*, Cmnd 1599, London: HMSO.

Clarke, J. (2005) 'The people's choice? New Labour and public service reform', *Renewal*, vol 13, no 4, pp 52-8.

Clarke, J., Smith, N. and Vidler, E. (2006) 'The indeterminacy of choice: political, policy and organizational dilemmas', *Social Policy and Society*, vol 5, no 3, pp 1-10.

Clarke, J., Newman, J., Smith, N., Vidler, E. and Westmarland, L. (2007) *Creating citizen-consumers: Changing publics and changing public spaces*, London: Sage Publications.

Clegg, N. (2008) 'Clegg calls for radical grassroots reforms in public services', 12 January (www.libdems.org.uk/news/clegg-calls-for-radical-grassroots-innovation-in-public-services.13707.html).

Conservative Party (2007) *Raising the bar, closing the gap* (www.conservatives.com/tile.do?def=news.story.page&obj_id=140513).

Coulter, A., Le Maistre, N. and Henderson, L. (2005) *Patients' experience of choosing where to undergo surgical treatment – Evaluation of the London Patient Choice Scheme*, Oxford: Picker Institute.

Curtis, P. (2008) 'Schools choice for all parents impossible, says minister', *The Guardian*, 17 January.

DCA (Department for Constitutional Affairs) (2005) *The future of legal services: Putting consumers first*, Cmnd 6679, London: DCA.

DCLG (Department for Communities and Local Government) (2006) *Strong and prosperous communities*, Local Government White Paper, Cmnd 6939, London: The Stationery Office.

DETR (Department of the Environment, Transport and the Regions) (2000) *Quality and choice: A decent home for all*, Housing Green Paper, London: The Stationery Office.

DfES (Department for Education and Skills) (2005) *Higher standards: Better schools for all*, Cmnd 6677, London: The Stationery Office.

DH (Department of Health) (1999) *Saving lives: Our healthier nation*, Cmnd 1523, London: The Stationery Office.

DH (2007a) *Our NHS, our future: NHS next stage review: Interim report*, October, London: DH.

DH (2007b) *Report of the National Patient Choice Survey*, England, May, London: DH.

Farrington-Douglas, J. and Allen, J. (2005) *Equitable choices for health*, London: Institute for Public Policy Research.

Frew, C. (2006) 'Direct payments for social care: the management of power and risk', Paper presented at the Association of American Geographers Annual Conference, Chicago, 10 March.

Giddens, A. (1991) *Modernity and self-identity: Self and society in the Late Modern Age*, Cambridge: Polity Press.

Giddens, A. (1994) *Beyond Left and Right: The future of radical politics*, Cambridge: Polity Press.

Giddens, A. (2003) 'Introduction: neoprogressivism: a new agenda for social democracy', in A. Giddens (ed) *The progressive manifesto*, Cambridge: Polity Press.

Goss, S. (2007) 'Re-imagining the public realm', in G. Hassan (ed) *After Blair: Politics after the New Labour decade*, London: Lawrence and Wishart, pp 107-19.

Greener, I (2003) 'Who is choosing what? The evolution and impact of "choice" in the NHS, and its importance for New Labour', in C. Bochel, N. Ellison and M. Powell (eds) *Social Policy Review 15*, Bristol: The Policy Press, pp 49-68.

Greener, I. (2005) 'The role of the patient in healthcare reform: customer, consumer or creator?', in S. Dawson and C. Sausman (eds) *Future health organisations and systems*, Basingstoke: Palgrave, pp 227-45.

Hall, P.A. (1993) 'Policy paradigms, social learning and the state: the case of economic policy making in Britain', *Comparative Politics*, vol 25, no 3, pp 275-96.

Hall, S. (2003) 'New Labour's double shuffle', *Soundings*, issue 24, pp 10-24.

HM Treasury (2007) *Comprehensive Spending Review*, London: HM Treasury.

Independent Living Institute (1996) 'Direct payments campaign in the UK' (www.independentliving.org/docs2/enildirectpayment.html).

Jordan, B. (1989) *The common good: Citizenship, morality and self-interest*, Oxford: Blackwell.

Klein, R. (2001) *The new politics of the NHS* (4th edn), Harlow: Prentice Hall.

Labour Party (2005) *Britain: Forward not back*, London: Labour Party.

Lawrence, F. and Quarmby, K. (2005) 'Private deals block Jamie's school dinners', *The Guardian*, 25 April.

Le Grand, J. (2006a) 'The Blair legacy? Choice and competition in public services', Public Lecture, London School of Economics, 21 February.

Le Grand, J. (2006b) 'Why is which? Helping critics of the less well-off?', *Financial Times*, 28 February.

Le Grand, J. (2007) *Delivering public services through choice and competition: The other invisible hand*, Princeton: Princeton University Press.

Lent, A. and Arend, N. (2004) *Making choices: How can choice improve local public services?*, London: New Local Government Network.

Lister, R. (2003) 'Investing in the citizen-workers of the future: transformations in citizenship and the state under New Labour', *Social Policy and Administration*, vol 37, no 5, pp 427-43.

Marquand, D. (2004) *Decline of the public*, Cambridge: Polity Press.

Milburn, A. (2001) *Reforming public services: Reconciling equity with choice*, London: Fabian Society.

Milburn, A. (2008) House of Commons debate, 16 January.

Miliband, D. (2006) 'Putting people in control', Speech to the National Council of Voluntary Organisations, 21 February, London.

Millar, F. and Benn, M. (2006) *A comprehensive future: Quality and equality for all our children*, London: Compass.

Ministers of State for Departments of Health, Local and Regional Government and School Standards (2004) *The case for user choice in public services*, Joint Memorandum to the Public Administration Select Committee Inquiry into Choice, Voice and Public Services.

Murray, R. (1989) 'Fordism and post-Fordism', in S. Hall and M. Jacques (eds) *New times: The changing face of politics in the 1990s*, London: Lawrence and Wishart, pp 38-53.

Needham, C. (2003) *Citizen-consumers: New Labour's marketplace democracy*, London: Catalyst.

Needham, C. (2004) 'Customer-focused government', *Soundings*, vol 26, Summer, pp 73-85.

Needham, C. (2007) *The reform of public services under New Labour: Narratives of consumerism*, Basingstoke: Palgrave.

Needham, C. (forthcoming) 'Policing with a smile: narratives of consumerism in New Labour's criminal justice policy', *Public Administration*.

O'Neale Roach, J. (2000) 'Milburn signs concordat with the private sector', *British Medical Journal*, 4 November.

Osborne, G. (2007) 'The emerging battle for public service reform', 30 May (www.conservatives.com/tile.do?def=news.story.page&obj_id=136952).

PASC (Public Administration Select Committee) (2005) *Choice, voice and public services*, Fourth Report of Session 2004-05, London: The Stationery Office.

PMSU (Prime Minister's Strategy Unit) (2006) *Strategic priorities for the UK: The policy review*, London: Cabinet Office, November.

Pollock, A. with Leys, C., Rowland, D. and Gnani, S. (2004) *NHS Plc*, London: Verso.

Reid, J. (2005) 'Social Democratic politics in an age of consumerism', Brough Lecture, Paisley University, 28 January.

Revill, J. (2008) 'Digital world creates a new underclass', *The Observer*, 6 January.

Rossiter, A. and Byrne, L. (2007) 'From choice to control: empowering public services', in P. Diamond (ed) *Public matters: The renewal of the public realm*, London: Politico's, pp 63-75.

Rowland, D., Price, D. and Pollock, A. (2004) 'Implications of the draft European Union services directive for health care', *The Lancet*, vol 364, no 9441, 1 October.

Schwartz, B. (2004) *The paradox of choice: Why more is less*, New York: HarperCollins.

Simmons, R. (2009, forthcoming) 'Understanding the "differentiated consumer" in public services: implications for choice and voice', in R. Simmons, M. Powell and I. Greener (eds) *The consumer in public services: Choice, values and difference*, Bristol: The Policy Press.

Sylvester, R. (2004) 'New Labour makes for a bossy, useless nanny', *The Daily Telegraph*, 8 November.

Tempest, M. (2004) 'Blair pushes "choice" agenda', *The Guardian*, 27 September.

Thatcher, M. (1987) *The Independent*, 6 June.

Timmins, N. (2005) 'Hewitt warns that failing hospitals will be closed', *Financial Times*, 14 May.

Timmins, N. (2007) 'Private sector role in pioneering healthcare to be slashed', *Financial Times*, 13 November.

Ungerson, C. (2004) 'Whose empowerment and independence? A cross-national perspective on "cash for care" schemes', *Ageing and Society*, vol 24, pp 189–212.

Warde, A. (1994) 'Consumers, consumption and post-Fordism', in R. Burrows and B. Loader (eds) *Towards a post-Fordist welfare state?*, London: Routledge.

Watt, N. and Wintour, P. (2007) 'Blair regrets over three wasted years', *The Guardian*, 30 April.

TWELVE

The conditional welfare state

Peter Dwyer

Introduction

This chapter utilises the work of Hall (1993) and 6 and Peck (2004) (see Chapter One, this volume) to explore welfare conditionality under New Labour. Hall's (1993) discussion of policy learning and paradigm shift is useful for analysing the wider importance of the conditional welfare state that has been mapped out by the Blair administrations. Certainly, his discussion of three key policy variables (that is, goals, instruments and settings) provides a useful way for considering the wider significance and long-term impact of New Labour's welfare reforms. Likewise, consideration of 6 and Peck's (2004) work highlights that several elements of New Labour's 'modernisation' agenda are also relevant here.

The concept of a welfare claim requiring some form of prior recognisable contribution became increasingly significant under the Blair governments of 1997–2007 and the much-quoted mantra that 'rights come with responsibilities' has long been a distinctive feature of New Labour's welfare reform. Increasingly, a principle of *conditionality* (Deacon, 1994), which holds that eligibility to certain basic, publicly provided welfare entitlements should be dependent on an individual citizen meeting particular compulsory duties or patterns of behaviour, has assumed central importance. As early as 1993, while in opposition, Blair was emphatically stating that a 'modern notion of citizenship gives rights but demands obligations, shows respect but wants it back, grants opportunity but insists on responsibility' (Blair, 1996, p 218), and a concern with duty rather than rights was clearly central in Blair's thinking when setting the tone for future governments. 'Duty is the cornerstone of a decent society. It defines the context in which rights are given.... The rights we receive should reflect the duties we owe' (Blair, 1995, p 5). Similarly, New Labour's first major statement of welfare policy intent, the welfare reform Green Paper (DSS, 1998), was couched directly in terms of modernising the welfare contract between the individual citizen and the state, and much subsequent policy has been concerned to set out details of 'the responsibilities that must be accepted in return for social rights' (Buck et al, 2006, p 1).

The notion that a citizen's right to social welfare should be linked to personal responsibility has a long heritage and did not, of course, begin with the ascent of New Labour. For example, Freud (2007) makes explicit reference to the Beveridge report (1942), and emphasises that a person's eligibility for unemployment benefit in the 'old' welfare state, established following the Second World War, was underpinned by a requirement that they should actively seek work or attend training centres. The introduction of restart interviews, stricter availability of work tests and 'actively seeking work' requirements were also a distinct feature of Conservative welfare policy under Thatcher and Major (for example, the 1989 Social Security Act and the 1995 Jobseekers Act). This leads some to argue that the emergence of welfare-to-work policies in the 1980s and 1990s can be regarded as a move 'back to Beveridge', and, indeed, also to T.H. Marshall's vision of social citizenship (Rees, 1995; Powell, 2002). Arguably, then, the conditionality at the heart of New Labour's welfare reforms may share a degree of continuity with the founding principles of the post-Second World War welfare state. However, building on Thatcherism's legacy, the subsequent New Labour decade under Blair has seen the instrumental application of the principle of conditionality in an ever-increasing number of welfare arenas.

The ongoing shift from the so-called 'passive' welfare state of the past to the 'active' welfare state of today (Walters, 1997) and the conditionality at the heart of welfare-to-work policies in the UK has attracted extensive comments (Clasen, 2002; Wright et al, 2004; Dean et al, 2005). Central to this shift has been the requirement that citizens should become active agents in their own welfare by seeking paid work rather than relying on social benefits. However, New Labour has been keen to extend its rights and responsibilities agenda into other policy areas, including housing, education and health (rf Dwyer, 2000, 2004a, 2004b; Stanley and Asta Lohde, 2004), pensions (Mann, 2007) and the management of anti-social behaviour (Rodger, 2006; Squires, 2006) and 'problem' families (Respect Task Force, 2006; Travis, 2007). Across all these areas New Labour has set out policies that utilise a variety of carrots and sticks to variously encourage, cajole or compel citizens to behave in certain ways. A common feature across the sectors is that those citizens who fail to behave in the prescribed responsible manner are likely to have their rights to public welfare reduced or even removed.

To consider more fully the extent to which conditionality has become an integral part of New Labour's welfare modernisation project, the next section outlines in more detail the particular arenas where rights and responsibilities have become unambiguously linked. As more recent statements (Johnson, 2005; Freud, 2007; Hutton, 2007) and reforms (the 2007 Welfare Reform Act) illustrate, constructing and extending the conditional welfare state remains very much a work in progress. While it is important to describe change, it is also vital to assess the significance of New Labour's welfare project in relation to broader questions about the lasting impact of 'Blairism' on the principles and practice of the UK welfare state. Questions concerning the Blair governments' legacy and whether or not the shift towards more conditional welfare has fundamentally altered the welfare relationship between citizen and state are therefore subsequently considered. In conclusion, it is argued that the changes instigated by the Blair governments have enduring consequences for citizens.

1997–2007: constructing an increasingly conditional welfare state

The wholehearted endorsement of a highly conditional welfare state by a British Labour government would once have been unthinkable, but within the past decade conditionality has become fundamental to the government's vision of a 21st-century welfare state (Deacon, 2002). Conditionality has become an accepted part of debate and policy across a range of welfare sectors. For brevity, discussions below concentrate on developments in policy concerned with social security and the management of anti-social behaviour, However, the varying degrees of conditionality that have been incorporated in the healthcare and education sectors are also noted.

From social security to conditional entitlement?

Since 1997 the link between rights and responsibilities for the young and long-term unemployed has been clearly defined within the New Deal. Failure to take up one of the four work/training options offered results in punitive benefit sanctions. The fifth option, of a passive right to benefit, has long since been removed. In subsequent developments under the Jobcentre Plus initiative, conditionality has been consistently applied to more and more people outside the paid labour market (PLM). From April 2002 eligibility to claim the overwhelming majority of working-age benefits became dependent on individuals attending a work-focused interview (WFI) with an adviser to explore options for paid work or training (Treolar, 2001).

In the UK in the past decade New Labour has presided over a 'rapid spread of a new emphasis on matching entitlement to obligation in the provision of social assistance' (Lødemel, 2001, p 311). It has built on the agenda of its Conservative predecessors by extending the reach of conditionality. Where previously the largely unconditional rights to benefit of lone parents and people with disabilities were recognised (either because, as lone parents, they were seen as making socially valid contributions as carers, or because the labour market inactivity of people with disabilities was seen as a consequence of individual impairment or illness), New Labour has challenged their exemption from participation in the PLM (Trickey and Walker, 2001).

While participants in the New Deal for Lone Parents are not yet compelled to seek work, the social welfare benefits available to lone parents are becoming more conditional. Since October 2005 all lone parents claiming out-of-work benefits with children aged 14+ have been required to attend compulsory WFIs at three-monthly intervals (Stanley et al, 2004). The government has also reiterated that lone parents have 'a responsibility to engage more intensively with our employment advisers' (DWP, 2005, p 8). Involvement in the New Deal for Disabled People also remains voluntary; however, the government has made clear its desire to end the 'sick note culture' (Johnson, 2005), and activating people with disabilities by threatening benefit sanctions is seen as increasingly legitimate. A 'significant extension of labour market conditionality for incapacitated claimants', which subjects them to 'a workfare-style regime' (Allirajah, 2005, p 4) has occurred.

Recent developments further illustrate New Labour's commitment to extending the reach of conditionality to encompass groups that in the past, for various reasons, were regarded as having legitimate claims to social welfare benefits. In March 2007 the Secretary of State for Work and Pensions, John Hutton, re-endorsed the 'fundamental principle of rights and responsibilities; of something for something', and denounced condition-free systems of welfare as exclusive (2007, p 9). Similarly, the Freud report (2007), established by the government to review welfare reform and to consider further ways of reducing work inactivity, noted:

> The government has made a commitment to rights and responsibilities a central feature of policy.... The report recommends maintaining the current regime for the unemployed, introducing stronger conditionality in line

with the Jobseeker's Allowance for lone parents with progressively younger children and moving to deliver conditionality for other groups (including people already on incapacity benefits). (Freud, 2007, p 9)

Arguing for a 'strengthened framework' that 'rebalances the system' away from unconditional welfare, Freud believes that a clear consensus has now emerged (in the minds of the public and politicians alike), whereby those who are supported to return to work must accept greater responsibility to help themselves or tolerate the possibility of benefit sanctions. Freud recommends an increase in the frequency of state interventions and the extension of the rights and responsibilities agenda to cover all economically inactive benefit recipients in future. This would include lone parents, many people with impairments, the partners of benefit claimants and those people with complex needs due to 'chaotic lifestyles'.

New Labour has shown its willingness to continue expanding the boundaries of the conditional welfare state through two significant changes included in the 2007 Welfare Reform Act. First, building on the Pathways to Work scheme, and Freud's (2007) call for greater conditionality, increasing numbers of people with disabilities will have to attend WFIs. In future those with less severe impairments will be required to be actively involved in seeking work (Corden and Nice, 2007). Employment Support Allowance (ESA) will replace Incapacity Benefit and Income Support paid in relation to sickness or incapacity. During an initial 13-week 'assessment phase', all new ESA claimants will be paid a basic allowance at Jobseeker's Allowance (JSA) rates and expected to undergo a revised personal capability assessment (PCA). Once PCA requirements are satisfied the majority of claimants will be able to access a work-related activity element of ESA. However, receipt of this Employment Support component (paid at a higher level than basic allowance) is conditional on clients drawing up individual return-to-work action plans, attending regular WFIs, routinely undertaking 'reasonable steps' to manage their condition and/or accepting specified training or basic skills support to facilitate their return to paid work. Refusal carries the threat of benefit sanctions and an enforced return to the lower basic benefit. Disqualification from ESA for up to six weeks is possible where someone is:

> ... limited in their capability for work because of their own misconduct, because they remain someone who has limited capability for work through failure, without good cause, to

> follow medical advice, or because they fail, without good
> cause, to observe specified rules of behaviour. (2007 Welfare
> Reform Act, s 18)

The small number of people who (following their PCA) are identified as having severe conditions and 'limited capability for work-related activity' will qualify for a Support Component. This will be set at a higher level than the work-related activity element of ESA and such claimants will not need to participate in work-related activities (CPAG, 2007).

Management of anti-social behaviour

The Conservative government's 1996 Housing Act brought about significant changes that linked the right to reside in social housing to specific behavioural responsibilities, most notably probationary tenancy periods which render tenants who behave in an 'anti-social' manner within a 12-month trial period liable to eviction. While such moves may enhance the rights of some tenants to live in peace (Deacon, 2004), as Hunter notes, a corresponding outcome of the 1996 Act is that it targets offenders living in social housing and 'reduces and limits the rights of such people, and ultimately takes away one of their most basic rights, the right to live in their home' (2001, p 228).

Since 1997 New Labour has endorsed and expanded the approach of its predecessors and has looked to limit the rights of citizens engaged in irresponsible behaviour. A range of instruments are now available to social landlords, and the exclusion of nuisance neighbours via the denial of a tenancy is an established part of policy. Definitions of anti-social behaviour encompass a wide range of conduct, for example, children's play annoying neighbours, serious criminal activity, racial harassment and violent attack (Flint, 2002), and linking rights to responsible behaviour is far from straightforward. Nonetheless, a series of Acts and initiatives clearly indicate New Labour's sustained enthusiasm for advancing a rights/responsibilities agenda in managing the problematic behaviour of certain citizens.

The 1998 Crime and Disorder Act introduced Anti-Social Behaviour Orders (ASBOs). These civil court orders grant local authorities or the police the power to prohibit an individual from acting in a specified anti-social manner and/or the power to exclude an individual from their home or other specified locality. It is a criminal offence (potentially punishable by imprisonment) to break the conditions set out in an order. ASBOs have subsequently been used in neighbourhood disputes, to tackle youth crime and to ban individuals from a particular area to combat street crime such as drug dealing and prostitution. New Labour has further developed this approach in the 2003 Anti-Social Behaviour Act and the 2003 Criminal Justice Act. This legislation introduced a host of new instruments including dispersal orders, parenting contracts, demoted tenancies, individual support orders and acceptable behaviour contracts to promote good behaviour (rf NAO, 2006, for details).

The 'personalisation' of rights and responsibilities has also been identified as one of the five guiding principles for those citizens who are identified as suffering multiple disadvantage (Social Exclusion Task Force, 2007). While the government promises individualised support packages to provide opportunities, and it recognises that a range of issues (for example, a lack of basic skills, mental health problems, substance misuse, debt homelessness) may play a part in people's lives, the message is again clear. Where 'contact with services is instead frequently driven by problematic behaviour resulting from their chaotic lives – such as anti-social behaviour, criminality and poor parenting', the government is willing to apply tough 'sanctions such as prison, loss of tenancy and possible removal of children' (Social Exclusion Task Force, 2007, p 74).

Likewise, the *Respect action plan* (Respect Task Force, 2006) contains an abundance of initiatives aimed at tacking anti-social behaviour, many of them focused on addressing the lifestyles of 'problem families' and the most excluded individuals. Measures include enhanced personal support schemes for individuals with specific or multiple issues, the linking of government regeneration funding to systems of behaviour management, and sanctions for problem families. Making good on the government's earlier commitment, section 31 of the 2007 Welfare Reform Act also allows for non-payment (or reduction) of Housing Benefit when a person is evicted on the grounds of anti-social or criminal behaviour, or has failed to comply with a local authority warning to improve behaviour. Sanctions range from an initial four-week, 10% reduction, to total loss of entitlement (for up to a five-year period) for those who continue to behave in an anti-social manner and who fail to engage with rehabilitation services (CPAG, 2007).

Conditionality in other sectors

In response to a significant number of violent/abusive acts against healthcare professionals a zero tolerance policy towards violent and disruptive patients has become an established part of UK health policy. Guidelines state that refusing treatment is a last resort. Nonetheless, the government has committed to support staff who (under the threat of immediate danger) take decisions to refuse treatment for violent patients (DH, 2002). The Queens Medical Centre in Nottingham took things a step further, and used court injunctions and ASBOs to ban three highly disruptive people from entering hospital grounds, unless in need of life-saving treatment (Carvel, 2001).

Elements of conditionality were also introduced to the Sure Start Maternity Grant (SSMG) in 2001 and the Welfare Food Scheme (2002). In both cases New Labour made substantial improvements in the level of grant and range of foods available to mothers of young children in receipt of means-tested benefits. However, access to the enhanced SSMG and healthy food vouchers became conditional on parents meeting with specified healthcare professionals to receive advice and support. This is an example of the least punitive type of conditionality; however, in the period 2001–02, over 8,000 claims for the SSMG were refused for non-compliance (DWP, 2002).

In a series of pilot projects established across England, conditionality also informed New Labour's policy for tackling adult illiteracy. Under the government's Skills for Life strategy nine localised schemes were established to test the effectiveness of a variety of 'carrot and stick' approaches in persuading JSA claimants to learn basic skills. In certain areas claimants were rewarded with enhanced benefits for successful completion of a full-time basic education scheme. Elsewhere, benefits were cut if claimants refused, or dropped out of, a compulsory basic skills programme (Treolar, 2001). The value of more limited conditionality in other education settings has not gone unnoticed:

> Increasingly, service providers are seeking to make the compact between service provision and citizen more explicit. For example, many schools are introducing pupil–parent 'contracts' and these are also used in relation to Educational Maintenance Allowances. Even where these contracts are not legally binding, they can have a powerful effect by simply making explicit what is expected of each party involved. (Social Exclusion Task Force, 2007, pp 39-40)

Perhaps the most controversial conditionality discussions to emerge under New Labour were proposals in April 2002 for the withdrawal of Child Benefit from parents whose children persistently truant from school and/or engage in anti-social behaviour (Hinsliff, 2002). In the face of intense debate and criticism from both within and beyond the

Labour Party this idea was subsequently dropped. However, in what amounted to a policy U-turn, the government became committed to the idea of removing Housing Benefit for perpetrators of persistent anti-social behaviour: a commitment which, as noted above, has now been acted on. Discussions above indicate that conditionality has been a central element of welfare reform in the past decade. Questions about the character and importance of such 'creeping conditionality' (Dwyer, 2004b) now require further consideration.

Tinkering or transformation: towards a new conditional welfare state?

Having described the emergence and consolidation of the conditional welfare state under the Blair governments it is now important to consider the significance of their legacy in relation to the UK welfare state more generally. How important is this influx of welfare policies that have linked citizens' access to certain social rights to specified responsibilities? Should this process be seen as New Labour merely tinkering around the edges, or has something more fundamental occurred? Has a more radical process of transformation in the welfare contract between citizen and state been played out? The work of Hall (1993) and 6 and Peck (2004) offers some insights here.

Significant change?

Hall (1993) identifies three important variables that may change as policies evolve. The first is *the goals of policy*, which in relation to this discussion can be identified as New Labour's attempt to change people's expectations vis-à-vis the welfare state. The old welfare state of the past built around 'passive' welfare rights has been deemed outdated. A key part of New Labour's task is, therefore, to convince people of the future need for citizens to take more active responsibility for their own welfare. Second, the *instruments of policy*, that is, the techniques used to achieve this goal, have changed somewhat. In the new conditional welfare state, 'carrots and sticks' are to the fore. Incentives are used to 'activate' the inactive (including ever increasing numbers of people with disabilities and lone parents), and benefit sanctions are employed against those who continue to behave irresponsibly. Third, Hall identifies that the details of policy instruments may be open to incremental modification and so change often occurs in a range of *policy settings*. This is certainly the case within New Labour's conditional welfare state.

Linked to the above, Hall also argues that when change occurs it may happen on three levels. First order change involves incremental alterations, for example, changing benefit levels and tinkering with eligibility criteria. Second order change is said to occur when the essential goals of policy remain the same but (often due to dissatisfaction on the part of policy makers about past policy performance) the techniques used to achieve those goals are altered. Third order change signifies a rarer but more radical shift in the ideas that underpin policy and its goals:

> First and second order change can be seen as cases of 'normal policymaking', namely of a process that adjusts policy without challenging the overall terms of a given policy paradigm....Third order change, by contrast, is likely to reflect a very different process marked by the radical changes in the overall terms of policy discourse associated with 'paradigm shift'. (Hall, 1993, p 279)

Has such change occurred in respect of New Labour's welfare reforms and, if it has, how has it come about? At the centre of Hall's ideas about policy change is the view that legacies matter.

As New Labour came to power in 1997 it inherited a world in which old ideas about the role and efficiency of the post-Second World War welfare state had been emphatically challenged. In the 1970s growing welfare costs, rising unemployment and the apparent emergence of a welfare-dependent 'underclass' all served to undermine the rationale for extensive welfare rights (Cox, 1998). An alternative right-wing vision (see, for example, Murray, 1984; Mead, 1986), critical of collectivised welfare, emerged under the Conservative administrations of the 1980s and 1990s. The authority of the 'old' welfare state was thus eroded. To use Hall's phrase, it appeared to have become an 'anomaly'.

Elements of the right-wing critique, alongside aspects of new communitarianism (Heron, 2001), have subsequently informed New Labour's thinking. The old 'passive' unconditional welfare system was to be replaced with a new 'active' welfare state in which social rights come with attendant responsibilities. To paraphrase Hall (1993, p 279), active welfare and the presumption of a principle of conditionality is now the 'prism' through which politicians and the public view the state's welfare role. New Labour under Blair has either distorted – for those who favour the 'old' largely unconditional Marshallian (cf Powell, 2002, for an alternative reading) approach to welfare citizenship – or (according to right-wing or communitarian critics) corrected our collective vision of social citizenship. The era of the old welfare state has passed and a new highly conditional welfare contract has been written. In short the 'overall terms of the policy discourse' (Hall, 1993, p 279) have moved significantly. In Hall's terms we have seen a 'paradigm shift' in the primacy of ideas that underpin the UK welfare system. New Labour's project has been about constructing a new type of social citizenship in which individual responsibility and duty take precedence over rights to welfare. Third order change has occurred.

This assertion is further supported by the work of Clasen and Clegg (2005). Echoing Hall (1993) they highlight three levels of conditionality in which changes may occur. Level one changes are concerned with the rules that 'govern membership of a given socially defined category of support' (2005, p 6). At this level change may be concerned with redefining the rules that govern access to benefits within a specific category of claimant or the reworking of eligibility criteria. Level two changes are about 'conditions relating to the distributive principles' on which different benefits and services are based. For example, in their discussion of unemployment benefit Clasen and Clegg highlight that the period 1980–96 saw an erosion of the contributory principle in favour of less generous, means-tested, social assistance benefits. Level three change is characterised by the introduction of conditions of continuing benefit receipt involving a certain form of prescribed behaviour or action on the part of benefit claimants, that is, the application of a 'principle of conditionality'. They conclude:

> The new British conditionality logic is both wider than previously (beyond unemployment) and focused on work-tests and employability criteria, ie behavioral aspects. Over the past twenty-five years, an overall pattern can be observed as a gradual progression through the levers of conditionality. (Clasen and Clegg, 2005, p 13)

A modernising project?

Debates about whether or not the conditionality at the heart of New Labour's reforms constitutes a modernisation of the UK welfare state are harder to pin down. Certainly, from the outset of New Labour's term in office ministers in Blair's governments have consistently emphasised the need to break from the past and to construct a new modern welfare state fit for the challenges of contemporary society (Heron and Dwyer, 1999). Similarly, the 'Third Way' philosophy popular in Blair's first and second terms of office was enthusiastically promoted as the shiny, new,

Table 12.1: A consideration of Hall's orders of change against examples of New Labour's conditional welfare state

Welfare arena	First order Levels or settings changed	Second order Policy instrument altered, goals unchanged	Third order 'Paradigm shift'
Social security Young and long-term unemployed	Jobcentre Plus – compulsory work-focused interviews (WFIs) introduced for majority of social benefit claimants (2002)	Compulsory New Deals for Young (18–25) and Long-term (6 months) Unemployed (from 1997)	From 'passive' to 'active' welfare state
Lone parents	Ongoing gradual reduction in age of child at which lone parent must attend WFI	Introduction of WFI for lone parents (2001) Voluntary New Deal for Lone Parents (1998)	From rights to rights explicitly linked to individual responsibilities Challenge in principle to the right to benefit of lone parents and disabled people who are 'inactive' in respect of primary labour market (PLM)
Disabled people	Link between work and entitlement to Incapacity Benefit strengthened; 'all work test' becomes 'capability assessment' (1999)	Voluntary New Deal for Disabled People (1998) Introduction of Employment Support Allowance with 'actively seeking work requirement' (1997)	
Management of anti-social behaviour		Introduction of ASBOs (1998); consolidation and expansion of ASBOs eg dispersal orders, parenting contracts (2003) Reduction/removal of right to Housing Benefit for persistent anti-social behaviour (2007)	Rights to housing and freedom of movement linked to responsible behaviour
Healthcare	Significant increases in the value of Sure Start Maternity Grant (SSMG) and improvements to the Welfare Food Scheme	Principle of conditionality introduced alongside means testing for these benefits	Rights now linked to receipt of appropriate professional advice/ notion of parental responsibility

modern pragmatic approach to politics required to renew UK society's institutions post-Thatcherism (Powell, 1999).

Several aspects of 6 and Peck's (2004) discussion of modernisation are relevant when analysing conditionality and its effects. In respect of *central standard setting*, the state has retained much of its power in setting out the behavioural requirements that are an essential feature of the conditional welfare state (for example, work and training requirements as set out in legislation). However, for New Labour, in looking to extend its approach and apply conditionality to people with disabilities, hard-to-reach groups and problem families and so on, *personalisation*, rather than standardisation, appears to have increasing relevance. In future, front-line service providers are to be empowered to negotiate individualised support packages and good behaviour contracts (Freud, 2007; Social Exclusion Task Force, 2007). These will meet standard state-prescribed requirements of 'activation' and/or responsible behaviour but allow for consideration of a client's particular situation when setting out individual obligations and compacts. This personalised case management approach has long been part of social work practice but is a relatively new development within the wider world of welfare.

Area-based initiatives also have some relevance to current discussions. For example, in January 2007 the government announced that resources and particular policies to tackle anti-social behaviour are to be targeted at 40 designated 'Respect Areas' (Home Office, 2007). Likewise, the New Deal for Communities focused resources on certain deprived neighbourhoods and also invoked a principle of conditionality by linking 'spending on "renovating" estates conditional on [the] "good" behaviour' of local residents (Wallace, 2007, p 4). Flint (2002) has also argued that the anti-social behaviour agenda is about targeting and controlling poor citizens living within particular geographically defined areas.

6 and Peck use the notion of *earned autonomy* to describe the institutional relationship between government and the plethora of agencies it seeks to regulate and monitor. Those agencies that meet their performance targets and/or successfully deliver improvement are granted greater independence. The idea of earned autonomy has some salience in respect of conditionality, in that individual citizens who demonstrate a willingness to improve their behaviour or enter paid work are set free from the everyday regulation of their lives by welfare state officials. Citizens who attempt to meet their responsibilities, to keep their side of the welfare bargain, are recognised and rewarded both with enhanced support and the right to manage their own affairs once again. Those who fail or refuse to improve their behaviour remain

subject to the routine management and day-to-day scrutiny of welfare state officials and continue to face the possibility of removal of their social rights.

An *extended role for private capital* is clearly part of New Labour's plans for the future conditional welfare state. The strong case made for extending the role of the private sector in delivering and managing welfare-to-work services (Adams, 2005; Freud, 2007) appears to have been heeded in the 2007 Welfare Reform Act. Work Directions UK, a subsidiary company of an Australian multinational, has just been awarded six contracts worth £85 million to deliver the Pathways to Work programme (Hencke, 2007). 6 and Peck are, however, mistaken to suggest that New Labour has presided over only a *modest increase in citizen obligations*. As previous discussions indicate, the increase in citizens' responsibilities that is central to the government's modernisation of welfare is modest in neither scope nor impact, particularly when the rights of poor citizens are considered (Dwyer, 1998, 2002). Rather than placing 'great emphasis on increasing access to services' (6 and Peck, 2004, p 13), the new conditional welfare state built by Blair's administrations seeks to purposefully exclude those who cannot, or who will not, play by the new rule of reciprocity.

Those most likely to be charged with modernising the welfare state in the immediate future appear unlikely to challenge this approach. Gordon Brown, Blair's successor as Prime Minister, has stated that New Labour had 'not done enough to promote a philosophy which emphasises rights and responsibilities together' (2006, p 5), and more recently that 'we will combine tough sanctions for those who refuse to work or train with better and more targeted support for those in most need to give them the skills and advice they need to get back onto the jobs ladder' (DWP, 2008, p 2). Similarly, in his 2007 Conservative Party conference speech, David Cameron has made explicit reference to the tough welfare-to-work programmes in Wisconsin, US, and stated that those who refuse 'fair' work should be denied rights to welfare. In moves that mirror the government's recent reforms private companies are also set to play a key role in Conservative plans to activate Incapacity Benefit claimants (Revill, 2008). Peter Hain (2008) (then Secretary of State for Work and Pensions) remained convinced that real differences remain between the current government's 'human capital' approach to activation (which emphasises training and opportunity) and what he sees as Cameron's more punitive 'work first' option (see Levy, 2004, for further discussions regarding such distinctions). Conditionality is, however, a non-negotiable element of both visions; those who refuse to take up work or training options will face sanctions and a reduction or loss of benefit.

Conclusion

New Labour under Blair has institutionalised a new form of social citizenship in which conditional entitlement now dominates (Dwyer, 2004b). The principle of conditionality is firmly embedded at the core of New Labour's modernised welfare state and, as the more recent policy developments discussed in this chapter indicate, an enthusiasm for extending its reach further clearly exists. Some shifts in emphasis appear to be emerging in the early days of Gordon Brown's leadership. For example, the Prime Minister appears to have pushed the 'Respect Agenda', with its focus on anti-social behaviour, into the background, while simultaneously looking to explore how 'for the first time the rights and responsibilities associated with an entitlement to NHS care' (Brown, 2008, p 2) can be codified in an NHS constitution. Nonetheless, the principle of conditionality per se remains unchallenged.

Conditional welfare rights are openly endorsed by politicians and commentators, from across the mainstream political spectrum including the centre-left (White, 2007), as a necessary element of the 21st-century 'active' world of welfare. A new consensus about the role and purpose of the welfare state has emerged. As this conditional welfare state, with its stress on individual responsibility, becomes embedded and institutionalised there is a danger that the social, economic and political causes of unemployment, poverty and family breakdown will cease to be recognised (Dwyer and Ellison, 2007). Influenced by right-wing ideas about the causes of welfare dependency, the principle of conditionality emerged as a key theme in welfare reform under the Conservative administrations of Thatcher and Major. The subsequent consolidation and expansion of the conditional welfare state under New Labour may yet prove to be one of Tony Blair's most enduring legacies.

References

6, P. and Peck, E. (2004) 'Modernisation: the ten commitments of New Labour's approach to public management?', *International Public Management Journal*, vol 7, no 1, pp 1-18.

Adams, J. (2005) *Towards full employment*, London: Institute for Public Policy Research.

Allirajah, D. (2005) 'Incapacity – into the melting pot', *Welfare Rights Bulletin*, no 185, April, pp 4-5.

Blair, T. (1995) 'The rights we enjoy reflect the duties we owe', Spectator Lecture, 22 March, Queen Elizabeth Conference Centre, Labour Party Press Release, London: Labour Party.

Blair, T. (1996) *New Britain: My vision of a young country*, London: Fourth Estate.

Brown, G. (2006) Speech by the Chancellor of the Exchequer, to the Donald Dewar Memorial Lecture, 12 October, Press Release 74/06, London, HM Treasury (www.hm-treasury.gov.uk/newsroom_and_speeches/press/2006/press_74_06.cfm).

Brown, G. (2008) 'PM's New Year message to staff', London, Department of Health (www.dh.gov.uk/en/DH_081585).

Buck, R., Phillips, C.J., Main, C.J., Barnes, M.C., Aylward, M. and Waddell, G. (2006) *Conditionality in context: Incapacity benefit and social deprivation in Merthyr Tydfil* (www.epolitix.com/NR/rdonlyres/03C6EAF4-BACB-40A2-9461-7775C7742ABC/0/ConditionalityinContext.pdf).

Cameron, D. (2007) 'Call that election. We will fight. Britain will win', Speech to the Conservative Party Conference, 3 October (www.conservatives.com/tile.do?def=news.story.page&obj_id=139453).

Carvel, J. (2001) 'Violent patients may be refused care', *The Guardian*, 28 December, p 9.

Clasen, J. (2002) 'Unemployment and unemployment policy in the UK: increasing employability and redefining citizenship', in J. Goul Andersen, J. Clasen, W. van Oorschot and K. Halvorsen (eds), *Europe's new state of welfare: Unemployment, employment policies and citizenship*, Bristol: The Policy Press, pp 59-74.

Clasen, J. and Clegg, D. (2005) 'Restructuring welfare states: a conditionality approach', Paper presented at the conference 'Exploring the dynamics of reform: the dependent variable problem in comparative welfare state analysis', Stirling University, 13/14 May.

Corden, A. and Nice, K. (2007) 'Qualitative longitudinal analysis for policy: incapacity benefits recipients taking part in Pathways to Work', *Social Policy and Society*, vol 6, no 4, pp 557-69.

Cox, R.H. (1998) 'The consequences of welfare reform: how conceptions of social rights are changing', *Journal of Social Policy*, vol 27, no 1, pp 1-16.

CPAG (Child Poverty Action Group) (2007) 'The Welfare Reform Act 2007', *Welfare Rights Bulletin 198*, London: CPAG.

Deacon, A. (1994) 'Justifying workfare: the historical context of the workfare debates', in M. White (ed) *Unemployment and public policy in a changing labour market*, London: Public Services Institute, pp 53-63.

Deacon, A. (2002) *Perspectives on welfare: Ideas, ideologies and policy debates*, Buckingham: Open University Press.

Deacon, A. (2004) 'Justifying conditionality: the case of anti-social tenants', *Housing Studies*, vol 19, no 6, pp 911-26.

Dean, H., Bonvin, J., Vielle, P. and Faraque, N. (2005) 'Developing capabilities and rights in welfare-to-work policies', *European Societies*, vol 7, no 1, pp 3-26.

DH (Department of Health) (2002) *Withholding treatment from violent and abusive patients: Resource guide*, London: DH (www.nhs.uk/zerotolerance/wh_treatment/index.htm).

DSS (Department of Social Security) (1998) *New ambitions for our country: A new contract for welfare*, Green Paper, Cm 3805, London: DSS.

DWP (Department for Work and Pensions) (2002c) *Social Fund: Sure Start Maternity Grants. Request for information*, Report provided in response to enquiry from P. Dwyer, London: Information and Analysis Directorate and DWP.

DWP (2005) *Department for Work and Pensions five-year strategy: Opportunity and security throughout life*, Cm 6447, London: DWP.

DWP (2008) *Transforming Britain's labour market: Ten years of the New Deal*, London: DWP.

Dwyer, P. (1998) 'Conditional citizens? Welfare rights and responsibilities in the late 1990's', *Critical Social Policy*, vol 18, no 4, pp 519-43.

Dwyer, P. (2000) *Welfare rights and responsibilities: Contesting social citizenship*, Bristol: The Policy Press.

Dwyer, P. (2002) 'Making sense of social citizenship: some user views on welfare rights and responsibilities', *Critical Social Policy*, vol 22, no 2, pp 273-99.

Dwyer, P. (2004a) *Understanding social citizenship: Themes and perspectives for policy and practice*, Bristol: The Policy Press.

Dwyer, P. (2004b) 'Creeping conditionality in the UK: from welfare rights to conditional entitlements', *Canadian Journal of Sociology*, vol 29, no 2, pp 265-87.

Dwyer, P. and Ellison, N. (2007) '"We nicked stuff from all over the place": exploring the origins and character of active labour market policies in the UK', Paper to the annual Social Policy Association Conference, University of Birmingham, July.

Flint, J. (2002) 'Return of the governors: citizenship and the governance of neighbourhood disorder in the UK', *Citizenship Studies*, vol 6, no 3, pp 245-64.

Freud, D. (2007) *Reducing dependency, increasing opportunity: Options for the future of welfare to work. An independent report to the Department for Work and Pensions*, London: DWP.

Hain, P. (2008) 'Fight poverty not the poor', *The Guardian*, 2 January, p 26.

Hall, P.A. (1993) 'Policy paradigms, social learning and the state: the case of economic policy making in Britain', *Comparative Politics*, vol 25, no 3, pp 275-96.

Hencke, D. (2007) 'Controversial company hired to get people off benefit', *The Guardian*, 24 September, p 29.

Heron, E. (2001) 'Etzioni's spirit of communitariansim: community values and welfare realities in Blair's Britain', in R. Sykes, C. Bochel and N. Ellison (eds) *Social Policy Review 13*, Bristol: The Policy Press/SPA, pp 63-87.

Heron, E. and Dwyer P. (1999) '"Doing the right thing": Labour's attempt to forge a new welfare deal between the individual and the state', *Social Policy and Administration*, vol 33, no 1, pp 91-104.

Hinsliff, G. (2002) 'Parents face benefits axe over unruly children', *The Observer*, 28 April, p 1.

Home Office (2007) 'Forty areas appointed to lead Respect programme', Press Release, 22 January, London Home Office.

Hunter, C. (2001) 'Anti-social behaviour and housing – can law be the answer?', in D. Cowan and A. Marsh (eds) *Two steps forward: Housing policy into the millennium*, Bristol: The Policy Press, pp 221-37.

Hutton, J. (2007) 'Improving employability for disadvantaged groups', Speech to the Welfare to Work seminar organised by Institute for Public Policy Research North, Manchester, Friday 2 March.

Johnson, A. (2005) 'Fit for purpose – welfare to work and incapacity benefit', Speech by the Secretary of State for Work and Pensions, Cardiff University, 7 February 2005, London: DWP.

Levy, J.D. (2004) 'Activation through thick and thin: progressive approaches to labour market activation', in N. Ellison, L. Bauld and M. Powell (eds) *Social Policy Review 16*, Bristol: The Policy Press, pp 187-208.

Lødemel, I. (2001) 'Discussion: workfare in the welfare state', in I. Lødemel and H. Trickey (eds) *'An offer you can't refuse': Workfare in international perspective*, Bristol: The Policy Press, pp 295-344.

Mann, K. (2007) 'Activation, retirement planning and restraining the "third age"', *Social Policy and Society*, vol 6, no 3, pp 279-92.

Mead, L.M. (1986) *Beyond entitlement*, New York: Free Press.

Murray, C. (1984) *Losing ground*, New York: Basic Books.

NAO (National Audit Office) (2006) *The Home Office:Tackling anti-social behaviour*, Report by the Comptroller and Auditor General, London: The Stationery Office.

Powell, M. (ed) (1999) *New Labour, new welfare state? The 'third way' in British social policy*, Bristol: The Policy Press.

Powell, M. (2002) 'The hidden history of social citizenship', *Citizenship Studies*, vol 6, no 3, pp 229–24.

Rees, A.M. (1995) 'The other T.H. Marshall', *Journal of Social Policy*, vol 24, no 3, pp 341-62.

Respect Task Force (2006) *Respect action plan*, London: Respect Task Force, Home Office.

Revill, J. (2008) 'Cameron's U-turn on jobless plan', *The Observer*, 6 January, p 13.

Rodger, J.J. (2006) 'Anti-social families and withholding of welfare support', *Critical Social Policy*, vol 26, no 1, pp 121-43.

Social Exclusion Task Force (2007) *Reaching out: An action plan on social exclusion*, London: Cabinet Office.

Squires, P. (2006) 'New Labour and the politics of anti-social behaviour', *Critical Social Policy*, vol 26, no 1, pp 144-68.

Stanley, K. and Asta Lohde, L. with White, S. (2004) *Sanctions and sweeteners: Rights and responsibilities in the benefits system*, London: IPPR.

Travis, A. (2007) 'Sin bins scheme for 1,500 anti-social families a year', *The Guardian*, 12 April (www.guardian.co.uk/society/2007/apr/12/socialexclusion.uknews).

Treolar, P. (2001) 'Compulsion creeps up', *Welfare Rights Bulletin*, no 164, October, London: CPAG (www.cpag.org.uk/cro/wrb/wrb164/compulsion.htm).

Trickey, H. and Walker, R. (2001) 'Steps to compulsion within the British labour market', in I. Lødemel and H. Trickey (eds) *'An offer you can't refuse': Workfare in international perspective*, Bristol: The Policy Press, pp 181-214.

Walters, W. (1997) 'The active society: new designs for social policy', *Policy & Politics*, vol 25, no 3, pp 221-34.

Wallace, A. (2007) '"We have had nothing for so long that we don't know what to ask for": New Deal for Communities and the regeneration of socially excluded terrain', *Social Policy and Society*, vol 6, no 1, pp 1-12.

White, S. (2007) 'Taking responsibility: a fair welfare contract', in J. Bennett and G. Cooke (eds) *It's all about you: Citizen centred welfare*, London: Institute for Public Policy Research, ch 2.

Wright, S., Kopač, A. and Slater, G. (2004) 'Continuities within paradigmatic change: activation, social policies and citizenship within the context of welfare reform in Slovenia and the UK', *European Societies*, vol 6, no 4, pp 511-34.

THIRTEEN

The stages of New Labour

Ian Greener

Introduction

When Labour came to power in 1997 it appeared to represent a mix of the modern, with its promise to reinvigorate the constitution, and the traditional, declaring itself to be guardian of the welfare state and promising to 'save the NHS'. How much has Labour's approach to policy changed in the past 10 years? Has policy under Blair and now Brown formed the basis of a new social policy settlement, or has change been less radical than the government has often claimed?

This chapter uses frameworks from 6 and Peck (2004a, 2004b) and Hall (1990, 1993) to examine the extent of change that has taken place since 1997. The key policy question Hall's framework asks of Labour is whether or not its approach to public reform represents an approach with a new hierarchy of goals in place, a new policy 'paradigm', or is it instead a variant of the Conservative approach that preceded it? Can Labour policy be divided into a series of stages or moments (Greener, 2004b) that show changes in Labour's approach?

6 and Peck organise their analysis around a series of headings derived from Labour policy documents: inspection, central standard setting, area-based initiatives, coordination and integration, devolution but limited decentralisation, earned autonomy, an extended role for private capital, a modest increase in citizen obligations, improved public access and e-government. Each of these has a role to play in exploring the extent of change. Hall's work on policy 'paradigms' suggests that the dominant ideas of government follow the path of a punctuated equilibrium in which periods of relative stability are followed by violent change, after which, once again, equilibrium is restored. This follows the path of scientific discovery suggested by Kuhn (1970), but also has clear links with more contemporary work examining how ideas and institutions constrain actor behaviour within them (Mahoney, 2000; Greener, 2006a). Policy change can be: first order, where the settings of policy instruments are changed, but within the same overarching

policy framework; second order, where policy instruments are changed, but the same underlying policy framework still exists; or third order, where the goals of policy are significantly changed, and where a policy paradigm shift occurs (Oliver, 1996, 1997; Greener, 2001).

When Labour returned to power, it claimed to be eschewing an ideological approach to policy, suggesting it would be taking a pragmatic, evidence-based approach instead (Labour Party, 1997). Its intellectual underpinning was based on 'Third Way' (Giddens, 1998) notions that the state should become a kind of super-risk adjuster, investing in skills in periods when people might be out of work, and expecting them to become self-reliant where they had found a place in the labour market. Public services had to become both more efficient and more customer-focused than they had been in the past, and an investment in them would generate a return for the country. Education was particularly regarded as being a key area that had to be considerably improved in the era of the knowledge-based economy.

However, ideas do not automatically make policy, and a change in policy alone does not automatically lead to reform (Majone, 1989). It is necessary to examine what exactly New Labour did during its first 10 years to explore what ideas appear to have driven its policy, and whether or not it is possible to identify a new approach to government (a new 'paradigm') after 10 years of its reforms. However, before examining Labour's policy, its immediate predecessor's approach must be considered in order to try and differentiate (or not) Labour's approach from it.

The Conservative approach to public reform, and Labour 1997–2000

The 'policy paradigm' at the end of the Conservative era can be characterised by the favouring of market means to achieve managerial ends. Management, specifically private management, was portrayed as the answer to the public policy problems of the past (Clarke and Newman, 1997). The fundamental problem was seen as the public sector's lack of profit motive, creating a lack of incentive to be either efficient or customer-focused, with reforms being geared towards those ends, particularly by trying to give greater scope for public managers to challenge entrenched professionals (Gabe et al, 1994).

Public management was given a greater legitimacy through the introduction of market mechanisms, leading to a logic where public managers could attempt to challenge high-status professional groups such as doctors and teachers in the name of organisational survival (Ferlie, 1994a, 1994b; Mannion and Smith, 1998). There is clearly an element of ideology in this in the selection and favouring of market mechanisms and private management to reform public services. Formerly public services were privatised during the 1980s in the name of achieving the Conservatives' goals (George and Wilding, 1994), but the core public services such as healthcare and education remained very much within public ownership. This showed a degree of pragmatism at the heart of Conservative policy – indeed accounts of the last significant Thatcher-era public reform demonstrate it was Secretary of State Ken Clarke rather than Margaret Thatcher who drove the process, with Thatcher favouring a more conciliatory approach because of its potential electoral consequences (Timmins, 1995a, 1995b).

This pragmatism at the heart of government contrasts with Labour's claims, on returning to government, that the Conservatives had put in place inefficient market solutions to replace the sclerotic bureaucratic forms of the 'command and control' system of the postwar period (Secretary of State for Health, 1997). Labour instead claimed that *their* policy was a return to pragmatism, and what counted was 'what worked'. Labour described public sector markets as inefficient because they created red tape and duplication, as well as a host of administrators to oversee the complex contracting processes that were necessary to make them work. The Third Way would take the best of previous organisational forms and combine them in new ways (Hay and Watson, 1999; Bevir, 2000; Fairclough, 2000)

Labour demonstrated an increased concern for fairness as a policy goal, at least in terms of trying to create greater equality of access, but also a concern for trying to achieve greater equality of outcome by wishing to narrow health inequalities, for example. However, public reform had to be achieved with a commitment to remain within Conservative spending limits for their first years in government, and so was initially a zero-sum game, with any budget increases for services having to be financed from reductions in others. Labour policy makers appeared to believe that once public professionals were back under their control, the difficulties of the past could be dealt with and a new era begun (Timmins, 2002).

Tony Blair famously claimed the top three priorities for his new government would be 'education, education, education', and his Chancellor was known to be rather taken by endogenous growth theory (Keegan, 2003). The combination of these factors suggested that the future affluence of the country would be about increasing the skill base of the population so that Britain could become a leader in the 'knowledge-based economy' (Jessop, 2002). Investment in education was therefore a significant concern, but expenditure limits meant it would be a struggle to make policy distinctively different (see DfEE, 1997). Policy was focused instead around goals such as the introduction of the literacy hour (Barber, 2007). There were early reforms in the NHS presented in terms of improving efficiency by abolishing the inefficiencies of the market, but the market itself remained (Powell, 1998). There were also attempts to get primary care organisations to take a more coordinated approach to creating a 'modern' healthcare system (Secretary of State for Health, 1997), and the use of area-based initiatives such as Health and Education Action Zones.

It is difficult to characterise Labour's approach on returning to government as representing a new direction in policy from their predecessors. The hierarchy of policy goals inherited from the Conservatives remained largely the same, but with an additional concern over fairness. The use of public markets was no longer as well regarded, with instead a more collaborative, longer-term approach proposed (Maddock and Morgan, 1998), suggesting a greater faith in public professionals than the Conservatives had displayed. In terms of 6 and Peck's modernisation framework, limited progress had been made in terms of inspection, central standard setting, coordination, devolution or earned autonomy. Labour did attempt to achieve 'joined-up' government through area-based initiatives such as Health and Education Action Zones, but these appeared to flounder when public funding was withdrawn from such projects. There was also greater potential for an increased role for private capital coming through Labour's embrace of the private finance initiative (PFI), although it took time for significant projects to begin to appear.

Labour policy 2000–04

Within a relatively short period of time, and certainly by 2000, Labour's public service reform plans began to become more ambitious. Freed from the shackles of the commitment to adhere to Conservative expenditure plans, and presiding over a successful economy, Labour made increased funds available for public investment. Increased public expenditure was, however, directly linked to service improvement. *The NHS Plan* is perhaps the clearest statement of this with its subtitle, *A plan for investment, a plan for reform* (Secretary of State for Health, 2000). Whereas in 1997 the word 'reform' was avoided in government discourse, Labour now made clear that increased sums for the NHS would only be made available if significant reform was delivered. The theme of modernisation from 1997 persisted, with continuing demands for services to become more responsive and user-focused. It became common for the government to claim that service users expected to be able to behave in public services in the same way as they did while in the private sector (Baldock, 2003; Shaw, 2003; McAteer, 2005; Newman and Vidler, 2006; Clarke et al, 2007).

Labour also persisted with its goal of increased fairness, but through a different policy mechanism. Whereas in 1997 the aim was fairness through collaboration with public professionals and improvement to be negotiated through them, by now a series of centrally imposed targets were appearing (*The Economist*, 2000). Regulatory bodies that were notionally independent of the government were taking an increased role in examining the day-to-day activities of public services (Salter, 1999). Within three years of declaring that its approach to public organisation would not be based around 'command and control', it appeared as if this was exactly what Labour was attempting to achieve. The justification for this centralisation was that high-performing organisations would be granted 'earned autonomy' (Mannion et al, 2003), with greater freedoms from inspection. However, it seemed as if the only freedom available was to do whatever the government told organisations to do (Hoque et al, 2004). When combined with the creation of semi-autonomous inspection agencies, the burden of control accountability on public organisations appeared to have increased dramatically (Broadbent and Laughlin, 1998; Peckham et al, 2005).

Labour's second phase of policy was about trying to extract as much gain from public services as possible through the imposition of stronger inspection and standard-setting bodies, and the devolution to managers and public professionals of the responsibility of meeting centrally set goals. PFI projects began to come to fruition, causing significant concerns about their value for money (Andalo, 2004) and lack of public accountability (Monbiot, 2001). This was the era, in 6 and Peck's terms, of inspection, central standard setting, devolution and earned autonomy. These instruments were second order changes in Hall's terms, as they did not represent a new hierarchy of policy goals.

The return of markets 2003–07

Before Labour's centralising phase reached its conclusion, a third phase of policy began to appear by the end of 2003. According to the former head of the Prime Minister's Delivery Unit, there was a growing realisation that top-down pressure to improve public productivity further was subject to definite limits, and, instead, systemic reform was necessary (Barber, 2007). The two means to achieve this were to move markets back to centre-stage, and to attempt to try and get the public more involved in the organisation and running of public services (Needham, 2003).

Markets were reintroduced in the apparent belief that they would improve the fairness of public provision (Greener, 2004a) by greater equality of access to public services. In education, choice policies were combined with proposals to move children around towns in US-style yellow buses to reach good schools (DfES, 2005). However, the problems of how popular schools were meant to expand to take on more students, and what to do about unpopular schools that fail to attract students, remained largely unresolved. In healthcare, funding changes were made to attempt to make resources follow patient referrals (DH, 2003). However, it is still less than clear exactly how patients are meant to choose between providers of care (Greener, 2005). In addition, because of the inherent complexity of many healthcare decisions, there is strong evidence that patients may simply attempt to refer the decision back to their general practitioner (GP) rather than making it themselves (Schwartz, 2004). While many of us would argue for increased choice prospectively (that is before we are ill), rather fewer of us seem to want it in practice (when actually ill). Despite these problems, former government advisers advocate the extension of Labour's most radical market-based experiment, the use of direct payments and individual budgets in social care, into areas such as healthcare, to achieve greater patient empowerment and supplier responsiveness (Le Grand, 2007).

The use of markets was accompanied by increasingly frantic demands from the government for evidence of service change (Greener, 2004b), with a particular concern that investment by the government generate a sufficient return (Giddens, 2007). This resulted in the re-establishment of the economy as being a central goal of public services – after a period where expansion has occurred in public funding (especially in healthcare), a period of increased parsimony appeared to be asserting itself with managers facing severe penalties for running up deficits in their organisations (Carvel, 2005).

Managers appeared to be moving from having roles primarily as the implementers of policy under a centrally imposed system of performance management, to having instead more of an entrepreneurial role. This change fitted neatly with management ideas around 'public value' in which managers are freed from the rigidities of public delivery in the name of creating better services for users (Moore, 1997), creating the possibility for public organisations to offer differentiated levels of service to their users and to charge extra for premium services.

The devolution associated with entrepreneurship also meant that the government was able to blame local managers when things went wrong (Greener and Powell, 2008).

In education, schools were encouraged to become more diverse, with in England a whole range of new organisational forms appearing including the new and controversial academies (Chitty, 2004; DfES, 2005). Diversity was meant to create choice, and school leaders were told to find private sector partners to help finance service improvements. In healthcare doctors were encouraged to consider themselves as being able to provide their services in a range of new settings, to relocate provision into community settings in order to move services closer to the public and away from the high overheads of hospitals.

The creation of new markets had the effect of dramatically increasing the role of the private sector in public services. This has come through two main routes – through finance and provision. PFI has continued to expand, and a range of public capital projects has been completed that would never have seen the light of day under previous public capital project systems. New schools and hospitals have been particularly visible. However, the long-term value of PFI remains a contentious topic, with public organisations being committed to maintenance payments running long into the future that often seem to offer private partners extremely high rates of return (Pollock, 2004). In terms of the extension of private sector provision, in healthcare a range of treatment centres have appeared that compete directly with public facilities, and not-for-profit organisations such as the Nuffield Trust have now reached a point where their hospitals provide NHS contract care only. On the railways private companies have been encouraged to invest considerably in rolling stock in order to compete with other providers using the same railway lines. Services formerly thought of as needing only to break even now generate substantial surpluses, emphasising the government's view of public services as an investment subject to economic appraisal, evaluation and even return.

Labour's attempts to overcome its reputation as centralising led to an increased use of public participatory mechanisms. In education parents are encouraged not only to be involved in the running of their child's school, but also to actively lobby locally for better provision where necessary (DfES, 2005). In healthcare the public are asked to become 'members' of foundation trust hospitals, to represent their local communities in participatory forums, and to get involved in national and local listening events. As well as being asked to be involved as 'choosers' of local services, the public are being asked to participate as citizens, representing themselves and their local communities in the running of health services. Some commentators suggest that this will create a remarkable experiment in local democracy (Birchall and Simmons, 2004), but others that public participation is likely to be confronted by the usual problems of participation, self-selection and an accountability structure that is so complex as to be unworkable (Klein, 2003). Whereas greater patient choice and public participation can be a means of achieving greater decentralisation of policy and management, if the strong centralisation tendencies of second phase Labour are not changed then they may come to nothing.

From 2007, and the changeover of Prime Minister from Blair to Brown, there appears to be something of a becalming of policy. Brown initially wished to present himself as 'getting on with business', and, especially when it became apparent there would be no election in 2007, appeared to be deliberately going against the hyperactivity of policy announcements in the Blair years. There were some signs that market-based solutions were no longer as favoured, particularly in healthcare, and the planned extensions of the private sector appear to have slowed. It is a little early to say that policy has undergone a change, but there is certainly something of a slowing down. Fourth phase Labour policy so far appears to be about consolidating the gains of the past rather than introducing radical new policies. The systemic reform of public services planned for the third term of the Labour government has slowed, as has the almost manic citizenship of third phase Labour. The language of Brown shows a preference for participation through public volunteering rather than through involvement in the governance of public organisations.

Table 13.1 summarises the four phases of Labour policy, and compares it with the Conservative approach that preceded it.

Discussion

A number of conclusions appear to follow from this analysis. First, Labour has been more radical in its policy than the preceding Conservatives. It has introduced private finance and competition on a scale far exceeding that of anything the supposedly ideological Conservative governments of the 1980s and 1990s did, but without the professional-led protests of the previous decade (Greener, 2006b). Perhaps public professionals are less likely to speak out against a Labour government, or perhaps the Conservatives, despite the lack of radicalism in their later years, actually managed to 'break' the professional groups, at least in terms of their expectation of involvement in the policy-making process, during the 1980s and 1990s. If this is the case, it would

Table 13.1: Goals and mechanisms for the Conservatives and Labour

Government and period	Policy goal and key mechanisms for achieving it	6 and Peck elements emphasised
Conservative 1992–97	Efficiency, economy Managers legitimated by the market	
First period Labour (1997–99)	Efficiency, fairness (but within economic constraint) – 'joined-up' government Collaboration within a network of provision	Area-based initiatives Private capital Access Coordination
Second period Labour (2000–03)	Efficiency, conformity, fairness (within expanding resources) Performance management, bottom-up involvement	Inspection Central standard setting Devolution Earned autonomy Private capital Access (equality of access)
Third period Labour (2002–07)	Efficiency, economy, responsiveness, fairness (with gradual reassertion of resource constraint) Markets, performance management, bottom-up involvement	Devolution (new markets) Central standard setting Inspection Earned autonomy Private capital Access (equality of access) Citizenship participation
Fourth period Labour (2007–)	Efficiency, responsiveness, fairness Markets, but with limited growth, performance management, 'bedding down' of previous reforms	Devolution (markets, but unclear whether they will continue to be expanded) Central standard setting Inspection Earned autonomy Private capital Access Citizenship participation through volunteering

be among their most significant legacies, alongside recasting services towards a more managerialist/customer-oriented model and away from the trust and professional dominance of the past.

In these terms the Conservatives used markets primarily as an instrument to aid managers in bringing public professionals under greater control. They had an ideological bias towards market solutions, but only used them in the public sector as giving managers greater leverage, rather than treating them as an intrinsic good. The exception to this, rail privatisation, was rushed and incoherent, the act of a government that knew its time was nearing the end. Labour, in contrast, appears to use markets because it believes they will improve service delivery, but also because it believes they are fairer (see, for example, Reid, 2004). Third phase Labour policy does not consider markets as one possible tool among many for the improved delivery of public services, but instead carries an assumption that markets are nearly always best. During their time in office the Conservatives were considered to be producing policy that was ideological (Taylor-Gooby, 1985), but in retrospect they appear to be remarkably pragmatic. From 2003 to 2007 Labour appeared to pursue policies with little idea as to how they were meant to work, but that were based instead on a simple faith in the market to deliver, with managers and professionals not trusted unless they worked under competitive disciplines. There is therefore an inversion – whereas the Conservatives appeared to use markets as a means of achieving greater managerial ends, Labour appeared to use managers as a means of achieving greater market ends.

Markets in the Conservative era were internal in that they were between public providers, whereas for Labour they are external, involving a mix of different kinds of providers. Labour believes it is the private sector mechanism, the market, that is more important than the managers. The Conservatives celebrated the chief executive officer, but Labour celebrate the entrepreneur – the one who successfully works within the private market mechanism. The Conservatives wanted private-sector style management to rule, and used market mechanisms to try and achieve this aim. Labour appears instead to use markets as the tool to try and achieve private (entrepreneurial) management. As such, managers are arguably more sacred to the Conservatives, whereas for Labour they are expendable, hence the frequent threats to remove managers who fail under its performance management systems. Under the Conservatives, bureaucrats and professionals were the enemies, whereas Labour is prepared to mobilise against others on a more wide-ranging basis; anyone who blocks (or even questions) market-based reform is portrayed as out of touch. For the Conservatives professionals did have a place, as principals acting on behalf of their customers/agents. For Labour, however, nothing other than directly empowering service users will do, through a range of choice and voice mechanisms. It is not clear how either of these is meant to work exactly.

The Labour focus on attempting to achieve greater fairness and access is a key distinguishing feature from the Conservative policy of the 1980s and 1990s, and manifests itself with particular initiatives. Labour prefers to extend existing policies to give greater access to groups previously discriminated against – hence its change to the Right to Buy to also allow same-sex couples to purchase their own social housing (DETR, 2000). Its attempts at achieving greater public consultation can be read as a cynical attempt to get buy-in, or a genuine concern to try and hear what individuals and groups have to say, even if they do not always appear to make a great deal of difference – perhaps Labour was sure it could convince everyone of the benefit of a market-based solution (Leys, 2003). In either case, there has certainly been a great deal more in terms of consultation going on under Labour than there ever was under the Conservatives, and also a great deal more means for individuals to participate, although, again, how serious these participative mechanisms turn out to be is another matter. Equally, the use of strong central performance management systems and targets in public services has been justified as a means of improving the fairness of public services by guaranteeing minimum standards. Labour is concerned with fairness, but appears to believe this can be achieved through a mixture of strong central intervention, equality of access to the market and increased public consultation.

Conclusion

Labour's approach to public reform appears to have incrementally reordered the hierarchy of goals the Conservatives had in place rather than creating a distinctively new set. They represent, even at their most radical, a series of second order changes, particularly based around inspection, performance management and the increased use of the market, rather than a third order or paradigmatic change. Labour's distinctive goal is that of trying to improve fairness, but the extent to which it has achieved this is open to question, with commentators arguing that Labour policies will take a significant time to have an impact (Giddens, 2007). The reticence of the Brown government to embrace the emerging market radicalism of his predecessor means that third order change now seems less likely. Were the public sector to become more organised on market-based terms, as Le Grand (2007) suggests, and choice to dominate service provision, this would lead to a dramatically new dynamic in public services, and so potentially a policy paradigm shift.

The means Labour has used to achieve its policy goals are significantly more radical than the Conservatives'. Labour has not rejected the Thatcher settlement (Jenkins, 2006), putting aside universal, standardised and professional-centred delivery in favour of differentiated, personalised, user-centred services instead. It has, however, gone rather further down the road of reform than the Conservatives ever attempted, especially in its use of private finance and market mechanisms. Perhaps Labour is best regarded as taking the Conservatives' approach to public reform to its logical conclusion rather than having a significant new approach in its own right.

References

6, P. and Peck, E. (2004a) 'Modernisation: the ten commitments of New Labour's approach to public management', *International Public Management Journal*, vol 7, no 1, pp 1-18.

6, P. and Peck, E. (2004b) 'New Labour's modernization in the public sector: a neo-Durkheimian approach and the case of mental health services', *Public Administration*, vol 82, pp 83-108.

Andalo, D. (2004) 'Hospitals charged high premiums for PFI projects', 23 December (http://society.guardian.co.uk/privatefinance/story/0,8150,1358757,00.html).

Baldock, J. (2003) 'On being a welfare consumer in a consumer society', *Social Policy and Society*, vol 2, pp 65-71.

Barber, M. (2007) *Instruction to deliver: Tony Blair, the public services and the challenge of achieving targets*, London: Politico's Publishing.

Bevir, M. (2000) 'New Labour: a study in ideology', *British Journal of Politics and International Relations*, vol 2, pp 277-301.

Birchall, J. and Simmons, R. (2004) *User power: The participation of users in public services*, London: National Consumer Council.

Broadbent, J. and Laughlin, R. (1998) 'Resisting the "new public management". Absorption and absorbing groups in schools and GP practices in the UK', *Accounting, Auditing and Accountability Journal*, vol 11, pp 403-35.

Carvel, J. (2005) 'Hewitt tells hospitals with deficits to delay operations', *The Guardian*, 7 December, p 4.

Chitty, C. (2004) *Education policy in Britain*, Basingstoke: Palgrave Macmillan.

Clarke, J. and Newman, J. (1997) *The managerial state*, London: Sage Publications.

Clarke, J., Newman, J., Smith, N., Vidler, E. and Westmarland, L. (2007) *Creating citizen-consumers: Changing publics and changing public services*, London: Sage Publications.

DETR (Department of the Environment, Transport and the Regions) (2000) *Quality and choice: A decent home for all*, London: The Stationery Office.

DfEE (Department for Education and Employment) (1997) *Excellence in schools*, London: The Stationery Office.

DfES (Department for Education and Skills) (2005) *Higher standards, better schools for all*, London: The Stationery Office.

DH (Department of Health) (2003) *Building on the best: Choice, responsiveness and equity in the NHS*, London: DH.

Economist, The (2000) 'Target mad', 29 July, p 32.

Fairclough, N. (2000) *New Labour, new language?*, London: Routledge.

Ferlie, E. (1994a) 'The creation and evolution of quasi markets in the public sector: early evidence from the National Health Service', *Policy & Politics*, vol 22, pp 105-12.

Ferlie, E. (1994b) 'The evolution of quasi-markets in the NHS: early evidence', in W. Bartlett, C. Propper, D. Wilson and J. Le Grand (eds) *Quasi-markets in the welfare state*, Bristol: SAUS Publications, University of Bristol.

Gabe, J., Kelleher, D. and Williams, G. (1994) *Challenging medicine*, London: Routledge.

George, V. and Wilding, P. (1994) *Ideology and social welfare*, London: Harvester Wheatsheaf.

Giddens, A. (1998) *The Third Way: The renewal of social democracy*, Cambridge: Polity Press.

Giddens, A. (2007) *Over to you, Mr Brown*, Cambridge: Polity Press.

Greener, I. (2001) 'Social learning and macroeconomic policy in Britain', *Journal of Public Policy*, vol 21, pp 133-52.

Greener, I. (2004a) 'Changing words, changing times: what difference has the change in Health Secretary made?', *British Journal of Health Care Management*, vol 10, pp 86-8.

Greener, I. (2004b) 'The three moments of New Labour's health policy discourse', *Policy & Politics*, vol 32, pp 303-16.

Greener, I. (2005) 'The role of the patient in healthcare reform: customer, consumer or creator?', in I.S. Dawson and C. Sausmann (eds) *Future health organisations and systems*, Basingstoke: Palgrave, pp 227-45.

Greener, I. (2006a) 'Path dependency and the creation and reform of the NHS', in N. Smyth (ed) *Health care in transition, Volume 3*, New York: Nova Science.

Greener, I. (2006b) 'Where are the medical voices raised in protest?', *British Medical Journal*, vol 330, p 660.

Greener, I. and Powell, M. (2008) 'The changing governance of the NHS; reform in a post-Keynesian health service', *Human Relations*, no 61, pp 617-36.

Hall, P.A. (1990) *The power of economic ideas*, Princeton, NJ: Princeton University Press.

Hall, P.A. (1993) 'Policy paradigms, social learning and the state: the case of economic policy making in Britain', *Comparative Politics*, vol 25, no 3, pp 275-96.

Hay, C. and Watson, M. (1999) 'Labour's economic policy: studiously courting competence', in G. Taylor (ed) *The impact of New Labour*, London: Macmillan, pp 149-61.

Hoque, K., Davis, S. and Humphreys, M. (2004) 'Freedom to do what you are told: senior management team autonomy in an NHS acute trust', *Public Administration*, vol 82, pp 355-76.

Jenkins, S. (2006) *Thatcher and sons: A revolution in three acts*, London: Allen Lane.

Jessop, B. (2002) *The future of the capitalist state*, Cambridge: Polity Press.

Keegan, W. (2003) *The prudence of Mr Gordon Brown*, London: John Wiley and Sons.

Klein, R. (2003) 'Governance for NHS foundation trusts', *British Medical Journal*, no 326, pp 174-5.

Kuhn, T. (1970) *The structure of scientific revolutions*, Chicago, IL: University of Chicago Press.

Labour Party (1997) *New Labour because Britain deserves better*, London: Labour Party.

Le Grand, J. (2007) *The other invisible hand*, Princeton, NJ: Princeton University Press.

Leys, C. (2003) *Market-driven politics: Neoliberal democracy and the public interest*, London: Verso.

McAteer, M. (2005) 'The government's choice agenda', *Consumer Policy Review*, vol 15, pp 79-84.

Maddock, S. and Morgan, G. (1998) 'Barriers to transformation: beyond bureaucracy and the market conditions for collaboration in health and social care', *International Journal of Public Sector Management*, vol 11, pp 234-51.

Mahoney, J. (2000) 'Path dependency in historical sociology', *Theory and Society*, vol 29, pp 507-48.

Majone, G. (1989) *Evidence, argument and the policymaking process*, New Haven, CT: Yale University Press.

Mannion, R., Goddard, M., Kuhn, M. and Bate, A. (2003) *Earned autonomy in the NHS: A report for the Department of Health*, London: Department of Health.

Mannion, R. and Smith, P. (1998) 'How providers are chosen in the mixed economy of community care', in W. Bartlett, J. Roberts and J. Le Grand (eds) *Quasi-market reforms in the 1990s: A revolution in social policy*, London: Routledge.

Monbiot, G. (2001) *Captive state: The corporate takeover of Britain*, London: Pan.

Moore, M. (1997) *Creating public value: Strategic management in government*, Cambridge, MA: Harvard University Press.

Needham, C. (2003) *Citizen-consumers: New Labour's marketplace democracy*, London: Catalyst Forum.

Newman, J. and Vidler, E. (2006) 'Discriminating customers, responsible patients, empowered users: consumerism and the modernisation of health care', *Journal of Social Policy*, vol 35, pp 193-209.

Oliver, M. (1996) 'Social learning and macroeconomic policy in the UK since 1979', *Essays in Economic Business History*, vol 14, pp 117-31.

Oliver, M. (1997) *Whatever happened to monetarism? Economic planning and social learning in the United Kingdom since 1979*, Aldershot: Ashgate.

Peckham, S., Exworthy, M., Greener, I. and Powell, M. (2005) 'Decentralizing health services: more local accountability or just more central control', *Public Money and Management*, vol 25, pp 221-8.

Pollock, A. (2004) *NHS plc: The privitisation of our health care*, London: Verso.

Powell, M. (1998) 'New Labour and the "new" UK NHS', *Critical Public Health*, vol 8, pp 167-73.

Reid, J. (2004) 'Managing new realities – integrating the care landscape', Speech given on 11 March.

Salter, B. (1999) 'Change in the governance of medicine: the politics of self-regulation', *Policy & Politics*, vol 27, pp 143-58.

Schwartz, B. (2004) *The paradox of choice: Why less is more*, New York: HarperCollins.

Secretary of State for Health (1997) *The New NHS: Modern, dependable*, London: The Stationery Office.

Secretary of State for Health (2000) *The NHS Plan: A plan for investment, a plan for reform*, London: The Stationery Office.

Shaw, I. (2003) 'Introduction: themed section on consumerism and social policy', *Social Policy and Society*, vol 2, pp 33-4.

Taylor-Gooby, P. (1985) *Public opinion, ideology and state welfare*, London: Routledge and Kegan Paul.

Timmins, N. (1995a) *The five giants*, London: Fontana.

Timmins, N. (1995b) 'How three top managers nearly sank the reforms', *Health Service Journal*, 29 July, pp 11-13.

Timmins, N. (2002) 'A time for change in the British NHS: an interview with Alan Milburn', *Health Affairs*, vol 21, pp 129-35.

FOURTEEN

Social Democratic reforms of the welfare state: Germany and the UK compared

Martin Seeleib-Kaiser

Introduction

Social Democrats regained power in the UK and Germany in the late 1990s, after long periods spent in opposition. This chapter takes stock of welfare state reforms in both countries and aims to answer whether, and how far, 10 years of Social Democratic governments have left their *modern* imprints on the institutional set-up of the welfare state, based on Hall's categorisations of change (1993; see also Chapter One, this volume). As the dimensions of 'modernisation' identified by 6 and Peck (2004) are largely peculiar elements of the UK modernisation process, I will refrain from operationalising these in comparative analysis here. A common thread of 'modernising' welfare state arrangements in both countries, however, has been the focus on reducing the dependency ratio and increasing employment rates, while at the same time highlighting the need for social justice. This approach to modernisation is in accordance with some of the elements outlined by Esping-Andersen et al (2002). After briefly sketching out the socioeconomic conditions and institutional design of the two welfare states in the late 1990s, this will serve as a reference point for further analysis. I will elaborate in greater detail on the main elements of the common modernisation themes, before addressing the various reforms in the domains of (un)employment, pensions and family policies. This chapter is limited to these three domains because, firstly, they constitute the core dimensions of mainstream comparative welfare state regime analyses (cf Esping-Andersen, 1990, 1999), and, secondly, space limitations do not allow for a more comprehensive analysis. In conclusion I aim to assess these reforms in the light of the research question.

Socioeconomic conditions and institutional welfare state design in the late 1990s

According to widely accepted categorisations, Germany and the UK are said to have very different forms of capitalism and welfare state arrangements. Germany belongs to the Conservative/Christian-Democratic welfare regime, relying primarily on social insurance, while the UK is usually characterised as a Liberal welfare state, relying primarily on the market and means-tested benefits (Esping-Andersen, 1990, 1999). While the main aim of the German unemployment and old-age pension schemes has been to achieve social stability and cohesion (mainly through guaranteeing the individually achieved living standard for unemployed [male] workers as well as pensioners), the main aim of the largely means-tested UK transfer system has been to alleviate poverty (cf Goodin et al, 1999). Despite these differences, both countries have promoted the strong male breadwinner model, which has had significant implications for female labour force participation and the provision of childcare (Lewis, 1992).

As a consequence of economic collapse following German unification and the subsequent steep increase in unemployment, extending the West German welfare state to the East, while continuing to rely on social insurance contributions as the main financing mechanism, led to an unprecedented increase in social insurance contributions. These subsequently not only exerted pressure on those German companies engaged in the global economy, but overall increased the tax wedge, primarily limiting the growth of jobs in the less exposed service sectors (Scharpf, 1995). From a social policy perspective the expansion of the social insurance system to the East was successful in the short term, as it provided quite generous financial means to those who had become unemployed or retired (early) as a result of the severe labour market adjustments after 1990, thereby effectively limiting the extent of poverty. However, sharply increased social insurance contributions and the reluctance to raise income taxes to finance the adjustment costs associated with German unification triggered retrenchment policies in the domains of the unemployment and old-age insurance system only a few years later. For the unemployed the reforms meant a reduction in replacement rates and a tightening of conditionality rules. Whereas benefits for current pensioners were largely left unchanged, the Conservative–Liberal coalition government significantly reduced the replacement rate for future pensioners of the baby boom generation. Thus both policy areas saw a withdrawal from the once guiding principle of publicly guaranteeing the achieved living standard. At the time, these reforms were vehemently opposed by the Social Democrats, who characterised them as unnecessary and unfair (Bleses and Seeleib-Kaiser, 2004).

With regard to family policies, the Christian Democrats have pursued an expansionary policy since the mid-1980s. The various measures included the introduction and subsequent expansion of parental leave and a parental (leave) benefit, as well as child-rearing credits in the old-age social insurance scheme. Furthermore, the introduction of an entitlement to a place in a childcare facility for every child between the ages of three and six led to a significant expansion of services in the second half of the 1990s (Bleses and Seeleib-Kaiser, 2004). Although we witnessed a steep and almost continuous increase in unemployment (with an increasingly high percentage of long-term unemployed), the poverty rate (based on 60% of median income) only increased marginally, from 12% (1993) to 13.1% (1998), despite the huge structural adjustments associated with German unification (Seeleib-Kaiser, 2007, p 28).

During the long tenure of the Conservatives in government, the British welfare state became (more) Liberal. Within pension policies the earnings-related programme was more or less eliminated and the benefit level of the universal Basic State Pension continued to be insufficient to lift pensioners out of poverty. After deregulating the labour market in the 1980s (Howell, 2006), the Conservative government in 1996 eventually replaced the earnings-related unemployment insurance benefit with a flat-rate Jobseeker's Allowance, with benefits set at the social assistance level and conditional on accepting basically any legal job offer (Clasen, 2005). In order to strengthen work incentives, in 1988 the government introduced the so-called 'family credit' that provided in-work benefits for poor families (Funk, 2007). Overall, an explicit family policy going beyond the provision of child allowances or tax credits was not perceived to be within the responsibility of the state. Partly as a result of these social policies, the socioeconomic situation in the UK differed remarkably from that in Germany at the time when Social Democrats gained power in the late 1990s. Although unemployment had started to decline in the mid-1990s, a significant proportion of the workforce was occupied in low-paying jobs;[1] poverty, and especially child poverty, increased significantly during the Conservative tenure in government. In the mid-1990s, the UK was one of the most unequal societies in the OECD (Organisation for Economic Co-operation and Development) world; its Gini coefficient was higher than in any other rich country except for the US. Its overall poverty rate (defined as 60% of median income) stood at more than 20% (LIS, 2007).

Modernising the welfare state

Despite these socioeconomic and institutional differences, both Social Democratic parties developed similar themes with regard to 'modernisation', as they repositioned and rebranded themselves 'New Labour' and the 'New Centre' (*Die Neue Mitte*) (see also Hudson et al, 2008). In the election campaigns both parties pledged that they would be fiscally 'responsible', while at the same time they aimed to achieve a more just society through greater opportunity. Although the state was said to play an important role in achieving this goal, both parties emphasised the potential benefits of the market and market mechanisms. While increasing the employment rate was a key element, the state should mainly function as an enabler by ensuring that 'work pays' and reducing non-wage labour costs through structural reforms. In accordance with the emphasis on activation instead of compensation and the promotion of greater self-reliance, all benefit recipients were to be assessed for their potential to earn. Finally, both parties highlighted the need to help parents balance work and family life (cf Labour, 1997; SPD, 1998; Blair and Schroeder, 1999).

An analysis of the 1998 party manifesto of the Social Democratic Party (SPD) clearly shows that it did not intend to expand the welfare state in the medium term, despite promises to revoke some policy changes of the prior Conservative coalition government in the short run. Social Democrats committed themselves to 'budgetary discipline' and the aim of reducing the public debt. Within such an environment there would be no room for deficit-financed employment policies. The Social Democrats had made it explicit in their election manifesto and later stated it again in their coalition agreement with the Alliance90/ The Greens that they would reform the old-age insurance system with the goal of expanding private and company-based pension plans as key elements. This approach was part of their broader strategy towards self-reliance, which also included a call for 'work instead of assistance', that is, a reform of the various support programmes for the (long-term) unemployed and an increased emphasis on activation. In addition, they called for a reduction of social insurance contributions as a means to promote job growth. Finally, in terms of family policy the party manifesto proposed improvements of parental leave provisions, an expansion of the child allowance and tax credits, as well as an expansion of childcare facilities. Instead of using the term 'modernisation', German Social Democrats used the term 'innovation' as their buzzword (SPD, 1998; cf Seeleib-Kaiser, 2004).

Going beyond the pledge of German Social Democrats, New Labour not only limited itself to refrain from a Keynesian approach to full employment and to stress the need for sound public finances, but explicitly committed itself to the spending limits set by the Conservative government for the first two years. Although the manifesto was very vague on specific commitments with regard to tackling the high levels of poverty, it did mention it in relation to reducing welfare dependency by reforming the tax and benefit system as well as helping people into jobs (cf Stewart and Hills, 2005). As Toynbee and Walker (2005, p 7) put it: 'social justice had barely been mentioned at election time, for fear of alarming middle England'. The key theme of New Labour's social security reform initiatives has been the promotion of paid employment, that is, to create incentives for employment and to 'make work pay' (Kemp, 2005, pp 17-18). This also included a National Childcare Strategy to help parents balance family and work life (Labour Party, 1997). After two years in government, Prime Minister Tony Blair unexpectedly announced: 'ours is the first generation to end child poverty forever. It is a twenty year mission but I believe it can be done' (quoted in Stewart and Hills, 2005, p 11). In addition to fighting child poverty, reducing poverty among pensioners became a priority (Stewart and Hills, 2005, p 11). However, it must be emphasised that Labour did not intend to pursue a comprehensive redistributive approach despite the internationally very high levels of inequality and poverty. As Blair stated: 'justice for me is concentrated on lifting incomes of those that don't have a decent income. It's not a burning ambition of mine to make sure that David Beckham earns less money' (quoted in Sefton and Sutherland, 2005, p 233).

The various elements of the Social Democratic approach towards 'modernisation' in both countries are summarised in Table 14.1.

Table 14.1: Social Democrats' aims and instruments of 'modern' welfare states

Aims	Instruments
Achieve 'sound' public finances	No new Keynesian investment programmes; limit overall public spending; no income tax increases; reduction of income tax rates and social insurance contributions (Germany)
Increase employment	Activation (through welfare-to-work programmes); reduction of social insurance contributions (Germany)
Improve support for families	Revision of transfer and tax systems; introduction/expansion of work–life balance policies
Reduce poverty	Increase employment (UK)

Social Democratic welfare state reforms in Germany and the UK

Welfare state reforms in Germany

During the first four years of the Red–Green coalition government no *major* reforms were enacted in the areas of active labour market policy, unemployment insurance or social assistance. The work on a comprehensive pension reform proposal, however, started very early in the tenure of the Red–Green coalition government. The main aim was to limit future social insurance contributions for pensions to a maximum of 20% of gross wages in 2020 and 22% in 2030. This limitation was accomplished by a significant reduction in the net replacement ratio from 70% to about 64% for a standard pensioner in 2030. Additional changes in the benefit calculation enacted in the subsequent years will further reduce the net replacement rate to 52% (Schmähl, 2007).[2] To mitigate poverty among pensioners, the coalition government introduced a de facto means-tested minimum pension. In addition, workers are encouraged through public subsidies to voluntarily enrol in certified private or collective occupational pension schemes. As a result of these reforms, inequality among pensioners is likely to increase and 'a remarkable percentage of pensioners will receive a pension only just above or even below social assistance level' (Schmähl, 2007, p 330). In other words, these reforms will over time lead to a withdrawal from the principle of publicly guaranteeing the achieved living standard. Through processes of re-commodification and marketisation the future German pension system will most likely have more in common with ideal Liberal approaches to welfare, than 'Conservative' approaches that dominated in the past.

In the realm of labour market policies, the Red–Green government by and large sustained the approach pursued by the previous Conservative government during its first term, that is, retrenchment of benefits and incremental reforms towards activation. Yet, after scandalous practices within the Public Employment Service (PES) became public in 2002, Chancellor Gerhard Schroeder appointed the Hartz Commission to develop proposals to reform the PES. The most significant element of the Hartz reforms enacted in 2003 and 2004 is the integration of the unemployment and social assistance schemes into one benefit scheme for the long-term unemployed (so-called 'Hartz IV'). Before the reform those long-term unemployed workers who had exhausted their unemployment insurance benefits were entitled to unemployment assistance benefits – a benefit scheme which combined earnings-related and means-tested elements; for long-term unemployed workers with previously well-paying jobs the unemployment assistance benefit was generally higher than the social assistance benefit.

Since the Hartz IV legislation became effective in 2005, all needy unemployed people not in receipt of the earnings-related unemployment insurance benefit are entitled to this new means-tested and tax-funded 'basic security for jobseekers' benefit (ALG II). Central objectives of this new scheme are the fast (re)integration of the unemployed into the labour market and a reduction of benefit dependence. To facilitate job take-up a wage subsidy for a maximum duration of 24 months can be made available. In addition, earning disregards for ALG II recipients were improved, that is, low-income workers can receive ALG II benefits in addition to their wages. Any legal job is now considered suitable for claimants of ALG II. Conceptually integrated with the new ALG II, the maximum duration of the regular unemployment insurance benefit was reduced to 12 months (and 18 months [instead of 32] for those aged 55 and older).[3] These changes effectively turned the unemployment compensation benefit for the long-term unemployed, which in the past to a considerable extent built on the objective of status maintenance (especially for the older, long-term unemployed), into a fully means-tested system along the lines of the general social assistance scheme. In parallel the government retrenched traditional measures of active labour market policies, such as job training and direct job creation (Seeleib-Kaiser and Fleckenstein, 2007). To make work pay, the parties of the Grand Coalition wrangle with the introduction of minimum wages for various industrial sectors and in December 2007 Parliament enacted an hourly minimum wage of €9.80 for the postal sector (FAZ [*Frankfurter Allgemeine Zeitung*], 20 December 2007).

With regard to family policies, the Red–Green coalition continued the expansionary trajectory of the prior Conservative government, albeit at an accelerated speed. As a first step, it improved the flexibility of the existing parental leave scheme. Since 2001, parents working full time are legally entitled to reduce their working time (Leitner, 2003). Furthermore, the child allowance was significantly increased, rising from €112 per month in 1998 to €154 in 2002 (Bleses and Seeleib-Kaiser, 2004); parents with a low income are entitled to an additional monthly supplement of €140 (introduced in 2005). This expansionary trajectory was further accelerated and changed direction after the 2005 elections and the formation of a Grand Coalition government between Christian Democrats and Social Democrats. Starting on 1 January 2007, parents are entitled to an earnings-related parental leave benefit with a net wage replacement ratio of 67% (capped at a maximum of €1,800 per month) for the duration of 12 months (with an additional two months if the other partner takes these; in Scandinavia these are often referred to as 'Daddy Months'). Under the new regulations all those parents not previously employed will continue to be entitled to a flat monthly benefit of €300 (BMFSJ, 2006).

Since January 2005, municipalities are as a first stage required to provide daycare for all those children under the age of three whose parents work or are enrolled in education and training. This programme is estimated to cost €1.5 billion and is to be financed through 'savings' for municipalities achieved by the merger of the unemployment and social assistance programmes for the unemployed (BMFSFJ, 2004). In a second stage, based on a compromise between the political parties of the Grand Coalition government in spring 2007, publicly financed/ subsidised care for children under the age of three will fully meet the demand by 2013, at which time the government will also introduce an individual entitlement to childcare for every child. Late in 2007, the federal government has allocated an additional €2.14 billion to support the expansion of childcare facilities by the *Länder*. It is estimated that the number of places will reach 750,000 by 2013, increasing coverage for that age group from approximately 14% in 2005/06 to 35% (FAZ, 15 May 2007, 20 December 2007).

Welfare state reforms in the UK

The New Labour government started quite early in its first term to enact measures (the so-called New Deals) to bring various groups of unemployed or workless people into work. These measures were designed to encourage people without employment, especially benefit claimants, to take up work through assisting with job search and work preparation. For certain groups, such as unemployed youth, receipt of benefits was made conditional on the participation in the New Deal programmes. The aim was fast (re)integration into the labour market, and not to provide extensive training to significantly improve skills (Clasen, 2005). Thus, it can be argued that these 'activation' measures are at least indirectly and partially coupled to a low-wage strategy. However, to make work pay New Labour introduced the National Minimum Wage and expanded the pre-existing system of tax credits in 1999. The National Minimum Wage was subsequently increased several times and in 2007 stood at £5.52 per hour. The Family Credit of the previous Conservative government was replaced by the more generous Working Families' Tax Credit, which in 2003 was divided into the Working Tax Credit and the Child Tax Credit. In order to be eligible for the tax credit people are required to work at least 16 hours per week. The maximum combined benefit from the two tax credits in the tax year 2005/06 was £8,475 per annum for a household with a joint annual income of £8,000 and three children. Someone aged 25 or over and working 30 hours a week at the National Minimum Wage would have earned £7,566 during that tax year. Further credits were introduced for people with disabilities and previously unemployed people aged 50 and older on returning to work after receiving benefits for a duration of six months or more (McNight, 2005).

However, New Labour did not change the unemployment benefit itself, which had been transformed by the previous Conservative government from an earnings-related benefit to a flat-rate benefit; its level has remained equivalent to the means-tested social assistance benefit (cf Clasen, 2005). In the UK context it is important to note that Incapacity Benefits were used in some economically depressed regions to support unemployed workers. Overall the number of Incapacity Benefit recipients exceeds the number of those claiming unemployment benefits. Thus it is not surprising that the government has decided to reform the scheme with the aim of moving many of the claimants back into the labour market (cf Kemp, 2008).

The UK pension system is very complex and only understood fully by few experts. It consists of a contributory Basic State Pension, with a benefit level below the social assistance level, a means-tested pension benefit (since 2003 called the guarantee element of the Pension Credit), a State Second Pension and occupational pension schemes. Continuing on a Liberal trajectory the New Labour government proclaimed early in its tenure to reverse the existing mix between public and private pension provision to 40% public and 60% private. In order to achieve that goal and specifically to increase the enrolment of workers with low to medium earnings in private pension plans, the government introduced the Stakeholder Pension in 2001 (Meyer and Bridgen, 2007, pp 9–10). In parallel the government focused on improving the income of poor pensioners, for whom it has increased spending by an estimated £8.5 billion between 1998/99 and 2003/04 (Evandrou and Falkingham, 2005, p 170). One key element has been the increase in the guarantee element of the Pension Credit, which rose from £69 per week in 1997 to £119.05 in 2007 (cf Kemp, 2005, p 19). After the Turner Commission, appointed by the government to assess the occupational and private pension system in 2002, 'concluded that voluntarism was "in serious and probably irreversible decline"' (cited in Meyer and Bridgen, 2007, p 11), and proposed a number of recommendations in 2005, the government accepted that voluntarism had not worked and policy change was needed. According to the 2006 pension White Paper the British pension system will be significantly reformed within the near future. The two main reform elements are: (a) the introduction of a national pension savings scheme for all those who are not enrolled in an employer scheme on an auto-enrolment basis in 2012, to be financed primarily through employees' and employers' contributions (total 8% of earnings); and (b) a change in the cost-of-living adjustment mechanism of the Basic State Pension, to be linked to earnings increases, instead of price increases, after 2012. It is expected that these reforms will lead to fewer pensioners having to rely on means-tested pension payments (DWP, 2006).

Since 1997, incremental reforms with regard to family policies, especially work–family balance policies, have cumulated to 'a significant policy change in the sum of its parts' (Lewis and Campbell, 2007, p 378). A core element of lifting families out of poverty was employment. Thus, the most important elements with regard to improving family incomes are tax credits (see above).[4] However, to make employment more attractive for both parents, improvements were necessary with regard to the provision of childcare, leave and flexible working time arrangements. Since 1998, New Labour has consistently aimed at improving childcare provision. Measures included the introduction of free nursery care for children aged three for 12.5 hours per week in 1998 and its subsequent expansion to four-year-olds. By 2010, 15 hours of free childcare per week will be provided (early years learning). Similar to other area-based initiatives the government launched the Sure Start programme to improve the situation of children in disadvantaged areas. Overall, the government has significantly increased the value of childcare subsidies for low-income parents from £46 million (1998) to £884 million (2004) (cf Lewis and Campbell, 2007, pp 372 f). According to figures from the Daycare Trust (2006, p 4), 644,000 net new places have been created since 1997, and about a quarter of children under the age of three were enrolled in childcare during 2004 (OECD, 2007c).

With the implementation of the European Directive on parental leave New Labour introduced the entitlement to parental leave for every employee in the UK with children under five, who had worked for their employers for at least one year. Furthermore, maternity leave has been extended from 26 to 39 weeks (and is expected to be further extended to 52 weeks), while maternity pay has risen from £55.70 to £112.75 per week since 1997. So far New Labour has not significantly increased the leave for fathers, who have been entitled to only two weeks' statutory paid leave since 2003 (Ben-Galim and Gambles, 2008).[5] Finally, New Labour has introduced *the right* for employees with children under the age of six *to request* from their employer to work flexible working patterns; this right has been extended to carers of adults through the 2006 work and families legislation (Lewis and Campbell, 2007, p 374).

Comparing 'Social Democratic' reforms: the outcome dimension

The welfare state reforms in Germany and the UK did not follow the lines of an ideal-typical Social-Democratic welfare state trajectory, as could be expected from the various theories building on partisanship or the power resources model (Stephens, 1979; Korpi, 1983; Garrett, 1998). Moreover, both countries pursued policies that were in accordance with key elements of their approach towards 'modernisation'. While overall employment rates increased in both countries, the UK witnessed especially strong increases in the female employment rate (age 25-34)[6] and among older male workers, the latter also being particularly strong in Germany since 2003[7] (see Figure 14.1).

Figure 14.1: Employment rates

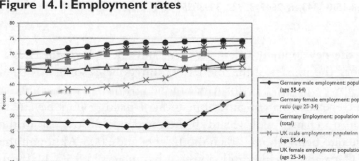

Source: OECD Labour Force Survey (data retrieved 20/12/07 from www.oecd.org/document/15/0,3343,en_2649_33927_38938959_1_1_1_1,00.html)

The remarkable decline in unemployment in the UK, which had started in the mid-1990s, continued until 2001 and the unemployment rate has been more or less stable, at around 5%, since. In Germany, the unemployment rate continued to decline during the first two years of the Social Democratic-led government, before rising sharply until 2005. The youth unemployment (age 15–24) rate was significantly lower in Germany than in the UK until the early 2000s, before rising sharply. While the UK youth unemployment rate saw a significant decline in the late 1990s, it once again rose sharply in 2005 and 2006 (see Figure 14.2). However, if we look at youth (age 15–19) not in education, employment or training in 2004, the picture changes significantly, as the UK rate stood at 10%, growing annually by 5% between 1995 and 2004, while the German rate was clearly below 5% (OECD, 2007c).

Figure 14.2: Unemployment rates

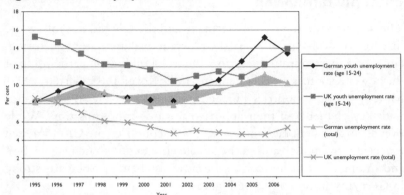

Source: OECD Labour Force Survey (data retrieved 20/12/07 from www.oecd.org/document/15/0,3343,en_2649_33927_38938959_1_1_1_1,00.html)

Taking the development of employment and unemployment rates as indicators, the impact of the 'modernisation' policies so far has been mixed; however, overall performance in the UK has been much better than in Germany. Analysing the dimension of 'making work pay' there has been no change with regard to the incidence of low pay in the UK, the rate being about 20% in both 1995 and 2005. Although the rate in Germany is significantly lower, it has increased from 11.1% in 1995 to 15.8% in 2005 (OECD, 2007a, p 268).

The story would be incomplete without a closer look at the development of poverty. In Germany the poverty rate among the unemployed increased from 33% to 41% between 1998 and 2003, while the overall poverty rate increased from 12.1% to 13.5% over the same period. The poverty rate among pensioners remained more or less stable at 11.8%, but is expected to increase in the future as a result of the recent pension reforms (cf Seeleib-Kaiser, 2007, p 28).[8] New Labour has been successful in so far as the overall poverty rate has dropped by two percentage points, from 20% (1997/98) to 18% (2005/06), which continues to be one of highest rates in the European Union (EU). The poverty rate for children has declined from 27% to 22% and the rate for pensioners from 25% to 21%, whereas the poverty rate for working-age adults has remained constant, at about 15% (DWP, 2007).[9]

How successful have both governments been in achieving sound finances? Taking annual budget deficits as indicators, we witness significant improvements in the late 1990s, before budget deficits once again increased significantly, especially in Germany. While in the UK the increase in the deficit might be at least partially related to increased investments in various public services, especially healthcare, the increase in Germany was largely the result of economic recession coupled with the effects of tax cuts (cf Seeleib-Kaiser, 2004). Due to the very positive economic development in Germany since 2005, the budget deficit has once again significantly declined (see Figure 14.3). The latest figures for 2007 even show a small surplus and experts expect the budget to stay in the black for the next couple of years (FAZ, 30 November 2007). However, the Red–Green government and the Grand Coalition have not been able to reduce significantly the level of social insurance contributions; the combined employees' and employers' contributions have declined from 42.1% (1998) to 40% (2007) of gross wages (BMAS, 2007, Table 7.7).

Modern Social Democrats' imprints on welfare state institutions

How far has 'modernisation' led to significant changes in the institutional design of the two welfare states? According to Hall (1993), we can

Figure 14.3: Budget deficit (per cent of GDP)

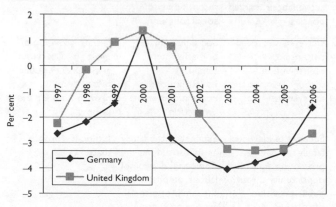

Source: Eurostat, Government Finance Statistics (http://epp.eurostat.ec.europa.eu/portal/page?_pageid=2373,47631312,2373_58674404&_dad=portal&_schema=PORTAL, 19/12/07)

differentiate between three orders of change along the dimensions of adjusting the settings of existing instruments (first order change), the change of settings as well as the choice of new instruments (second order change) and simultaneous changes of settings, instruments as well as policy goals (third order change). To assess whether the 'modernisation' processes have led to *significant* changes in the Liberal UK and Christian–Democratic German welfare states, we first have to briefly summarise the instruments and goals of the three worlds of welfare (see Table 14.2). In order to be able to speak of a significant or third order welfare state change, we would have to be witnesses to changed aims and moves along the various policy dimensions.

The German Social Democrats followed and accelerated a welfare state reform trajectory that has led to a greater reliance on means-tested

Table 14.2: Ideal aims and policy instruments in the three worlds of welfare

	Social–Democratic welfare state	Christian–Democratic welfare state	Liberal welfare state
Political aims	Social justice, autonomy and full employment within a capitalist economy	Social capitalism; promotion of social stability and cohesion; insurance against social risks	Economic growth; equal opportunity; poverty alleviation
Employment policy	Keynesian demand management; coordinated wage policies; comprehensive active labour market policies	Emphasis on supply-side measures; no explicit commitment to full employment (primarily the responsibility of social partners)	Emphasis on supply-side measures; no direct interference of the state
Social policy	Universalism; social citizenship; vertical redistribution through transfer and tax system	Social insurance; primarily inter-temporal redistribution; occupational status protection	Private provision of most social services and transfers; public means-tested programmes for the poor
Family policy	Support of individual family members; promoting equal opportunity through public provision of social services and parental leave schemes	Support of the family as an institution; traditional division of labour; emphasis on the family as a social service provider	No policy; private matter

Source: Cf Seeleib-Kaiser (2002a); Seeleib-Kaiser et al (2008)

benefits for the unemployed[10] and a significant percentage of pensioners will do so in the future. Instead of publicly guaranteeing the achieved living standards based on the principles of social stability and cohesion, social transfer programmes increasingly aim at poverty alleviation. Thus we could speak of a clear trend towards a more Liberal welfare state approach. However, reforms with regard to childcare, parental leave and working-time arrangements follow more closely a Social Democratic trajectory, although keeping clear elements of communitarianism. I have characterised this development as a 'dual transformation' of the Christian-Democratic German welfare state, leading towards a Liberal-Communitarian trajectory of welfare (Seeleib-Kaiser, 2002b; Bleses and Seeleib-Kaiser, 2004; Seeleib-Kaiser et al, 2008). In a nutshell, we can argue that the 'modernisation' of the German welfare state by Social Democrats has significantly contributed to and accelerated the process of welfare state transformation that was set in motion through many seemingly incremental first and second order changes since the 1980s. These incremental reforms, however, have cumulated over time to produce a 'third order' or paradigmatic change.

Although reforms by New Labour surely had an impact on the livelihood of many poor people, they did not change the overall Liberal welfare state trajectory; the recent changes in family policies, however, deviate somewhat from that trajectory. Despite the fact that New Labour has coined elements of its approach as 'progressive universalism', it is indeed a policy that relies primarily on means testing and targeting to improve the situation of the poor. Thus, one can argue that New Labour primarily adjusted the settings and introduced new instruments without changing the overall aims. Although the work–family balance policies do not fit the expectations of a Liberal approach and clearly differ from the policies pursued by the previous Conservative government, they are nowhere nearly as comprehensive as those pursued by Social Democrats in Northern or Continental Europe. This evaluation is largely based on the rather residual rights for working parents with regard to flexible working times and parental leave schemes.[11] The first and second order changes in the domains of employment, pension and family policies can be characterised as leading to a more social-liberal approach. Nevertheless, from a comparative perspective the welfare state changes seem quite limited and do not qualify to be categorised as a third order change.

Conclusion

Both countries have indeed 'modernised' their welfare states in (re)focusing policies on increasing the employment rate and supporting parents. In Germany the 'modernisation' process that had begun under Christian-Democratic rule in the 1980s has significantly changed the institutional design of the welfare state. The *outcomes* of the modernisation processes have been rather mixed. In Germany they have clearly contributed to increased inequality, while in the UK the reduction in poverty could be characterised as rather marginal after 10 years of Social-Democratic rule. On balance, working parents (especially mothers) and children seem to be the clear winners of welfare state 'modernisations' in both countries.

Notes

[1] According to Organisation for Economic Co-operation and Development (OECD) data, 20% of the workforce experienced low pay in 1995. Low pay is defined as earning less than two thirds of median earnings (OECD, 2007a, p 268).

[2] These comparably 'bleak' estimations are confirmed by recent simulations of the OECD, estimating that the median earner of the future will only be entitled to a net replacement rate of 51%, whereby the pre-reform replacement rate for this earner would have been 67.5% (OECD, 2007b, p 129).

[3] In late 2007, the Grand Coalition agreed to once again extend the duration of unemployment insurance benefit receipt for older workers to a maximum of 24 months.

[4] In addition, the government has increased the weekly universal child benefit from £14.40 (1999) to £18.10 (2007).

[5] Based on the 2006 Work and Families Act mothers will be able to transfer parts of their maternity leave to fathers by 2010 (cf Lewis and Campbell, 2007, p 373).

[6] Since time-series data for maternal employment is not available, I have used the female employment rate for the age group 25–34 years as a proxy.

[7] This largely seems to be a result from changes in the early retirement scheme enacted in the 1990s and the Red–Green unemployment benefit reforms (cf Kettner and Rebien, 2007).

[8] All figures relate to a poverty threshold defined as less than 60% of median income. Observers expect that poverty rates have further increased during the past couple of years, especially since the reform of the unemployment insurance system through the Hartz IV legislation is expected to have had a significant impact on the poverty rate. Unfortunately, the government will only make the figures available later in 2008.

[9] All figures relate to a poverty threshold defined as less than 60% of median income, before housing costs.

[10] This convergence towards a Liberal model obviously does not mean that all the differences between the British and German unemployment systems have been abolished. Significant differences remain, especially for those workers witnessing only short spells of unemployment. Since 2003, however, more unemployed workers are in receipt of means-tested assistance than earnings-related social insurance benefits (cf Seeleib-Kaiser and Fleckenstein, 2007).

[11] For a comprehensive discussion of the policies in Scandinavia see Ellingsaeter and Leira (2006).

References

In addition to the references listed below, I have relied on reporting in the *Financial Times* and the *Frankfurter Allgemeine Zeitung* (FAZ).

6, P. and Peck, E. (2004) 'Modernisation: the ten commitments of New Labour's approach to public management', *International Public Management Journal*, vol 7, no 1, pp 1-18.

Ben-Galim, D. and Gambles, R. (2008) 'The "public" and "private" of work-family reconciliation: unsettling gendered notions and assumptions', in M. Seeleib-Kaiser (ed) *Welfare state transformations*, Basingstoke: Palgrave Macmillan, pp 182-94.

Blair, T. and Schroeder, G. (1999) *Europe: The Third Way / Die Neue Mitte* (http//.labour.org.uk/views, 24/6/99).

Bleses, P. and Seeleib-Kaiser, M. (2004) *The dual transformation of the German welfare state*, Basingstoke: Palgrave.

BMAS (2007) *Statistisches Taschenbuch 2007. Arbeits- und Sozialstatistik*, Bonn: BMAS.

BMFSFJ (2004) *A bis Z zum Kindertagesbetreuungsausbaugesetz*, Berlin: BMFSFJ.

BMFSFJ (2006) *Das Elterngeld von A-Z*, Berlin: BMFSFJ.

Clasen, J. (2005) *Reforming European welfare states. Germany and the United Kingdom compared*, Oxford: Oxford University Press.

Daycare Trust (2006) *Childcare today. A progress report on the government's ten-year childcare strategy* (http://daycaretrust.org.uk/mod/fileman/files/Childcare_Today_Nov_2006.pdf, 11/10/07).

DWP (Department for Work and Pensions) (2006) *Security in retirement: Towards a new pensions system*, London: DWP (www.dwp.gov.uk/pensionsreform/pdfs/white_paper_complete.pdf, 11/10/07).

DWP (2007) *Households Below Average Income 1994/95–2005/06*, London: DWP (www.dwp.gov.uk/asd/hbai/hbai2006/chapters.asp, 11/10/07).

Ellingsaeter, L. and Leira, A. (eds) (2006) *Politicising parenthood in Scandinavia: Gender relations in welfare states*, Bristol: The Policy Press.

Esping-Andersen, G. (1990) *The three worlds of welfare capitalism*, Cambridge: Polity Press.

Esping-Andersen, G. (1999) *Social foundations of post-industrial economies*, Oxford: Oxford University Press.

Esping-Andersen, G., Gallie, D., Hemerijck, A. and Myles, J. (2002) *Why we need a new welfare state*, Oxford: Oxford University Press.

Evandrou, M. and Falkingham, J. (2005) 'A secure retirement for all? Older people and New Labour', in J. Hill and K. Stewart (eds) *A more equal society? New Labour, poverty, inequality and exclusion*, Bristol: The Policy Press, pp 167-87.

Funk, L. (2007) 'Convergence in employment-related public policies? A British-German comparison', *German Politics*, vol 16, no 1, pp 116-36.

Garrett, G. (1998) *Partisan politics in the global economy*, Cambridge: Cambridge University Press.

Goodin, R.E., Headey, B., Muffels, R. and Dirven, H.-J. (1999) *The real worlds of welfare capitalism*, Cambridge: Cambridge University Press.

Hall, P.A. (1993) 'Policy paradigms, social learning, and the state: the case of economic policy making in Britain', *Comparative Politics*, vol 25, no 3, pp 275-96.

Hills, J. and Stewart, K. (eds) (2005) *A more equal society? New Labour, poverty, inequality and exclusion*, Bristol: The Policy Press.

Howell, C. (2006) 'The state and the reconstruction of industrial relations after Fordism', in J.D. Levy (ed) *The state after statism – New activities in the age of liberalization*, Cambridge: Harvard University Press, pp 139-84.

Hudson, J., Hwang, G.-J. and Kühner, S. (2008) 'Between Ideas, institutions and interests: analysing third way welfare reform programmes in Germany and the United Kingdom', *Journal of Social Policy*, vol 37, pp 207-30.

Kemp, P.A. (2005) 'Social security and welfare reform under New Labour', in M. Powell, K. Clarke and L. Bauld (eds) *Social Policy Review 17*, Bristol: The Policy Press, pp 15-32.

Kemp, P.A. (2008) 'The transformation of Incapacity Benefits', in M. Seeleib-Kaiser (ed) *Welfare state transformations*, Basingstoke: Palgrave Macmillan.

Kettner, A. and Rebien, M. (2007) 'Hartz-IV-Reform: Impulse für den Arbeitsmarkt', *IAB Kurzbericht*, vol 1, pp 164-81.

Korpi, W. (1983) *The democratic class struggle*, London: Routledge.

Labour Party (1997) *New Labour because Britain deserves better* (www.psr.keele.ac.uk/area/uk/man/lab97.htm).

Leitner, S. (2003) 'Die Tour de force der Gleichstellung', in A. Gohr and M. Seeleib-Kaiser (eds) *Sozial- und Wirtschaftspolitik unter Rot-Grün*, Wiesbaden: Westdeutscher Verlag, pp 249-64.

Lewis, J. (1992) 'Gender and the development of welfare regimes', *Journal of European Social Policy*, vol 2, no 3, pp 159-73.

Lewis, J. and Campbell, M. (2007) 'Work/family balance policies in the UK since 1997: a new departure?', *Journal of Social Policy*, vol 36, no 3, pp 365-81.

LIS (Luxembourg Income Study) (2007) *Key figures* (www.lisproject.org/keyfigures.htm, 3/10/07).

McNight, A. (2005) 'Employment: tackling poverty through work for those who can', in J. Hills and K. Stewart (eds) *A more equal society? New Labour, poverty, inequality and exclusion*, Bristol: The Policy Press, pp 23-46.

Meyer, T. and Bridgen, P. (2007) 'Unlikely alliances in liberal regimes: employers, occupational welfare and the state', Paper presented at the 2007 ESPAnet Conference, Vienna.

OECD (Organisation for Economic Co-operation and Development) (2007a) *OECD Employment Outlook*, Paris: OECD.

OECD (2007b) *Pensions at a glance: Public policies across OECD countries* (2007 edn), Paris: OECD.

OECD (2007c) *OECD family database. Version June 2007* (www.oecd.org/els/social/family/database, 11/10/07).

Scharpf, F.W. (1995) 'Subventionierte Niedriglohnbeschäftigung statt bezahlter Arbeitslosigkeit?', *Zeitschrift für Sozialreform*, vol 41, no 2, pp 65-82.

Schmähl, W. (2007) 'Dismantling an earnings-related social pension scheme: Germany's new pension policy', *Journal of Social Policy*, vol. 36, no 2, pp 319-40.

Seeleib-Kaiser, M. (2002a) 'Neubeginn oder Ende der Sozialdemokratie? Eine Untersuchung zur programmatischen Reform sozialdemokratischer Parteien und ihrer Auswirkung auf die Parteiendifferenzthese', *Politische Vierteljahresschrift*, vol 43, no 3, pp 478-96.

Seeleib-Kaiser, M. (2002b) 'A dual transformation of the German welfare state?' *West European Politics*, vol 25, no 4, pp 25-48.

Seeleib-Kaiser, M. (2004) 'Continuity and change? Red-Green social policy after 16 years of Christian-Democratic rule', in W. Reutter (ed) *Germany on the road to 'normalcy': Policies and politics of the Red-Green Federal Government*, Basingstoke and New York: Palgrave Macmillan, pp 123-43.

Seeleib-Kaiser, M. (2007) *From Conservative to Liberal-Communitarian welfare: Can the reformed German welfare state survive?*, Barnett Papers in Social Research 2007/4, Oxford: University of Oxford.

Seeleib-Kaiser, M. and Fleckenstein, T. (2007) 'Discourse, learning and welfare state change', *Social Policy and Administration*, vol 41, no 5, pp 427-48.

Seeleib-Kaiser, M., van Dyk, S. and Roggenkamp, M. (2008) *Party politics and social welfare*, Cheltenham: Edward Elgar.

Sefton, T. and Sutherland, H. (2005) 'Inequality and poverty under New Labour', in J. Hills and K. Stewart (eds) *A more equal society? New Labour, poverty, inequality and exclusion*, Bristol: The Policy Press, pp 231-49.

SPD (1998) *Arbeit, Innovation und Gerechtigkeit – SPD-Programm für die Bundestagswahl 1998*, Antrag 4 (in der Fassung der Antragskommission), Bonn: SPD Parteivorstand.

Stephens, J.D. (1979) *The transition from capitalism to socialism*, London: Macmillan.

Stewart, K. and Hills, J. (2005) 'Introduction', in J. Hills and K. Stewart (eds) *A more equal society? New Labour, poverty, inequality and exclusion*, Bristol: The Policy Press, pp 1-19.

Toynbee, P. and Walker, D. (2005) *Better or worse? Has Labour delivered?*, London: Bloomsbury.

FIFTEEN

Conclusion: the Blair legacy

Martin Powell

Introduction

There are a great number of terms used by supporters and critics to describe New Labour's social policy (Powell, 1999, 2002; Powell and Hewitt, 2002). They may not be relevant to all sectors, and may apply to different phases of the Labour governments, but they add up to a formidable list of claims:

- modern welfare state
- new welfare state
- Third Way
- new Social Democracy
- progressive agenda
- reformed public services
- world-class public services
- CORA (community, opportunity, responsibility, accountability)
- RIO (responsibility, inclusion, opportunity)
- social investment state
- positive welfare
- crossing the Rubicon (from universalism to means testing; from state to private provision)
- hand up, not a handout
- investor's Britain
- no rights without responsibilities
- post-industrial welfare society
- new egalitarianism
- conditional welfare state
- changing behaviour – encouraging desirable behaviour and discouraging undesirable behaviour
- joined-up government
- preventive government
- outcome-focused government

- ending the 'something for nothing' society
- asset-based welfare
- Anglicanised communitarianism
- progressive universalism (provides 'support for all and more help for those who need it most when they need it most')
- welfare with the lid on
- active welfare
- active, enabling system
- active modern service
- ACTIVE: Active services; Customer-focused services; Transformed services; Integrity and security against fraud; Valuing staff; Efficient services
- we want to rebuild the system around work and security. Work for those who can; security for those who cannot
- welfare 2020 will be built on three core values of work, security and opportunity
- to put the consumer first

As we have seen, many of these terms and phrases have some resonance regarding the modernisation of the welfare state. This chapter revisits the analytical framework of Chapter One of modernisation and orders of change in order to summarise the material presented. It first examines views of the Blair legacy, summarises the evidence of the type and extent of change in the welfare state, places this material in a wider context and concludes by considering whether we have a new political consensus of 'Camerownism' (Cameron/Brown).

The Blair legacy

There have been a number of analyses of the Blair legacy during and after his period as Prime Minister. Rawnsley (2001) concludes that, compared with many governments, New Labour has a well above-average record. However, by the measure of the expectations aroused by the size of the majority, New Labour's transformatory rhetoric and the ambitions that Blair had trumpeted, the government looks less impressive. According to New Labour pollster, Philip Gould: 'if I had gone to a focus group on April 29th 1997 and said that this Labour government is going to run the economy more competently than any other, it's going to invest unprecedented amounts in public services plus it will create a million jobs plus it will lift a million people out of poverty, they would have thought I was mad. It was difficult enough getting them to believe our five pledges. They would have called me a

Martian' (quoted in Rawnsley, 2001, p 383). Toynbee and Walker (2001, pp 238-40) claim that it is hard at the end of the day to compile a single balance sheet, as there were zigzag positives and negatives. However, the social account is full, and 'things did get better'. Giddens (2002) argues that, in Labour's first term, the successes were: marginalising the Conservatives, economic policy, welfare reform, or at least some aspects of it, high employment, redistribution and some key aspects of education policy. 'Halfway houses' included constitutional reform, the NHS, crime and punishment, relations with the European Union (EU) and the environment. Failures include the dismal saga of the Millennium Dome, public relations (PR) and communications and the promotion of corporate responsibility. Giddens claims that the New Deal, the Working Families' Tax Credit, the National Childcare Strategy and other innovations have proved their worth (2002, p 24). Powell and Hewitt (2002, pp 170, 184-5) state that the new welfare state is clearly still a work in progress, but its core is based on: active rather than passive, redistributing opportunities rather than income, pluralist rather than statist, enabling rather than providing, conditional rather than unconditional, process- rather than pattern-driven and inclusive rather than egalitarian. Toynbee and Walker (2005, p 44) assert that Blair's reputation was always going to stand or fall on whether huge amounts of extra health spending secured improved care. It did (2005, p 123). They conclude that by 2005 Britain was a richer and fairer society than in 1997. It was healthier, safer and in many respects better governed. If Britain was not exactly wiser, it was better educated. Fewer people lived in dire hardship. Crime kept falling, schools and hospitals were improving, work was plentiful. Many comparisons with European neighbours were positive and pleasing (for the first time in many cases). Blair's era was a better time to be British than for many decades. 'The second term started with a weak manifesto, but delivered more than it promised. We can only restate our conclusion on Labour's first term: good, but not good enough, with still time to do better in a third term' (Toynbee and Walker, 2005, pp 327-8). According to Giddens (2007, p 3), since coming to power, New Labour has managed to shift the framework within which politics in Britain is carried out. As a result the Conservatives have had to change ideological ground quite fundamentally in order to be taken seriously again. 'Overall, Labour has done a good job for the country, often in trying circumstances.' He asks 'What went right, what went wrong?' (2007, p 23), and responds that Labour won three consecutive elections for the first time in its history, and was the only left-of-centre party in the US and Europe to have stayed in government over the past decade (2007, p 24). The

UK has shifted in a more Social Democratic direction. On balance, Labour has been a successful government on the domestic front, so long as it is not measured against unrealistic expectations (Giddens, 2007, pp 27-8). The government has a good track record in education by any reckoning (2007, p 81). As in education, the government's achievements in reforming healthcare are formidable (2007, p 85).

With Blair's announcement of his resignation in May 2007 and his departure in June 2007, many newspapers carried features on the Blair legacy. Most of this was dominated by foreign policy, but discussion here focuses on social policy. Max Hastings ('Blair's legacy: 10 years that ruined Britain', *Daily Mail*, 28/04/07) got his retaliation in first. He claimed that the man who was swept into office in 1997 amid higher hopes and greater goodwill than any incoming British Prime Minister in modern times would 'leave it in a few weeks hence with his reputation in ruins. History will remember him at home for the yawning chasm between the rich promises which he made in 1997, and the sour fruits we are all harvesting today'. David Aaronovitch and Matthew Parris engaged in a debate ('Tony Blair: success or failure?', *The Times*, 11/5/07). Aaronovitch claimed that Britain was a better country for having had Tony Blair as its Prime Minister. He rejected the 'Clintonian disappointment' view, who 'campaigned in poetry and governed in prose'. He argued that paradoxically the main achievements probably came during the misunderstood and reviled twilight years of the Blair reign. Parris conceded that 'substantial increases in public spending have brought modest increases in some public services'. Alice Miles ('You wait: you'll be sorry when they're gone', *The Times*, 9/5/07) wrote that his temporary unpopularity would fade. She conceded his one huge failure on the domestic front was in the betrayal of that first promise: education, education, education, but from the Minimum Wage to civil partnerships, state-funded childcare to a well-resourced NHS, devolved assemblies and peace in Northern Ireland, this is a man who shifted the culture of Britain and the centre of gravity of its politics. Polly Toynbee (*The Guardian*, 11/5/07) termed Blair's resignation speech a 'tour de force from the moderniser who always thought it his destiny to pull the country into the 21st century. And so he did'. She continues, 'Make no mistake, at home he leaves a country far better than he found it – and unimaginatively better than it would have been under 10 more years of Conservative rule'. Blair's Britain is a better place to live in, especially for the least well-off. After Blair, no party can be elected without espousing Labour's progressive social policies. All must promise generous spending on health and schools, pensions, childcare and families. Blair has set benchmarks no future government dare retreat from: NHS waiting lists must keep falling, exam results must keep rising. His taste of grand institutional change distracted from what worked best – fine-tuned practical programmes such as Sure Start for under-fives, literacy and numeracy hours and NHS walk-in centres. These are his best monuments, not the ever-shifting furniture and nameplates on NHS doors. *The Guardian's* (18/05/07) 48-page supplement, 'How Blair will be remembered', contained views so polarised that it is difficult to believe that commentators are talking about the same person. Polly Toynbee pointed to 'that most extraordinary pledge in British living political history: to abolish all child poverty by 2020', and stated that 'let no one diminish his social achievements that outshine every government since Attlee'. In the *Daily Telegraph* ('The Blair years', 10/5/07), Toby Helm wrote that 'no one could argue that he had failed to earn his place alongside Margaret Thatcher as a giant of modern political history'. Philip Johnston claimed that 'the gap between rhetoric and achievement has defined this era'. The Blair years have been an avalanche of promised reforms that never did quite what they said on the tin, giving not a new dawn but a false one. In the *Sunday Telegraph* ('The Blair years', 13/5/7), Patrick Hennessy wrote of 'a decade of wasted opportunities'. Key reforms failed to materialise. It is fair to assume that many Britons will judge his achievements to be frustratingly slight. Matthew D'Ancona stated that 'Margaret Thatcher often said that her achievement was to transform two parties: her own and Labour'. With Mr Cameron's election as Conservative leader, Blair could claim to have pulled off a similar trick.

To conclude, we should let Blair speak for himself. In his resignation speech (*The Guardian*, 10/5/07) he claimed that 1997 was:

> a moment for a new beginning, for sweeping away all the detritus of the past. Expectations were so high. Too high. Too high in a way for either of us. However, only one government since 1945 that can say all of the following: more jobs, fewer unemployed, better health and education results, lower crime and economic growth in every quarter.

A modernising project?

This section summarises the elements of modernisation (6 and Peck, 2004a, 2004b; see Chapter One, this volume) noted by the contributors in the different themes and policy sectors.

Table 15.1 summarises the elements by policy sector according to 6 and Peck (2004a, 2004b). However, their 10 commitments have

Table 15.1: Modernisation: the 11 commitments

	Health (Chapter Two)	Housing (Chapter Three)	Social security (Chapter Four)	Social care (Chapter Five)	Education (Chapter Six)	Criminal justice (Chapter Seven)
Inspection	Establishment of the Commission for Health Improvement (CHI)/Commission for Healthcare Audit and Inspection (CHAI)	Housing Inspectorate	–	–	Increased role for Ofsted	Cross-agency inspectorates
Central standard setting	Increased role	Decent homes standard, performance indicators	Remains highly centralised	Centralised regime	Early years curriculum	More explicit standards set for the police
Area-based initiatives	Health Action Zones	New Deal for Communities, Housing Market Renewal pathfinders	Piloting, pathfinder	–	Education Action Zones	Some local variations as part of the Reassurance Agenda

Table 15.1 (continued)

	Health (Chapter Two)	Housing (Chapter Three)	Social security (Chapter Four)	Social care (Chapter Five)	Education (Chapter Six)	Criminal justice (Chapter Seven)
Coordination and integration	Partnership and joint commissioning	Neighbourhood Renewal Fund	–	–	*Every Child Matters* agenda	Joined-up public protection linked to multi-agency public protection arrangement (MAPPA), Youth Offending Teams (YOTs) and the National Offender Management Service (NOMS)
Devolution but limited decentralisation	Devolution to nations	Devolution to nations	–	Devolution to nations	Devolution to nations; some devolution to schools	Tension between national standards and localism
Earned autonomy	Foundation trusts, star ratings	Arm's-length management organisations	–	–	Reduced inspection for successful schools	'Lighter touch' inspection for better performing police forces
Extended role for private capital	Private finance initiative (PFI)	Stock transfer, expansion of private rented sector; PFI	Role for private and third sector for jobseekers	Extension of Conservative policies	PFI; private sponsors for academies	Continued expansion for private prisons

Table 15.1 (continued)

	Health (Chapter Two)	Housing (Chapter Three)	Social security (Chapter Four)	Social care (Chapter Five)	Education (Chapter Six)	Criminal justice (Chapter Seven)
A modest increase in citizen obligations	'Mostly rhetoric'	Rough Sleepers Initiative; conditional Housing Benefit	Strong increase	'User control' in direct payments	Attempts to introduce parental contracts	Continuing ethos of citizens' responsibility to protect themselves and their property. Enhanced role for reparation to victims from offenders
Access	Symbolic such as walk-in centres	Choice-based lettings, Neighbourhood renewal	Some moves, but some unsuccessful such as Child Support Agency	Care Direct	Lifelong learning, education in community	Drop-in surgeries; growing role for victims' information networks
E-government	NHS Direct, NHS information centre	Choice-based lettings	Limited	–	Schools become the vehicle for preparing all for the electronic age	Significant growth in CCTV and electronic tagging
Neoliberal/choice	Choose and Book	Choice-based lettings	–	Extension of direct payments	–	–

Note: See individual chapters for more details.

been expanded to 11. Calum Paton (Chapter Two) argues that the 10 commitments framework is dated as it fails to capture the neoliberal hard edge of later New Labour (New New Labour?), and omits arguably the most significant trend in New Labour health policy – the acceptance from 2002 of neoliberal approaches to steering the NHS. This dimension is also noted by Ian Greener (Chapter Thirteen) and Catherine Needham (Chapter Eleven). Mark Baldwin (Chapter Five) examines two further dimensions: on social justice and on prevention (compare with David Denney, Chapter Nine, on the precautionary principle).

It can be seen that most of the elements have some resonance in most of the policy sectors. Susan Martin and Yolande Muschamp (Chapter Six) claim that perhaps the process of modernisation is more visible in education than any other welfare services: nine out of ten elements are met time and time again in our analysis. The tenth element of coordination and integration is an aspect of modernisation which has been introduced but not yet achieved. Conversely, the least resonance appears to be in social care. Moreover, some initiatives such as choice based lettings cover more than one element of modernisation (see Brian Lund, Chapter Three).

Table 15.2 examines the wider themes. Catherine Needham (Chapter Eleven) gives a 'high score' for six of the ten elements. Mark Drakeford (Chapter Ten) sees resonances for all the elements, except coordination. Peter Dwyer and David Denney (Chapters Twelve and Nine, respectively) cover most of the elements.

Tinkering or transformation?

The magnitude of change is examined using Hall's framework (1993; see Chapter One, this volume), which points to three central variables of policy making: the overarching goals that guide public policy in a particular field; the techniques or policy instruments used to attain those goals; and the precise settings of those instruments. First order change on levels or settings (for example, to the annual budget) tends to occur frequently. Second order change of techniques or instruments and settings (for example, the development of 'cash limits' for public spending control in 1976) occurs less frequently. Third order change involving simultaneous change in all three components of goals, techniques and settings (for example, from Keynesianism to monetarism) is rare. First and second order changes can be seen as cases of 'normal policy making', namely of a process that adjusts policy without challenging the overall terms of a given policy paradigm, but third order or paradigmatic change is likely to reflect a very different

Table 15.2: The wider themes

	Choice (Chapter Eleven)	Risk (Chapter Nine)	Private welfare (Chapter Ten)	Conditionality (Chapter Twelve)
Inspection	High: Ofsted and Healthcare Commission generate service ratings to allow informed choice	Precautionary principle, inspection as central feature of risk management	Substantial expansion of private sector involvement in inspection	–
Central standard setting	High: different choices must all meet minimum standards	Central standard setting as a technique of avoiding risk	Services remain subject to strongly centralised standards	Behavioural requirements
Area-based initiatives	Low	Early intervention to avoid risk eg Sure Start	Includes strong representation from private sector interests	'Respect Areas'; New Deal for Communities
Coordination and integration	Low	Local partnerships	–	–
Devolution but limited decentralisation	High: devolution to nations extends choice and 'double devolution' increases local diversity	–	Devolution to nations	
Earned autonomy	Medium: need to avoid 'cherry-picking'	Arm's-length management organisations	Private sector management techniques deploy the rhetoric, but more rarely the reality	Rights and responsibilities as part of contract; 'hard working families who play by the rules'

Table 15.2 (continued)

	Choice (Chapter Eleven)	Risk (Chapter Nine)	Private welfare (Chapter Ten)	Conditionality (Chapter Twelve)
Extended role for private capita	High: increases competition	Increased insecurity and risk for some groups, PFI designed to share risk	Key theme – PFI/public–private partnership (PPP) and stock transfer	Greater role for private sector in eg 'Pathways to Work'
A modest increase in citizen obligations	Medium	Strong increase in obligation	Substantial increase	Strong increase in obligation
Access	High: one of the key mechanisms of choice	Increased access to crisis services	Growth in privately provided call centres	–
E-government	High: the main channel through which choices are expressed in a range of services	Use of technology to control risky populations	Many private providers	–

process, marked by the radical changes in the overarching terms of policy discourse associated with a 'paradigm shift' (see Table 15.3).

A number of the contributors point to third order or paradigmatic change. Stephen McKay and Karen Rowlingson (Chapter Four) consider that one of New Labour's main claims to radical change in the field of welfare and social security is to have put the term 'poverty' firmly back on the political, policy and public agenda. Mark Baldwin (Chapter Five) views prevention as a potential paradigm change. Brian Lund (Chapter Three) regards the Scottish Parliament as an *opportunity* for 'third order change', but sees limited divergence in the case of housing. Susan Martin and Yolande Muschamp (Chapter Six) see the end of the comprehensive school model as radical change. Sarah Charman and Stephen Savage (Chapter Seven) point to the

Table 15.3: Third order or paradigmatic change

	Third order change
Health (Chapter Two)	• (Tacitly) changing mission for the NHS, influenced by political economy • Tripartite NHS mission: services for middle classes, pro-poor and in support of the economy
Housing (Chapter Three)	• Post-2003 emphasis on supply culminating in 2007 housing Green Paper (issued under Brown) • Scottish Parliament
Social security (Chapter Four)	• Commitment to end child poverty by 2020 • Focus on reducing pensioner poverty • Asset-based welfare (second/third term) • New Deal (second/third term) • National Minimum Wage (second/third term)
Social care (Chapter Five)	• Prevention as 'potential paradigm change'
Education (Chapter Six)	• 'Diversity' marks abandonment of comprehensive school model
Criminal justice (Chapter Seven)	• Discourse: 'tough on crime...' • 'Rebalancing the criminal justice system in favour of the law-abiding majority' • Public protection
Risk (Chapter Nine)	• Increased responsibility for personal risk (eg financial security in old age) • The precautionary principle
Private welfare (Chapter Ten)	• Shifts from public provision and public responsibilities
Choice (Chapter Eleven)	• Individual choice in public services?
Conditionality (Chapter Twelve)	• From 'passive' to 'active' welfare state, with rights linked to responsible behaviour

'sea-change' in New Labour's approach to crime signalled by Blair's 'tough on crime; tough on the causes of crime' sound bite, and the paradigm shift of rebalancing the criminal justice system in favour of the law-abiding majority.

Alexandra Dobrowolsky and Ruth Lister (Chapter Eight) consider that the social investment state provides the combination of changes in goals, settings and techniques indicative of third order change. They point to policies aiming to change human, financial and social capital, but argue that enhancing human capital over the life course lay at the heart of Blair's social policy agenda. David Denney (Chapter Nine) writes that New Labour emphasised the precautionary principle, and some risk-led precautionary measures appear to mark a radical shift with the past. According to Peter Dwyer (Chapter Twelve), conditionality has become fundamental to New Labour's vision of a 21st-century welfare state. He argues that the consolidation and expansion of the conditional welfare state may yet prove to be one of Blair's most enduring legacies. Mark Drakeford (Chapter Ten) writes that the sense that the Blair years were marked by the purposeful pursuit of welfare pluralism is largely uncontested, and a substantial shifting of the balance of, and blurring of, the public and private sector amounted to a sustained, interconnected and comprehensive paradigm shift away from public services.

Modernising the welfare state

This section places the material on the type and magnitude of change into a wider perspective. First, it is far from clear that the elements of modernisation are new. For example, 'partnership' pre-dates the 'classic welfare state' (Glendinning et al, 2002; see also Chapter Two, this volume). This relates to the early debates on New Labour's 'Third Way' involving the extent to which policies reflected continuity or discontinuity with the preceding Conservative government (Powell, 1999). For example, Mark Baldwin (Chapter Five) writes that New Labour's social care agenda should not generally be seen as either modern, in the sense of new and improved, nor as constituting a paradigmatic shift in policy values as it reflects continuity with Conservative policies. Lund (2008, p 43) cites John Major, who wrote in 1999 that 'I did not appreciate at the time the extent to which Blair would appropriate Conservative language and steal their policies. The attractive candidate was to turn out to be a political kleptomaniac.' Lund argues that New Labour adopted many of Major's policies ('Blairjorism'), and then, from 2001, returned to the competitive quasi-markets initiated by Margaret Thatcher, and that there are sufficient policy comparisons to claim that a significant policy break came when Major became Prime Minister. This view, then, sees Major as proto-Blairism (Lund, 2008). Ian Greener (Chapter Thirteen) considers New Labour's policies as a series of second order rather than third order changes: perhaps New Labour is best regarded as taking the Conservatives' approach to public service reform to its logical conclusion rather than having a significant new approach in its own right (see below).

Second, as Stephen McKay and Karen Rowlingson (Chapter Four) note, Hall's (1993) framework does not cover policy outcomes or impact. This means that it may overplay rhetoric or discourse and underplay results – talking the talk rather than walking the walk. Sarah Charman and Stephen Savage (Chapter Seven) point to the difference between pronouncements and policy. For example, the pledge to abolish child poverty in a generation can be seen as third order or paradigmatic change, but the signs are that the government is not on track to achieve this. More attention is needed to examine any implementation gaps or failures (cf Marsh and Rhodes, 1992). Dostal (2008) points to 'the workfare illusion': workfare programmes pursued by various OECD (Organisation for Economic Co-operation and Development) countries do not amount to a fundamental change of policy, and questions whether the UK represents workfare discourse without workfare. A week rarely goes by without yet another 'crackdown on crime' or the parties attempting to see who can talk tougher on conditionality. Yet, there is a degree of 'Groundhog Day' about 'no option of life on benefit' (from 1997) or 'the end of the something for nothing society' (from 2001). Of course, evaluating policy impact 'on the ground' as opposed to 'on paper' is problematic (Powell, 2002; Boyne et al, 2003). For example, there appears to be some dispute between the contributors on the degree of conditionality. Peter Dwyer (Chapter Twelve) regards the conditional welfare state as third order change, but David Denney (Chapter Nine) views it as second order change. Dwyer states that 6 and Peck (2004a, 2004b) are mistaken to suggest that New Labour has presided over only a 'modest' increase in citizen obligations, as the increase is central to the government's modernisation of welfare, and is modest neither in scope nor impact. However, there appears to be a degree of 'symbolic politics' (Edelman, 1964) – words that succeed and policies that fail – about at least some policy areas (see, for example, Chapter Two, this volume; cf Jenkins, 2007, on 'devolution' and 'earned autonomy').

Third, modernisation does not appear to be an even or linear process. 6 and Peck (2004b, pp 90–1) noted different phases – phase I: 1998–2001 and phase II: 2000 to date. Ian Greener (Chapter Thirteen) points to a number of stages or moments of reform (cf Greener, 2004; see also Chapter Nine, this volume). In Chapter Two Calum Paton sees some signs of circularity and of a U-turn. In 1997 New Labour aimed to 'abolish' the internal market only to later reinvent and strengthen it. Paton writes that we have moved from the stage of 'the high noon of Milburn centrism' (1999–2002) to markets. Brain Lund (Chapter Three) claims that towards the end of New Labour's first term a specific 'Blair agenda' of choice and competition for public service 'modernisation' started to emerge. According to Catherine Needham (Chapter Eleven), 'strong' individual choice is one of the most distinctively Blairite strands of the reform programme, and the period after the 2001 election – the key period for the entrenchment of choice across the public services – is arguably the most characteristically Blairite.

The question of how these diverse strands fit together at one point in time or sequentially over time is far from clear. According to 6 and Peck (2004b, p 92), there are of course some potential tensions between some of these elements. Fairclough (2000, p 119) sees some contradictions such as modernisation by centralisation or decentralisation. The New Labour narrative is that there is a clear logic to the reform strands over time, but Calum Paton (Chapter Two) considers the 'rubbish bin model' a better explanation. It does appear difficult to explain why it was necessary to 'abolish' the Conservatives' internal market only to reinvent and strengthen it; to take one step backwards in order to go two forwards; or to cut the knot to then re-tie it (Jenkins, 2007).

Fourth, the Blair legacy of changing the welfare state appears to be less far-reaching than the Attlee and Thatcher governments. David Denney (Chapter Nine) argues that the Attlee and Thatcher governments achieved paradigmatic change, but suggests that Blair's changes were of more limited scope. Marr (2007) views the Thatcher government as 'the British Revolution', and represented 'the most nation changing premiership of modern British history' (2007, p 474). However, Jenkins (2007, p 5) argues that there were two Thatcher revolutions: the liberation of the 'supply side' (cutting taxes, freeing labour markets and blurring the boundaries between the public and private sectors), and of centralised government. He argues that subsequent Prime Ministers – Major, Blair and Brown – represent essential continuity, and are the 'prisoners of a revolution effected by Margaret Thatcher in the 1980s' (2007, p 1). Blair renamed Thatcher's foundation schools trusts and her trust hospitals foundations (Jenkins, 2007, p 289). Thatcher 'transformed the nation' and Thatcher's sons were convinced disciples, going even where their mistress had feared to tread (p 2). Marr (2007, p xxiv) regards all British postwar governments as failures, with the exceptions of Attlee and the first two administrations of Thatcher.

These judgements involve problems of context and counterfactuals, as these governments operated in very different times. Attlee built the welfare state in the aftermath of a world war and with a shattered economy. Thatcher inherited a broken country after the economic difficulties of the International Monetary Fund (IMF) and the 'Winter of Discontent'. Blair inherited an economy in broadly good shape, but with under-investment in public services – crudely, private affluence and public squalor. Thatcher paved the way for many of Blair's reforms, leaving him with the political equivalent of an open goal.

Fifth, Blair's reforms can be placed in a wider international comparative context. Martin Seeleib-Kaiser (Chapter Fourteen) regards the dimensions of modernisation identified by 6 and Peck (2004a, 2004b) as largely peculiar elements of the UK modernisation process. Governments in both the UK and Germany wished to modernise the welfare state (Blair and Schroeder, 1999), but instead of the term 'modernisation', the German Social Democrats used the term 'innovation' as their buzzword. In Germany, incremental reforms have cumulated over time to a 'third order' or paradigmatic change, while New Labour's reforms did not change the overall Liberal welfare state trajectory. From a comparative perspective the welfare state changes seem quite limited and do not qualify to be categorised as third order change.

'Camerownism': a progressive consensus?

Before addressing the question of whether Blairism will survive Blair, it is necessary to examine 'whose legacy?'. Stephen McKay and Karen Rowlingson (Chapter Four) point out that Brown had significant input on social policy, and Blair was never particularly concerned with the detail of social security policy. It might be argued that the chance of paradigmatic change was significantly reduced with the exit of Frank Field as Minister for Welfare Reform. Field 'thought the unthinkable', but the government could not 'do the undoable'. Calum Paton (Chapter Two) claims that most modernisation themes are more Brownite than Blairite, reflecting the fact that Brown drove most domestic policy from the Treasury between 1997 and 2007. Alexandra Dobrowolsky and Ruth Lister (Chapter Eight) argue that Brown, as Chancellor, was a pivotal player in this project and thus it can be expected that social investment will continue under his premiership. Whoever wins the next election, many of the priorities established under Blair and Brown's social investment perspective will continue to shape social policy.

There appears to be some uncertainty about Brown's trajectory. Brian Lund (Chapter Three) writes that Brown's 2007 housing Green Paper marked a partial return to 'Old' Labour's housing agenda: a concern with supply; new towns (eco-towns); public housing; and taxing planning gain – an agenda that can be seen as a paradigm shift. However, the 2007 Pre-Budget Report abandoned the proposed planning gain tax. According to Mark Drakeford (Chapter Ten), it is still unclear as to whether Brown represents the true fount of New Labourism or a reversion to the path of Old Labour. Ian Greener (Chapter Thirteen) suggests that there may be a becalming of policy under Brown. Catherine Needham (Chapter Eleven) points to the careful rhetoric of Brown of 'personalisation' rather than 'choice', weaker rather than strong choice, and more voice, but below the rhetoric, the expansion of provider choice continues.

Some commentators have addressed the issue of a post-Blair progressive consensus involving all three major parties and 'political cross-dressing' (Cable, 2007, p 119; cf Finlayson, 2007). Miliband (2007, p 111) wrote that this period of progressive rule was never going to be 1945–51: the 'big bang'. The model is surely closer to Scandinavian Social Democracy: sustained incremental change which knits progressive values deep into the fabric of the country. The ingredients of the progressive movement are ethos, clear priorities and political practice. He claimed that today an explicit agenda around tax cuts, shrinking the state, blaming the poor, and anti-environmental policy seems as out of the mainstream as nationalisation, penal tax rates and withdrawal from the EU did in 1997 (2007, p 118). Some of these claims may be a little thin. Given the chance to express a view, a large number would probably favour withdrawal from the EU. The pledge of tax cuts at the 2007 Conservative Party conference led to a significant rise in support in the opinion polls that probably prevented an early general election. Moreover, New Labour appeared to steal the Conservatives' clothes by announcing shortly afterwards their own tax cuts.

Some of the contributors see some differences between the parties. Brian Lund (Chapter Three) claims that Cameron has adopted Blair's choice agenda, but Brown has adopted a more structural, Social Democratic approach in housing. However, Stephen McKay and Karen Rowlingson (Chapter Four) write that it is highly unlikely that Brown will make any major changes in social security, and that there is a new consensus between Brown and Cameron. Peter Dwyer (Chapter Twelve) claims that conditionality is a non-negotiable element of Brown and Cameron's vision, contributing towards a new consensus about the welfare state. Catherine Needham (Chapter Eleven) points out that choice is favoured by all three major political parties.

Conclusion

The main focus was to examine the degree of change in the welfare state using the analytical template of modernisation (6, and Peck 2004a, 2004b) and Hall's orders of change (1993). However, as we saw in Chapter One, modernisation is difficult to define, and perhaps summed up best in Calum Paton's 'Morrisonian' definition of 'everything a New Labour government does' (Chapter Two). As the material in the chapters shows, many of the elements of modernisation were present in most of the policy sectors and themes. Some have been present over the whole period of government. Others have waxed and waned. Some, like choice, have become clearer over time. Indeed, having reduced some choices and market mechanisms in the first term, Blair reintroduced them and went further than the Conservatives in some policy sectors. It is difficult to discover a clear 'blueprint' such as the Beveridge report for the Attlee government or the quasi-markets for the Thatcher governments. The original 'Third Way' blueprint (Powell, 1999) has been changed significantly since 1997, with New Labour becoming 'New New Labour' or 'Even Newer Labour'. Although change was everywhere, third order or paradigmatic change was more difficult to detect. New Labour found it easier to invest than to reform. The manifesto promises of 'welfare reform', 'world-class public services' and a 'modern welfare state' have only been partially delivered. In this sense, the Blair legacy is incomplete and not easy to pin down. Blair reflected that 'every time I've ever introduced a reform in government, I wish in retrospect I had gone further' (quoted in 'The Blair Years', *Sunday Telegraph*, 13/05/07). However, while Blair does not cast such a long shadow as Attlee or Thatcher, it will be difficult for Blair's 'sons' (Brown or Cameron) to significantly change political course (cf Jenkins, 2007). The longest-serving Labour Prime Minister in history has certainly left his mark on the welfare state.

> 'There is a judgement to be made on my premiership and in the end that is for you, the people, to make.... I give my thanks to you, the British people, for the times I have succeeded and my apologies to you for the times I have fallen short. Good luck!' (Tony Blair's resignation speech, 10 May 2007)

References

6, P. and Peck, E. (2004a) 'Modernisation: the ten commitments of New Labour's approach to public management', *International Public Management Journal*, vol 7, no 1, pp 1-18.

6, P. and Peck, E. (2004b) 'New Labour's modernization in the public sector: a neo-Durkheimian approach and the case of mental health services', *Public Administration*, vol 82, no 1, pp 83-108.

Blair, T. and Schroeder, G. (1999) *The Third Way*, London: Labour Party.

Boyne, G. , Farrell, C. and Law, J. (2003) *Evaluating public management reforms*, Maidenhead: Open University Press.

Cable, V. (2007) 'Prospects for a post-Blair "progressive consensus"', *Public Policy Research*, June-August, pp 119-25.

Dostal, J.M. (2008) 'The workfare illusion', *Social Policy and Administration*, vol 42, no 1, pp 19-42.

Edelman, M. (1964) *The symbolic uses of politics*, Chicago, IL: University of Chicago Press.

Fairclough, N. (2000) *New Labour, new language?*, London: Routledge.

Finlayson, A. (2007) 'Making sense of David Cameron', *Public Policy Research*, March-May, pp 3-10.

Giddens, A. (2002) *Where now for New Labour?*, Cambridge: Polity Press.

Giddens, A. (2007) *Over to you, Mr Brown*, Cambridge: Polity Press.

Glendinning, C., Powell, M. and Rummery, K. (eds) (2002) *Partnerships, New Labour and the governance of welfare*, Bristol: The Policy Press.

Hall, P.A. (1993) 'Policy paradigms, social learning and the state: the case of economic policy making in Britain', *Comparative Politics*, vol 25, no 3, pp 275-96.

Jenkins, P. (2007) *Thatcher and sons*, Harmondsworth: Penguin.

Lund, B. (2008) 'Major, Blair and the third way in social policy', *Social Policy and Administration*, vol 42, no 1, pp 43-58.

Marr, A. (2007) *A history of modern Britain*, London: Macmillan.

Marsh, D. and Rhodes, R. (1992) *Implementing Thatcherite policies*, Buckingham: Open University Press.

Miliband, E. (2007) 'Centre-forward. What's left after Blair?', *Public Policy Research*, June-August, pp 111-18.

Powell, M. (ed) (1999) *New Labour, new welfare state? The 'third way' in British social policy*, Bristol: The Policy Press.

Powell, M. (ed) (2002) *Evaluating New Labour's welfare reforms*, Bristol: The Policy Press.

Powell, M. and Hewitt, M. (2002) *Welfare state and welfare change*, Buckingham: Open University Press.

Rawnsley, A. (2001) *Servants of the people*, Harmondsworth: Penguin.

Toynbee, P. and Walker, D. (2001) *Did things get better?*, Harmondsworth: Penguin.

Toynbee, P. and Walker, D. (2005) *Better or worse? Has New Labour delivered?*, Harmondsworth: Penguin.

Index

Note: Page numbers followed by *tab* indicate that information appears only in a table, e.g. 187*tab*.

A

Aaronovitch, David 258
academies programme 97, 98–9, 168, 185, 191, 225
access as theme of modernisation 11, 228–9, 262*tab*, 265*tab*
and choice 186, 187*tab*
and conditionality 212
and criminal justice 113*tab*
and education 93*tab*, 94
and housing policy 46*tab*
and NHS 20*tab*, 24–5, 27*tab*, 172
and private sector involvement 162*tab*, 167, 172
and risk 152, 153*tab*, 154*tab*
and social care 74, 78, 80, 82*tab*
and social security 65*tab*
accountability 10, 93–4, 223
see also inspection; regulation
active citizenship 130, 151, 154*tab*
'active' welfare 200, 207, 208, 210*tab*, 266*tab*
see also conditional welfare; welfare-to-work/active labour market policies
adult illiteracy and conditionality 206
affordable housing supply 44–6, 48–9
Age Concern 66
Allsop, A. 171
anti-discrimination legislation 74, 81, 85
anti-social behaviour
and criminal justice policy 106, 116–17, 165
and housing rights 41, 165
conditional welfare 204–5, 207, 210*tab*
'Respect Areas'/'Respect Agenda' 211, 213
Anti-Social Behaviour Act (2003) 205
Anti-Social Behaviour Orders (ASBOs) 165, 204–5, 206, 210*tab*
anti-terrorist legislation 105, 106, 147–8
area-based initiatives as theme of modernisation 11, 222, 260*tab*, 264*tab*
and choice 184, 187*tab*
and conditional welfare 211

and criminal justice policy 113*tab*
and education 93*tab*, 170
limitations of Sure Start 147
and neighbourhood renewal 37, 46*tab*, 47*tab*
and NHS 20*tab*, 23–4, 172
and private sector involvement 162*tab*, 165, 170, 172
and risk 146–8, 153–5, 155–6
and social care 82
and social investment 125
and social security 65*tab*
Arend, N. 191
assessment of young children 95–6
asset-based welfare 59–60, 60–1, 69, 266*tab*
social investment 126, 135–6
asylum seekers 81, 126
Attlee, Clement 144, 269, 270
Audit Commission 23, 169
autonomy *see* earned autonomy

B

Baggott, R. 171
Baker, Kenneth 168
Ball, S.J. 170
Balls, Ed 138
Barker, Kate 44
Barrientos, A. 12
Bartlett, W. 84
Beacon Schools programme 98, 100–1
Beck, Ulrich 143
benefits *see* social security
Bennett, F. 166
Better Regulation Commission/Task Force 145, 153*tab*
Bevan, Aneurin 170
Beveridge, William 53, 144, 162, 200
Blair, Tony
'Blair legacy' 1, 255–72
analyses 256–9
Blair on 259, 272
and Blair's successors 13, 43, 66
and modernisation 267–70
modernisation themes 259–63, 264–5*tab*

New Labour, new welfare state?
The 'third way' in British social policy
*Edited by **Martin Powell***

The New Labour government elected in May 1997 claimed that it would modernise the welfare state, by rejecting the solutions of both the Old Left and the New Right.

New Labour, new welfare state? provides the first comprehensive examination of the social policy of New Labour; compares and contrasts current policy areas with both the Old Left and the New Right; applies the concept of the 'third way' to individual policy areas and to broader themes which cut across policy areas. It is essential reading for students and researchers in social policy, politics and sociology.

PB £21.99 US$35.00 **ISBN** 978 1 86134 151 8
216 x 148mm 368 pages June 1999

To order copies of this publication or any other Policy Press titles please visit **www.policypress.org.uk** or contact:

In the UK and Europe:
Marston Book Services, PO Box 269, Abingdon, Oxon, OX14 4YN, UK
Tel: +44 (0)1235 465500
Fax: +44 (0)1235 465556
Email: direct.orders@marston.co.uk

In Australia and New Zealand:
DA Information Services,
648 Whitehorse Road Mitcham, Victoria 3132, Australia
Tel: +61 (3) 9210 7777
Fax: +61 (3) 9210 7788
E-mail: service@dadirect.com.au

In the USA and Canada:
ISBS, 920 NE 58th Street, Suite 300, Portland, OR 97213-3786, USA
Tel: +1 800 944 6190 (toll free)
Fax: +1 503 280 8832
Email: info@isbs.com